DEDICATED

To my mother,

Alvenues Marzett

My
Queen

December 29, 1932 – November 17, 2009

I miss my momma!

The
ANOINTING

A Novel Written
by

Cassandra Oakes

PREFACE

I always wondered what happens when a preacher says he was called to the ministry. What cosmic, glorious, indescribable event happened when the Lord God Almighty contacted them, to make known their destiny; that they would teach the word, serve the people, and spread the gospel?

Then there's the other kind of folk, the kind that from the time they were pushed in the world knew who they were and what they wanted to be. They had a burning desire to minister. So all their lives they lived and breathed and practiced preaching. Why were they like that? When I was young, I used to look at the boys and girls like that, who had similar spirits, and I thought something was wrong with them. Now I think . . . How awesome to live an entire life doing the will of God.

Well, I often wondered what kind of person does God call? I thought they must be so very special and lucky. Yeah, I said 'lucky' because that's how I felt. Just think, God was using them to do His work. To be 'Called by God,' Destined! Your whole life nurtured and protected, like rain falling from heaven cleaning your path so you don't get dirty . . . Couldn't be somebody like me.

I was disobedient and had an expeditious nature. I had a naïve desire for excitement. I hung out with men and women that were fast like me. We wanted to taste life, see the world and be a part of all its glitter, glamour and fame. We wanted to make the happenings, not just watch from the sidelines. Well, by my skewed outlook, we were it! We were the happening. We had it goin' on! So I thought.

When I started writing this book, I began researching and asking ministers, "When you got your calling to be a preacher, what exactly happened? What events transpired? When, where and how did God get your attention? I wanted the details.

Well, to my edification, I got all kinds of detailed accounts of that mind-blowing event. I was amazed. One day, if no one beats me to it, I would like to produce a documentary on just that, because there were all kinds of experiences. There were the dramatic thunder like phenomeral and then the humble voice. Some had witnesses that testified what happened, step by step. I don't use this word loosely, but their experience was miraculous.

Then I had to think about my life and the life of my friends, the fast and the furious; the ones that endured life's pains from self-inflicted wounds, the ones that bear the scars of the world and lived to tell about it. In a way, our lives could be a calling too. The fact that we lived through it all and we're able to have a new life shows the nature of God, His mercy and love for us. He gave us protection, resilience and healing. Healing when there was no hope, when the doctors gave up, He showed us a degree of grace that one could only describe as a miracle.

We could have a calling too, to give our testimony.

Chapter 1

It's Friday night, around eleven o'clock; it may be a little later. I'm up, watching late night news with my momma. I like having a little time with her before Lonnie, her boyfriend comes home from work. When he's home he takes over my mom. He won't admit it but, it irritates him when I'm around; so I'll go to my room. And he's so loud. He walks loud and talks loud. His voice carries, even when he's trying to whisper something in my momma's ear, and I really don't want to hear that. He's got a good job; he's at work when I'm home from school. . . Yeaaaa! Me and momma are home alone most of the time. We eat and talk before Petticoat Junction or Bonanza comes on the TV. On Bonanza, I like Little Joe Cartwright. He's so cute. Momma likes Adam, his older brother.

We used to do my homework together, but that was when I was a little kid. Now I'm fifteen years old and a freshman in high school; she doesn't know any of this stuff. Next year I'll be a sophomore. In three years I'll be finished with school. I'm graduating with the class of 1970; I can't wait.

I started a job already, working for Uncle Charlie's Barbeque Restaurant, and I get good tips. I can only work weekends when I don't have to get up so early in the mornings. Sometimes momma will let me work on Thursday nights . . . that's because I get good grades. I can always finish my homework at Uncle Charlie's. That'll give me four whole days with tips.

Anyway, momma's boyfriend Lonnie cleans the post office buildings downtown. I guess he's been there awhile. How in the world does he keep that job? I bet he don't do anything but look in the mirror and run his mouth. He's one of those guys that think because he's so high yellow and he's got pretty hair, that he's fine. He ain't fine to me. Lonnie talks over everybody and he think that he knows everything. By the time he's finished talking, all you want to do is get the hell away, before he starts on something else.

I can't believe they made him a supervisor. Well, that's what he says, that he's the supervisor. The way he talks, you would think he's running the whole post office. He's loud, he's obnoxious. I wouldn't let Lonnie run my bath water. My momma thinks we need him. We'll be just fine with or without Lonnie. I don't get it.

First thing he's going to do is get him a little nip. That's what he calls his scotch whiskey, a nip. Then he's going to take a shower and put on one of his crazy suits. He ought to be ashamed of himself leaving the house in those get ups, like he's cool. It's something you'd see those pimps wearing on the streets. You should see him. That man will wear anything. One time, I saw him in a purple, cat daddy suit, with a stupid cat daddy hat, with a big feather . . . it was purple too. If he wasn't my momma's boyfriend, I would have laughed my ass off. But, I didn't, I was so embarrassed.

Lonnie tries too hard to be cool, he ain't cool. Out of all the gamblers at Razz's gambling house, how did my momma pick Lonnie; the broke joke, that tries so hard to be a big shot. It's ridiculous, just watching him faking.

My momma is pretty, she has smooth dark skin; she's tall and built. My momma's got a good shape. She's got a little waist . . . Well it used to be little. She's getting thick, too thick if you ask me. I'm dark skinned and tall too, just like my momma. But her hair is long and wavy. She keeps it all wrapped up in a bun on top of her head. My hair isn't as pretty as momma's, and my mom has the prettiest teeth you ever want to see. She has dimples, she's pretty. I don't know how she got stuck with Lonnie Evans. He never has any money and for some reason, it doesn't bother momma. My momma make excuses for him because he comes home broke on payday; he has to pay that gambling debt at Razz's.

7

But my momma won't complain, she won't say anything bad about anybody.

"Now baby, you remember when I had to see Dr. Clark. Lonnie had to borrow money from his boss to get my prescriptions filled. Medicine is so high these days. I was glad he could do it. I guess being the supervisor has some good points. I don't know what I would have done. I can't go long without my sugar pills. No . . . I can't play with that sugar. That's how your grandma died. I'm taking care of my sugar. You know getting paid once a month is hard. Shoot, when we pay all the bills around here, there's nothing left to buy food. I sure appreciate that man. You know what I mean?"

"I know momma. How are you feeling now?"

"I'm alright. As soon as this place heal on my big toe, I'll be better." Patricia sat down on her bed and was rubbing around the sore spot . . . wanting to scratch it, but knew better.

"Let me see it." Marianne whispered. "Momma, is that the same sore as before . . . when you stomped it on the bed post. It got like that? I thought you said it was better. Look at it. It's worse, a lot worse."

"It was getting better, but working in that cafeteria, I keep hitting it. It's bad, huh? I can't afford taking off work, not right now. This summer, when school's out, it'll heal. Right now, it's just a little sore is all . . . it's alright."

"Momma, put your leg up on the chair so I can put something on it. You want me to use the peroxide or that other stuff? Where's that red stuff, momma?"

Marianne pulled up a chair close to her mother's bed. She got a towel, tucked it under her mother's foot, then began looking for the medications for her patient, mom."

"Marianne, look on my night stand, everything's there. It should be right there, baby."

"I got it. Momma, can I ask you something?" Marianne started laughing before she could get it out.

8

"What?" Patricia started laughing too.

"Why are you getting so fat? Momma, you don't look right with your face fat like that. Look at you. Your pants are ti-ight, look at your stomach. You're eating those butter cookies and cinnamon rolls in that cafeteria, aren't you? Don't eat that stuff, momma. I don't want to hurt your feelings, but momma, do you know how fat you look?"

"Yeah, I got to leave those sweets alone. My face is big, huh?"

Marianne was laughing and nodding. "Yeah momma, you got to stop it. You're gonna be one of those fat old ladies, with a big butt, and run over shoes, wearing one of those white suits working in the cafeteria. That's what you're gonna be."

"Naw . . . naw, naw. I can't do that. I'm getting too old and I'm slowing down. It sure ain't good for my diabetes. But those butter cookies. . .um um um! Baby, baby, they are goooood . . . I brought some home. I put some extra butter and sugar in these, just for us. You want some?" Patricia had a sly way of smiling; those dimples jumped out and twinkled. Marianne couldn't resist her mother's smile.

"Yeah I want some. Where are they?"

The screen door slammed shut like somebody just shot through the door. "Patricia . . . Pa-tri-shaaaa! I'm hungry girl. Fix my plate."

It was Lonnie. He's home.

"Have you seen my brown pin-striped suit? That slick-ass Stoney from Oklahoma City is in town. Yeah, that joker got me last time. He got my ass. I'm getting my money back this night. . , yeah, this night I'm getting paid. Hey Pat. You hear me. What's in there to eat? Did you cook? I got to eat something before I get out. I can't eat that high ass food they're serving at these nightclubs. I'm trying to make some money, not spend it at these damn clubs around here. Patricia, come here, woman. Now I know I hung that suit in here." Lonnie looked in his old closet where most of his clothes still hang from every color of the rainbow, bright yellow, sparkly white to jet black. "Let me see. You think my baby blue turtle neck will go good with my brown suit? Maybe, I should wear my purple shirt. Pat . . . Did you hear me?"

"Baby, I'm in here."

"Momma, you gonna give him some money tonight? I'm supposed to get my band uniform; I'm supposed to get it before Friday's game. Momma . . .momma, can you give me the money for my uniform, now. I'm supposed to have everything paid, the bus and hotel too. I want to go to the game in St. Louis. I promised everybody that I was going, momma. I'm the only one who hasn't paid for the trip. All I need is twenty-five more dollars. Man! I'm going to be the only one without a uniform."

"Hey Pat, where's my stuff? I got to calm down. I need a nip before I get out of here. Hi Marianne."

"Hi Lonnie"

Patricia was still rubbing her leg, trying to get some blood flowing to her foot.

"Marianne, baby, fix Lonnie some of those navy beans and ham. I want to keep my leg up for a few more minutes. Get a piece of that cornbread, if there's any left. We still have some kool-aid in the icebox. Fix him a plate for me, baby, we'll talk when I get up." Momma was whispering. "I'm going to rest a little while longer. I'm tired. I got to get up so early in the morning. I'm so tired."

"Okay momma."

* * * * *

We live in an old two story house. It has red, fake brick siding and lots of big windows. There's a few stairs, well, there's a lot of stairs, but we have a huge porch, with a swing. At night, we sit out there for hours, enjoying the breeze. I love my house. It's not the prettiest house in the neighborhood, but I love my house. We've lived here all my life. I have my own room; it used to be my grandma's room. I got all grandma's furniture too. My grandma's old bed is huge and soft. And I have my grandma's old vanity set. It's been in our family a long time. For me, it's just right. I'm wearing makeup now. I put all my lipstick and makeup in there. It's nice. My grandma's perfume bottles are still right where she left them. I still have some of her powder and perfume, I love it. I don't use any of it. I want to keep it forever.

Since I have a corner room, I can see everything on the block. There's a picture window on each side. Plus I'm upstairs. . . I can see everything that's happening.

My grandma Maxine knew everything that went on around our block. People told her all the news. They'd sit on the porch and talk about the neighborhood . . . who's going with whose husband. Who lost their job. What boy was in trouble and had to go to Vietnam. Everything was discussed with grandma. Who went on welfare; cause then their man had to move out. Grandma would just smile with those pretty gold teeth and tell them to come over a few days and help around our house. If needed, she'd feed the whole block. We looked after each other.

People were always talking about my grandma Maxine, and what she used to do. They say that back in the day, those soldier boys would come from Fort Riley and stay at our house cause they couldn't stay at any hotels in town. She let them stay the whole weekend and party, she fed them; then sent them back to the base early in the morning. She baked cakes and sometimes fried pies for them to take back on base. Ms. Shirley said they came every weekend and stayed at our house . . . my mom was just a little girl, then.

Grandma had a way about settling matters, too. She could iron out everything just right and people trusted her. Cause grandma wasn't going to put anybody's business on the

11

streets. She'd get calls in the middle of the night, somebody in trouble and wanting to borrow some money.

Ms. Shirley . . . Shirley Butler is our next door neighbor. She was fighting with her husband, Clarence. They'd have some bad fights. I felt sorry for Ms. Shirley. Mr. Butler has a girlfriend that's really young and Ms. Shirley came home from work and caught them together in her bed. Man, they had a bad fight. I thought they were going to kill each other. Somehow, grandma knew the right thing to say and the right thing to do. She asked Ms. Shirley to come over our house a few days . . . to help around the house. Clarence wasn't going up against grandma Maxine. He knew better. My grandma wasn't scared of anybody. So Ms. Shirley stayed with us two or three months. It was a long time. Clarence begged and begged her to come home . . . she finally gave in. All was fine until Clarence got another girlfriend. He's crazy. Ms. Shirley took it real hard when grandma died.

I remember my grandma always looking out the bedroom windows, just like I do now, watching the neighborhood. She'd stand right there so you know she saw everything that went on. People were glad to see her watching and guarding the block. They'd wave. She'd smile and wave back. Sometimes when I came home from school I'd look up at my window, I could almost see her standing there, smiling. When I go to my room, it sounds crazy, but sometimes I can smell her perfume, so clear, just like she had walked in the room. I sure miss my grandma. I know she's gone to a better place. We were safe when my grandma was alive. Our house has been in our family a long time, and I want to stay right here in it with my momma.

People used to rent rooms from us . . . not anymore. Lonnie used to rent a room too, that's how he got my momma. Lonnie convinced momma not to rent anymore rooms out. He promised he would help her and she didn't need people lying

around leaching anymore, trying to live for free. Yeah, right.
He's the main one. He ran off all our help. Now my momma's
hurt and she still has to work like a dog in that school cafeteria.
My mom is so tired when she comes home from work.

Lonnie thinks one day I'm gonna leave for college and
leave him here with my momma. So he'll finally have her all to
himself. Yeah . . . when I'm gone, he can take over our house.
But I'm not leaving, I'm not going anywhere. Nope, not while
he's here. Anyway my mom's not going to marry his ass. She
promised me that. She don't want anybody taking our house
from me. Yeah, I got to stay around here and watch out.

* * * * *

I ran upstairs. I didn't want to be around when Lonnie
asked my mother for some money, the money for my uniform.
He'll promise her everything; that he'll win tonight, that he'll
give her interest for using the money. She'll have it back
tonight. He always says that. Please mom, not this time. Don't
give it to him. I prayed that she wouldn't give in to his broke
ass. I don't ask for much from momma. I know how hard she
works.   But she promised to help me pay for my new uniform
for our school band. The band has new uniforms; all the football
players and cheerleaders got new uniforms. Man, they look
good too.

I was listening to Lonnie. He shouldn't be asking her
for money. But he was. In my heart, I was pleading . . . don't
do it momma . . . please not this time. Stand up to his ass.
Then I prayed that it wouldn't turn bad.

One time, Lonnie hit her when he wanted some money.
I grabbed a kitchen knife. I was going to stab him right in his
skinny little heart for hitting my momma. Momma made me
promise not to ever get involved again. That it was between
them. Yeah, momma got mad at me. So now, I won't say
anything else, even when he yells at her. He just better not ever
hit her in front of me again.

13

"Um! She gave it to him. She gave him the money." I don't know how my mom let little Lonnie run her like that. He would never do that if my grandma was still alive. Soon as grandma died, Lonnie started talking shit and taking over. He talked like he knew everything. He even told my mom that he would handle my grandma's funeral arrangements.

"Don't worry about a thang, Patricia. I'll handle it. She was like my momma too."

Oh Lord, I couldn't believe what I was hearing. Thankfully, my grandma had every detail worked out with Temple's Funeral Home long before she died. My grandma wasn't even in the ground before he moved into my momma's bedroom and was sleeping with her. It wasn't a week before he started trying to tell me what to do, but he didn't know me. Did Lonnie really think I would just let him take my momma from me and . . . oh, and he, be my daddy? Um! That's my momma, she belongs to me and he sure ain't my daddy. He said he wanted to protect us, he was gonna be there for the family. Shoot. I saw right through that mess. Lonnie wouldn't let me and momma have any time alone when my grandma died. I hate him for that.

* * * * *

Paseo High is the best school in Kansas City. Kids are cool, we dress good. We got the best band in Kansas City and the guys are fine. On Fridays there's always a fight, a girl fight and a boy fight. But it's not that bad. Nobody really gets hurt. I mean, Paseo High has its moments, but we're not bad kids. We took state in Math and Science two years straight. That's because of Mr. Blair with his fine self. He can explain things in a way that makes it clear and simple. He can sure turn on my lights.

I never thought I was very smart until I was in his class. When Mr. Blair explains, I understand everything. I'm even doing good in History. Since I started high school, I've gotten

14

straight A's. The kids that I grew up with can't believe it, because when we were in Jr. High I wasn't that smart. Now, I don't want to disappoint Mr. Blair. He's just smiles when he hands me my A's.

* * * * *

I was surprised when I woke up and Lonnie was standing over me. He was in my room.

"Hi Marianne."

"Hi, what are you doing in here, what time is it? Where's momma?"

"It's early little girl. I didn't think you would wake up this easily. I just wanted to give you some money. I was gonna put it on your table so you could see it, pay for your trip, and here's an extra five dollars for letting me use it. Buy you something nice, something real nice from me."

"Okay, thanks. Wow, I'll get to go to the game. Okay, thanks."

"Believe it or not, I used to be young. I want you to have fun. Don't spend it all on the trip. Save something for later. In fact, always keep you an extra dime or fifty cents for emergencies. You never know what can happen. At least you can make a call in case of an emergency."

Marianne nodded. "Okay Lonnie, thanks." She wondered why was he acting funny, why is he still in here . . . in her room. He's never came in her room before. She felt very uncomfortable and couldn't sleep with Lonnie standing there.

"Is there something else, Lonnie?"

"No, little girl. Go back to sleep. Thanks for letting me use your money. Have fun at the game."

He finally left and she drifted back to sleep. She slept peacefully, knowing she wouldn't be embarrassed that morning at school and be left behind for the most important game of the year.

* * * * *

15

First thing, after Marianne arrived at school, she headed toward the band room.

"Where's Mr. Jernigan?"

"I don't know, he's probably in the teacher's lounge." That was Taco, he plays the tuba in the band.

"There he is, talking with Ms. Hardimon." Just then Mr. Jernigan walked in the door. Rushing, trying to prepare for his next class.

"Hi Mr. Jernigan, I got my money for my uniform and I can pay for the trip too."

"Okay. That's good, baby. You know we plan on stopping at Big Boy's for a hamburger, but you can bring your lunch, I just want you know that we'll stop there."

"Okay, Mr. Jernigan. I like Big Boy's"

"Do you know who you'll be sharing rooms with?"

"Yes sir, me and Kim, will be sharing a bed, then Kathy and Stephanie will be sharing the other bed."

"That's fine, get your receipt from Ms. Adkinson, and write your name on the board. Find the square with the other girls names on it, make sure you pick the right square."

"Yes sir. Okay, thank's Mr. Jernigan." Marianne was happy

"You're welcome, baby."

Chapter 2

School is out next month; then I'll be working every day for Uncle Charlie. I want to buy some summer clothes and have money saved for school next year. Nothing fits. I've out grown everything. I grew my tits overnight. My breasts are so big now that my bras don't fit. I've been wearing my momma's bra. I'm taller, too, taller than my momma. I want some of those elephant leg pants, and some hip hugger bell bottoms. Next year I'm going to be ready. I'm going to get me some fishnets in every color. And some boots. I'm getting me an alfro wig . . . I want a big one. Momma can't buy me everything. Thank God I got a job, so I can buy my own stuff. I need new clothes, new underwear . . . . some shoes. Next Fall, I'll be ready.

Momma's been asking me about my future lately . . . What I want to do when I graduate? I don't know. She's been hinting at me to become a nurse. I don't want to do that. Being around sick people all the time, or sick babies . . . what if they die. I don't think I can do it. I got to start thinking about something, though. I'll be out of high school before I know it. Everybody's been grabbing scholarship applications. A couple of my friends are going to Job Corps during the summer. The Army has been enlisting the boys. A couple of boys enlisted and dropped out of school, they said they were leaving for boot camp. Their parents sign for them to enlist. Wow, can you believe that.

I'm going to apply for college. They said you should apply during your junior year. But, I was thinking of joining the Army like the boys, or the Peace Corps. I don't know what to do. I just want to do something good and help out poor people.

Women don't fight in a war, I'm glad of that, I'll probably work in the cafeteria if I join the Army, and work

17

somewhere in Nam or maybe Okinawa or Korea; wouldn't that be something. I wouldn't mind helping at a hospital overseas, I don't know, I'd like to travel a little bit. They say if I join the Reserves, then I won't be gone too much. They say only one week out of a month. That's not a bad idea. That's not bad at all. Then I can keep an eye on my momma.

I don't know what's happening with her. She's sick all the time and tired. She says she's not eating a lot of sweets, but she's getting bigger every day. She's getting older and momma has got to take care of herself.

"Marianne, baby, please leave me alone about my sugar. I'm taking care of it. I don't know why I'm gaining weight like this. I'm going through the change is what's happening. You know, that automatically makes you gain weight. I've been skipping my monthly visits. That's how menopause starts. My momma, your grandma, went through the change around my age. That's all it is, your momma's going through the change a little early."

"Well mom, you may need to see a doctor to make sure that's all it is, cause it could be something else. If you're going through the change, your medicine may be different now. You might need some stronger insulin or something . . . cause you're tired all the time."

"I don't know baby, I'm alright. If I don't feel any better when school's out, then I'll do something. I want Dr. Clark to check this place on my big toe anyway. I'm tired of it being sore all day long; everyday my foot hurts . . . Shoot! Well, I'll see about taking off tomorrow. They can do without me for one day."

"Momma, I wanna go. I can skip school . . . one day won't hurt anything. We're not doing anything. Everybody's doing makeup work and talking with the school counselors. They've been giving us grant applications. And people have been coming from all these colleges to talk to everybody. It's fun, but I don't want to go to college."

"What are you talking about Marianne?

"I don't want to go to college, not right now. I don't want to go."

"Well, what do you plan on doing with your life? I don't want you laying around here, waiting to have a baby on me. No ma'am. If that's what you think, you better think again. Marianne, are you pregnant? Don't tell me that. Please don't tell me you're pregnant"

"Mom . . . mom, stop . . . it! You are so uptight. You let your imagination work you all up. Momma, you're trying to curse me? Soon as somebody starts saying things like that, then it happens. That's what grandma used to say." Marianne put her fingers in a cross sign. "Please don't say the curse words around me. That's the last thing we need around here."

"Well you better explain cause I know you don't want me to start imagining things. You won't leave this house. I promise, you'll be locked in a room for the next ten years. Don't play with me, girl."

"First off, momma, I need sex to have a baby, isn't that right momma? Well . . . Okay then! I'm the only girl at Paseo High that's still a virgin." Marianne did a cursive bow like she was royalty. "And I like it, I like being the only virgin in school." She shook her hips with every word.

"Woo wee. Let me sit down. Um um um, I got dizzy thinking of that." Patricia fell on the couch, then put her foot up on the coffee table and starting rubbing her leg. "Soooo, what are you going to do, cause you got to do something, Marianne. I can go along with anything. any decision you make, but you got to make a decision with your life. It ain't nothing around this block."

"I know, I want to get out of Kansas City for a while. I got a few ideas, but I don't know. I'm not sure, I'm not sure, right now, is all"

"It's always good to move from home, get out of town; see what's out there. Live a little. I want you to do things and go places. I never did anything, I never went anywhere. I've never been a hundred miles out of this city; I don't want that for my baby girl. Just don't get stuck on boys, not right now. You got to live a little before all that. Listen to your momma, girl."

"I know mom, I was thinking of joining the Army Reserves or the Air Force or something. What do you think about me joining the military? I can get a job around here and join the Reserves."

"Baby, you might go to Vietnam. What about that? Why don't you want to go to college, Marianne?"

"I don't know. I want a break from school. I like the idea of traveling one week out of the month . . . and seeing the world. Don't that sound good mom. I want a career in something but I don't know what I want to be. So I'm thinking about doing four years in the military and maybe I can figure something out by then."

"You'll be alright. You got so many ways like your grandma. She was smart just like you. You're just like her."

* * * * *

It was time for momma's doctor appointment. Clouds were heavy and gray . . . rain was pouring down, it was a storm. Momma didn't want to go. I could tell she was feeling bad but she wasn't complaining. Mostly, her foot was hurting; she could hardly walk on it. Momma had been sick all morning and this rain wasn't helping. Finally, she was seeing the doctor and I was glad of that. We weren't talking much, so I turned on the radio, Cowboys to Girls was playing,

I remember, (I remember) when we use to play, shoot em up (shoot em up) bang bang baaaaby, and I remembeerrr . . . when we chase the girls and beat em up...

Rainy Night in Georgia was next, then Marvin Gaye singing, Ain't that Perculiar . . . music was good. We got there

20

a little early so we just listened to the music while the rain slowed down before we got out the car.

In the doctor's office, Nurse Helen Watson was sipping coffee, moving around, cleaning the office and getting ready for a full day. There were only two people in the waiting room; that was good. I grabbed a couple of magazines, Reader's Digest and The Jet.

"Ms. Robinson, can you update your records, the doctor will see you shortly" The nurse handed momma a clipboard with a few forms to fill out.

I want my mom to get better. She lays around all the time, that's not like my mother. Right now she takes oral medicine for her diabetes but maybe she needs to start taking the shots with this menopause thing happening.

Lonnie stays gone. He's not home an hour before he's out the door. These days, momma's been fussing. She's been real mean and he don't want to hear it. He can't do anything right. I've been kind of proud of momma. Lonnie's shocked. Goody! Maybe he'll leave.

"Patricia Robinson, the doctor will see you now." Nurse Helen announced, looking over her glasses and doing a quick scan of the other patients in the reception room.

Momma motioned her hand for me to wait there.

"Ms. Robinson, can you get on the scales for me?"

"Yeah . . . For the life of me, I don't know why I'm gaining so much weight. Wow, I weigh 205 pounds? When did all this happen?"

"It comes on fast, doesn't it? Now I'll need to get your blood pressure and temperature. How's everything with you?"

"I got this place on my big toe that won't heal . . . and I'm tired all the time. Plus, I'm going through early menopause. So I'm doing just fine." Patricia gave the nurse a pretty little smirk showing a few of her perfectly straight white teeth.

21

"Well the doctor will want some blood to check your sugar levels. When was your last cycle?"

"Let's see. My last cycle was in January. Before then, I was missing a lot. I would have a period about once every two or three months. My mother started her menopause in her early forties.

"But Pat, you're barely in your thirty's. What are you thirty-three, thirty-four?"

"Thirty-two, I've been skipping my period all my life. It stopped all together now. I'm doing the same thing as my momma."

"Patricia, I hope you're right . . . cause a lot of women get pregnant when they're going through the change, or they think cause they don't have a period, they can't get pregnant. Now I know the doctor is going to want some blood. It could be a little surprise in there."

"Girl, Ha ha ha, wouldn't that be something. I know that ain't it, cause I ain't doing nothing. Naw, I ain't doing too much these days. I don't feel like it. So, I'm not pregnant. It's been 16 years since I had a baby. Marianne tore me up so bad that I couldn't have anymore. I wish I could have had another child so Marianne could have a little sister or brother, but it didn't happen."

There was a knock on the door and Dr. James Clark came in with his smiling self. "Hey Patricia, how's everything, girl."

Dr. Clark has been the neighborhood doctor close to 20 years now. He delivered Marianne. He's delivered most of the babies around here. The doctor married his high school sweetheart. It's funny how guys like him always stay married. Well, one reason is he's a handsome man. He tall and has a little gray around his temples. He has a young-looking face, he's smart and got money, plus he's a doctor. What more do you need?

"Oh, everything's fine, doc. My toe won't heal. I've had this sore place over four months now. I've been keeping it clean and dry. I had some antibiotic that I was taking but I ran out. It was getting better when I had those antibiotics."

"Pat, why didn't you call me? Don't you know that you could lose your leg? Infection can set in it and I'll be taking that leg off. Let me see it." Dr. Clark was horrified when he saw Patricia's toe.

"What have you been doing Pat?" Dr. Clark threw a towel across the room.

"I've been washing it with peroxide and with that iodine. I keep it covered. When I see it might be getting bad, I make a paste with Arm and Hammer, put that on it. My mother use to do that when she had a sore place."

"Pat, are you crazy? Look at your toe? What's wrong with you? You know better. Don't you ever . . . go this long . . . with a sore like that. Girrrl . . . Patricia, you know me. I don't have a problem with writing you a prescription, all you have to do is ask." Doctor Clark started slamming drawers and cabinets. "What's wrong with the Negros around here? We got diabetes, high blood pressure, this sickle cell thing . . . I'm disappointed in you." Dr. Clark rubbed his head like he had a headache. "Have you been taking care of your diabetes? You taking your insulin . . . cause right now, I don't know about you, girl."

"Yes sir." Patricia straightened up Doc was mad and she knew it. "But, I'm gaining weight." Pat was trying to change the subject. "I must have a problem with my thyroid or something. I've gained over 30 pounds. I shouldn't be gaining weight like that."

The nurse then spoke up, "Doctor, Patricia said she was going through early menopause."

"Is that right? When was your last cycle?"

"Five months ago. Before that, I was having a cycle

every two to three months. Now it stopped all together."

"I'm going to order you some lab work, we can't be too careful. Dr. Clark started writing on his pad. He was really pissed off. "Get this prescription of antibiotics for your foot. Take all of it. Put this cream on three time a day. I want you back in my office, this Friday. We may have to change your insulin too."

The doctor looked at nurse, Helen. "Make Ms. Robinson an appointment for this coming Friday, before the weekend. I'll call to get her test on a fast track. I should have her results back by then."

The Doctor turned his attention back to his patient.

"Now Patricia, I want you to promise me, if your foot doesn't get better, call me. I'm really upset that you let it get this bad. . . It doesn't look good. Pat, you could lose your toe. Do you understand? I'm taking you off work; I want you to stay off it. Understand!" Dr. Clark looked hard at Patricia, giving her the evil eye. He was clearly upset.

Momma fussed all day. Dr. Clark called the school to make sure momma would be off the rest of the year. I was glad something was going to be done.

"That's why I wanted to wait till schools out for the summer. There's nothing I can do about it now. Dr. Clark made sure of that . . . Now he wants me to come back this Friday. For what! Sometimes James goes too far. Um um um."

"Well mom, at least your toe is going to get better."

"Yeah, stop at Rexall drugs off Main street; they're cheaper. I'll get my prescriptions filled there."

"Why do you have to come back Friday?"

"Girl, I don't know. He ran tests on my sugar. I know he wants to know if I'm keeping my diabetes under control. I told him that I'm really tired. I may be anemic or something. That nurse got him giving me a pregnancy test cause I'm going

24

through menopause."

"A pregnancy test! Are you kidding?"

"Oooooooo child, wouldn't that be a mess?"

"You'll run Lonnie off for sure."

"Marianne, why don't you like Lonnie? He's not a bad guy. I could do a lot worse than him. At least he's honest, he's faithful, he ain't chasing around all those old fast women that hang out at Razz's . . . I know he talks like he's a ladies man . . . bless his heart, but he's just talking. Yeah, that's Lonnie, he can talk." Patricia was smiling thinking about her man.

Marianne was rolling her eyes, being careful to hold her tongue.

"Momma, can you at least get him to stop buying those cheap suits? He can't dress." They were both laughing.

"I know. Bless his heart. He's had that stuff a long time. I can't get him to buy anything decent. He loves those cheap suits. He's been helping me save money for you . . . for when you graduate."

They gave each other a distrusting eye.

"Yeah, he just wants me to hurry up and get out the house."

"Marianne, believe it or not, he likes you. He thinks you're a good girl. He talks about you going to college."

"Momma, Lonnie likes you. He wants me to leave, that's all. Get out and go to college; all he wants is me to go . . . so I'll be out his way and he'll have you to himself."

Marianne thought about the night when Lonnie was in her room. She never mentioned it to her mother. Lonnie never had done anything like that before, maybe it was all innocent. Maybe he just wanted to leave money for her to go to the game. But she couldn't shake the feeling that he was up to something. After all, he could have put the money on the dresser and left, but he was watching her while she slept.

Marianne decided not to mention it to her mother. But if

anything like that ever happened again, she would take a hammer and threaten his skinny ass.

"Lonnie is scary. Sometimes he scares me, momma."

"Well, I don't know about all that. Now that we don't have renters anymore, the money he brings in takes us through the summer."

Marianne's voice was high and loud. She was more than a little irritated. "Momma, he ran off all our renters. He should help out and pay some bills around here."

Patricia was now ready to change the subject. "I was planning on getting you a little car, if I can find one reasonable. I thought that you might need something to drive if you were going to college. But since you're not . . ."

"Momma . . . mommy, I still need a car. You're getting me a car?"

"If I can find you a little car for around $500, I'll get it. You're such a good girl, always helping me. You've been keeping those boys off too. Now, I don't know, girl, I may need to get me a pistol with some of this money. Look at you. I ain't bragging but, my little girl is fine. You're beautiful, those boys are going to come after my baby, I might have to shoot one. If you bring any babies home, I promise, you will not get a car. You'll get diapers and milk . . . maybe." She was smiling "I mean it, Marianne."

"Don't worry about me. I don't even have a boyfriend. These boys around here ain't doing nothing. I want to meet somebody going to college or something. I'm going to wait and marry me a lawyer."

* * * * *

Friday was here and time to see Dr. Clark again. I was surprised that she wanted me there. Momma must be worried about something.

"Well, mom, your foot looks better. Man, that place is drying up, it's healing fast. You should have seen the doctor a

26

long time ago."

"Yeah. Marianne, are you almost ready? We need to get out of here."

"I'm ready. I was waiting on you."

"Okay . . . Okay, here I come. It sure is a pretty morning, isn't it? I don't know why I got to come back here to see Dr. Clark. He already gave me a refill on my antibiotics."

"Probably wants to tell you about your sugar."

"Shoot, he can do that on the phone. I hope I won't have to start taking shots. You think that's why he wanted me back in, to see him."

"Aww momma, it's not going to hurt you to see Dr. Clark. He can take another look at your toe. It got better fast."

"I know that's a blessing. Come on, let's go in and get it over with."

"Good morning. How are you Patricia? Hi Marianne."

"I'm doing good. It sure is a pretty day, isn't it?"

"Yes ma'am it is. The doctor hasn't made it in yet. He had a late night. Do you know the Williams, over off Post road?"

"Isn't he a preacher or something?" Momma asked. "Is he the one that got that little house over off 2nd street that they turned into a church? I heard they have night church in their basement." Momma was smiling at the thought.

"Yeah, that's it. Well people are working Sunday mornings, can't afford to take off."

"Helen, you are so right. Have you ever gone?"

"Naw, but I need to go. I heard they were pretty good folks. Anyway, that family, the Williams, had twins last night. Doc didn't know it was two of them. One was hiding in there. Two girls . . . they're identical. He's tired, but he's on his way. It shouldn't be too long."

Dr. Clark waltzed in the door.

"Speak of the devil." Ms. Helen eyed Pat and they both

27

laughed.

With a sly look in his eyes, "How are you Patricia?" Then he looked at Marianne with a fatherly smile and wink. "You've been keeping her out of trouble?"

Marianne spoke up. "I'm trying, Dr. Clark. It's hard, but I'm trying."

"Patricia, I'll see you in five minutes. Let me put my briefcase down, and grab your files. Matter of fact, why don't you come on back to my office. I've got your results." Dr. Clark motioned her toward the door. "Come on in and have a seat."

"Mom, you want me to come with you?"

"Noooo. It's okay."

Patricia sat down looking at the patterns on the walls, the room smelt like old pipe tobacco. Her right eye was jumping. Something was going to happen. "I hope Lonnie is okay. I've been so mean to him lately." Patricia was talking to herself.

It wasn't long before Dr. Clark rushed in the room where Patricia sat. She had a feeling all morning that something was up, her eye kept jumping, when that happens, Patricia learned to just brace herself.

"Patricia, you know I ran a few tests. Your sugar is high. What have you been doing?" Dr. Clark was looking at Patricia, very concerned but not waiting on an answer. "I'm going to start you on insulin shots, right away. You've got to start taking this diabetes thing very seriously. I want you to start this strict diet. It's very important." Dr. Clark pulled his chair closer to Patricia; he held her hands together in his. "You know why it's so important?"

"Of course I do, James. If I want to be around to see my grand babies, I'd better take care of my sugar. It's bad, isn't it?"

"Yes dear, it is. It's too high and we've got to get it under control right now. You need to be healthy for your little

28

baby that'll be here in the next few months."

"You're talking about Marianne? She ain't no baby. Marianne is more like my sister, these days."

"No Pat. From the looks of things, you're probably five to six months pregnant."

"You're shitting me? I can't be pregnant. I'm too old for that shit. Shoot, I've been menopausing, James. I haven't had a period in seven months. How can this happen, I'm too old. Marianne will be going to college in a few years. Oh my goodness. James, come on now, are you sure?" Tears started streaming down. "James, I can't have a baby. Marianne is sixteen years old; I'm thirty-two myself. I can't have a baby. I have diabetes, doctor, you got to help me. I can't have a baby. I'm too old and I got this sugar. A baby won't be healthy. Something might be wrong with it. I can't do it. I can't have a baby. What about?" Patricia couldn't finish.

"Patricia, it's too late to do anything about it now. You're nearly six months pregnant. Right now you need to be very careful. Your sugar is high, too high for this pregnancy. We will work together and get it under control. You'll need to maintain this diet that I'm giving you. You want a healthy baby don't you?"

Patricia was nodding her head yes and still crying. "What in the world am I going to do with a baby?"

"You'll be fine."

"I'll be fine, I'll be fine. James when was the last time you had a baby? I was a kid when I had Marianne. In fact, my mother raised her. She's more like my sister. I never really took care of a baby. Lord, what am I going to do? I can't do this." Patricia cried hard. "Having Marianne was a miracle."

"I want to schedule an appointment with you to check everything. I want to make sure our little baby is alright. I want to get some kind of timing." Dr. Clark was smiling and trying to be reassuring. "I'm going to prescribe some prenatal vitamins. Okay? You'll be alright. These things all work out just fine . . . Patricia, do you want to stay back here a few minutes? And stop all that crying. Should I ask Marianne to come back here? I know you two will have a lot to talk about."

Patricia nodded yes. "Oh my goodness. What am I going to do. Um um um . . . of all the things that could happen. Why me? This takes the cake."

Marianne came cautiously in the door. "Mom, what's wrong? Why are you crying?" Marianne started crying too. "Whaaat's wronnng?"

"Baby, Dr. Clark said I'm six months pregnant."

"That's it. Man I thought something was really wrong. You're kidding right?"

"No Marianne, Do I look like I'm kidding? He said I was pregnant."

"How far along, mom?"

"I just told you he said I was around six months pregnant. He thinks I'm six months pregnant. What am I going to do with a baby?"

Marianne's tears started smiling. "Mom, I'm going to have a brother or sister. I'm going to have a brother or sister. Momma, you don't look six months pregnant. I guess you're not all that fat after all."

Chapter 3

Lonnie's been mute. I've never seen him this quiet. He hasn't said a word since he's gotten the big news. Oh, he's sick. I can understand, Lonnie and my mom are too old to be having a baby. He's got to be forty-five or forty-six, and this will be his first child. Po-thang. Lonnie might be fifty years old and fixing to be a daddy. Um!

My mother's doing better. She finally knows why she's tired all the time. I know that's a big relief. She's been doing real good with her diet. She's faithfully taking her vitamins. Her toe is better, her toe is so much better. Matter of fact, it's healed. Everything is fine. She's gotten bigger. It's like once she found out about the baby, she started to look pregnant. At first, momma didn't want anybody to know about it. I guess she's ashamed of being pregnant. Um! She couldn't keep this secret, not for long anyway.

"Marianne baby, how's your momma doing?" Ms Shirley asked, waiting to see if I was going to confirm the news that she'd already suspected.

"Oh momma's fine Ms. Shirley."

"She and Lonnie's doing alright then?"

"Yeah, I guess."

"Girl, why is yo momma gaining all that weight? I know she ain't PG."

I thought I would just play dumb. "What's that, Ms. Shirley?"

"You know what I'm talking about. Girl, just tell me the trooff. Is your momma pregnant?"

I shrugged my shoulders, "You mean 'truth' Ms. Shirley. I don't know, why don't you ask her?"

"What is she doing now? I can come help around the house . . . if she needs me. Your family has been there for me, so many times. I don't mind helping ya'll. If it hadn't been for your grandma Maxine, I don't know what I would have done . . . all those years with me and Clarence fighting all the time. She was a real friend to me, during some real hard times. You're probably too young to remember everything, but I loved that lady. And if yo momma need me for anything, all ya'll got to do is ask. I want you to remember that, Marianne."

Looked like Ms. Shirley was getting ready to cry. I should be nicer to her. I know how much grandma meant to her. Momma was asleep and I know she didn't want to be bothered.

"Okay, I'll remember that Ms. Shirley, but momma was sleep when I left. Give her a call in a couple of hours. She should be awake by then."

"Well, I'll just come over in a bit and see how's she doing?"

Mom is about seven, maybe eight months down the road. It won't be long, now. It's happening so fast. I still can't believe it's true. I don't know about having a little brother or sister. It's been only me and momma for so long, I really don't know how to feel about the baby. I don't know if what I'm feeling is excitement or nervousness. I wonder what the baby's gonna look like. If it's going to be healthy, it'll probably be cute. My mom is beautiful, and Lonnie's not so bad. I guess it'll be alright. I want a brother. That's what I want. I want a little . . . baby . . . brother.

Shoot, I'll never get rid of Lonnie now. I'll have to accept the fact that he'll be a part of our lives forever. Damnit, I hate to think about that. Ummmmmmm! Maybe since he'll have a kid, he'll stop losing all his money at Razz's. He'll bring some home first, and help my momma with that baby. I know she won't be going back to work this Fall, not that soon, cause the baby is supposed to come in August. My mom won't be able to go to work till later on, probably in January. The baby will be too little for her to leave with somebody. Maybe Ms.

Shirley will babysit for us. She's home every day. Um, a baby! I still can't believe it. Oh yeah, and Lonnie will have to stop making all that noise at night.

* * * * *

Uncle Charlie's Rib House is fun. I love it. It's a lot of work, I got to wipe down the tables, mop the floor, wipe the stools where people sit, and refill the containers. But that's it. The boys, Victor Edwards and Calvin Veasley, wash dishes and clean the kitchen. Uncle Charlie has the boys seasoning the meats, and smoking everything, and they smell like smoke too. Then Ms. Rosie cooks all the side dishes. Ms. Rosie makes the best potato salad and coleslaw you ever had, and her macaroni and cheese, um! One thing about it, they're serious about their ribs . . . and the sauce.

I'm learning a lot about waiting tables too. I make five to ten dollars a night in tips. I've made over twenty dollars before; that's cash. I get paid every two weeks. I make .50 cents an hour, but my tips are good. Uncle Charlie says if I treat the customers good, then they'll want me to wait on them every time. And that's what I'm gonna do, treat'em good so I can get my tips.

A couple of times I took some dinners to Razz's gambling shack. I really got some good tips in there. I made ten dollars, right then, Johnny-on-the-spot. But Uncle Charlie don't want me delivering dinners to the gambling house. He wants the boys to do that. They don't make tips everyday like I do. But when they can't leave the restaurant, I get to deliver the ribs. Shoot, I don't mind at all. Uncle Charlie's wife, Ms. Rosie, drives me there; it's just around the corner on Prospect Street. All I do is carry the dinners to the door and get the tip. I don't see why that's such a big deal.

Uncle Charlie's niece, Deandra, will be here Wednesday. Dee's been coming here from San Angelo, Texas since we were five years old. She's my play sister. I'll be glad

33

to see her. She's been working at the restaurant a long time, I'd use to help her wipe the tables and sweep, but I didn't get paid. Yep, Dee's been working a while now.

Dee got me in so much trouble. She's so sneaky. Last year she was messing with those boys in the smoke house. Dee was only fourteen. Her Uncle and Ms. Rosie thought I was a bad influence on Dee, but it's her, Dee's already fast. She's probably been doing it already. Uncle Charlie and Ms. Rosie don't have any kids and Dee is like their daughter. So Ms. Rosie was ready and willing to blame me for everything that girl do.

Dee is real pretty. Her father is a Mexican and Dee can speak in Spanish. She talks so fast and she can act craaaazy. She gets hysterical when she's caught doing something she has no business doing. But she don't fool Uncle Charlie anymore. He's got her number. She'll tell her Aunt Rosie anything, but not Uncle Charlie. Ms. Rosie just couldn't believe her cute little niece was stealing money from them. She still don't know that she was kissing and going on with Victor and Calvin in the smokehouse, being fast with those ugly old boys. She said she was going with both of them.

"Marianne, girl, I got both those guys. They'll do anything I ask. Victor follows me around like a little puppy dog. I was in the smokehouse kissing Calvin and Victor almost caught us. We heard him coming. Girl, Calvin was trying to unbutton my blouse, then we heard Victor sneaking around."

"Unbutton your blouse? You let him do that?"

"Yeah girl. That ain't nothing. You should have been there. We were moving so fast, trying to button my blouse back up, it was fuunnnny. We were laughing soooo hard."

"What were you doing in the smokehouse with Calvin anyway. Dee, he's too old for you. He must be sorry to be messing with you and you're only fourteen. He's a grown man. Ain't no grown man gonna get me in no smokehouse playing with my titties." Marianne was shaking her head in disgust. "Naw, girl. Especially Calvin or Victor. They're ugly."

"They ain't ugly. I don't know what you're talking about, cause they ain't ugly."

"Yes they are ugly." Marianne laughed at Dee. "I can't believe you're getting mad cause I called them ugly. Calvin don't even comb his hair, his teeth are yellow, and he's too old for you. He shouldn't be messing with you, girl. That man is over twenty years old."

"He's not too old for me, I like old guys, cause in Texas, I got a man way older than that. He's older than both those guys. He's a manager at the Hamburger House and I can get anything I want."

"Have you ever did it?"

"Yeah! I almost did it with Victor, too."

"With Victor?"

"He was too big, I couldn't take it. I told him to get off me right now! And I wasn't playing. I know I was looking crazy. You know how crazy I can get. I start talking in Spanish. I think he got scared, anyway he got up. Girl, I wasn't playing with him. Girrrrl, he's big. I'm going to try again before I go home."

"Dee, don't you know what you look like, you can have any boy you want. Why waste your time with those guys. I'm waiting to meet a doctor or something. I'm not marrying anybody like Victor, Calvin or my momma's boyfriend, Lonnie. I want somebody that can take care of me. My momma's sick, and she's got to work anyway, I don't want no man that will make me work and I'm sick like my momma. Dee, girrrrl. Why you got to do it?"

"I don't know. I just do."

"What if you have a baby or something?"

"Marianne all you have to do is make them pull it out in time. You won't get pregnant if they pull it out in time."

"How do you know? You don't know. You don't need to be doing it anyway. You're too young. Ain't no boys getting any from me. I'm gonna stay a virgin till I get married."

Uncle Charlie put his foot down when it came to Dee. Yep, last year she stole some money from his wallet. He told her if he had to watch his money in his own house, she couldn't come back. I was so glad I wasn't around. Cause Ms. Rosie would have blamed me.

Yep, she'll be here Wednesday. Wait till she sees my alfro wig. I have eye shadow in every color. I finally got my ears pierced. I'm gonna wear my bell bottom jeans and a halter top. Wait till she sees me.

Wednesday finally came. I was so glad to see Dee. She's changed a lot too. She's short. Dee hadn't grown an inch but she looks all grown up. She wears her hair down her back. It's pretty. Dee's pretty, she looks like a little doll with really red lipstick.

"Hey girl, you finally made it in, I didn't think you would ever get here."

"Hi Marianne. You sure got tall since last summer. Girl, you're tall and skinny. But you look cute. Is that a wig? It looks good. Before I go back home, we're going shopping."

"Yeah, they got some good stuff here. I'll take you where I go. There's a skating rink. We can skate after we shop. It's fun."

"I brought you something from Texas. I thought they were cute . . . its earrings with a star hanging at the bottom. See the star. That's a Texas star. I got some too; we can get us matching outfits and go to the movies, and meet some boys."

"Thanks, they are cute."

"Here, put them on."

"Yeah, I like them. Thanks."

"Girl, do they have cowboys here? I want to meet some cowboys."

"In the country, there are whole towns full of cowboys. We can go to a rodeo this summer. Uncle Charlie knows everything that goes on around here. He'll take us to a rodeo. But why you like cowboys, Dee?"

Uncle Charlie let us catch up with each other before he started giving us our duties.

"Now, I think we're going to split the room in half. Marianne, you take the right, Dee, take the left and you keep the counter too. Marianne, since Dee won't be here that long, let her wait on the counter. I know you get your tips there. But she's here only three months . . . when she's gone, you'll get it back. Any questions? Good, now take care of those customers. They're ready to order."

* * * * *

Since Patricia's been pregnant, Ms Shirley was sticking close. Shirley already agreed to babysit for Pat. Shirley's so excited about the baby, she's happier than anybody, humming baby songs. She's been shopping, thinking of names. Whatever Pat needs for the baby, Ms. Shirley has already gotten it. Shirley started long before Pat admitted she was pregnant, buying t-shirts, diapers, bottles. Ms Shirley was ready.

"Girl, you don't know how much I appreciate you. Cause, as soon as I can, I got to go back to work. Marianne is graduating in a couple of years. I want my baby's graduation to be special, I never graduated from high school, but she will. I got to make some money, you know, let it be special for Marianne. She's such a good girl. Marianne, has everything all figured out. She's not going to college. She plans on joining the military . . . the Army or the Air Force. Have you ever heard of that, a girl like her wanting to join the Army. I don't know where she gets it all. It's like she's been here before. She's so much like my momma. I won't have to worry about that girl at all."

"I know what you mean. You should have heard the

way she tried to protect you. I kept asking her everyday about you, to see if she was going to tell me that you were pregnant. Shoot, I could look at you and see you were pregnant. Honey, that girl didn't give up nothing. I mean she's smart. She kept telling me to ask you, with her smart mouth. I wouldn't mind if she was my little girl. She's going to be something big one day."

"Marianne didn't tell you that I was pregnant?"

"Naw, that girl is like glue. Her lips are sealed tight."

"She's just like momma, isn't she."

"Just like Maxine, all over again."

* * * * *

Lonnie's been walking around the house like a shadow. He hasn't had much to say. It's like he's afraid he might break something. So he moves delicately, making sure Patricia don't need anything. He's not the same man at home.

Now at the gambling house, it's a different story. He's loud, he's proud, and he struts around like a rooster . . . happy that he's made a baby.

"Razz man, I think I'll marry her before this baby comes."

"Well you better hurry up."

"I know I'd better hurry up. You ain't telling me nothing I don't already know. That baby is going to be here any minute. Man I can't believe it. But ain't no baby of mine coming in this world illegitimate. What do you think of this ring, man? You think she'll like this rock? "

"Man, that's it. What did you do? You rob somebody? Where'd you get the money to buy something like that?"

"Believe it or not Razz, I got some things up my sleeve too. You ain't the only man in town with a little something going on. You'd be surprised about me. Seriously . . . I got family in North Carolina and I got a little money stashed if I need it. When Marianne goes to college, I'll probably move Pat

38

and the baby there, around my folks.

"Why's that, Lonnie?"

"My folks will help her with the baby. Patricia don't know much about caring for a baby. You should hear her, Razz. She's scared, man." Lonnie laughed. "Ms Maxine raised Marianne."

"Man, don't feed me that bull. She's a woman ain't she? That stuff comes natural."

"Not for Pat, Razz. She's really scared. Anyway, I want Patricia to meet my auntie and I got some first cousins that I grew up with, they're' all like brothers and sisters to me. Right now they don't believe that's my baby coming, so I want them to meet my lady. Yeah, in case something happens to me, I don't want any trouble with my property around there."

"Lonnie, now you're going to break Shirley's heart. Patricia is like her sister. That's her only family outside of Clarence."

"Shit man, I get tired of coming home with everybody at our house, in our business. Hell, Shirley is the main one."

"What's wrong with you? Pat can't have friends." Razz grabbed a towel and started wiping down the bar.

"Patricia is my ole lady and she don't need all those folks all over her, especially when the baby comes."

"Shut up Lonnie. You're gone to work all day, you're here all night; you ought to be glad Shirley looking after her."

"After the baby comes, I'll take her home to my family, let them help her. If she wants, she can stop working, too. It'll be easier in North Carolina."

"Man, Patricia ain't gonna move with you in the country, around those country folk and you shouldn't be asking her."

"Razz, if the post office will transfer the janitor, then we're skipping town."

"What you going to do, take her to the courthouse to

marry her?"

"I talked with Rev. Williams; he said he'll do it before the baby comes. I'm thinking this weekend sometime . . . or maybe next weekend. We can sign the papers and let the preacher marry us. I'll just have to wait till Marianne graduate before we move home to North Carolina."

"You know me and Patricia were school mates. I think she's a year or two older than me, but she was always a good girl. Some old funky stuff happened with one of those teachers, she got pregnant with Marianne. They never talked about it, but that teacher got taught a lesson, a real hard lesson. We never heard anything else from that dude."

"Man, I heard something about that. I never asked Patricia. So, what happened, Razz."

"It wasn't good, Lonnie. You don't want to know. Take care of Pat man, she deserves it. I've never heard her badmouth anybody. That's just the way she is. I wish you the best man."

"Thanks Razz, let me get on to work. It's getting late. I'll see you tonight. I'll stop by after work."

* * * * *

Ms. Shirley was home alone, working around the house. Clarence started staying out again. He goes through spells where he won't come home for nights at a time. She used to be jealous, go looking for him and fight him wherever she found him. She'd take his car so he wouldn't have a way home. Once she had planned on killing him, but decided not to, who would take care of her like Clarence. She wasn't the beautiful little bride anymore. She's gotten a few rolls around the middle, she's lost a few teeth, so now, she just let it go; he'll be back. He'll stay home for over a year or more; then out of the clear blue sky, he'll stay out all night for a few months. She was used to it.

After so long, it didn't bother her as long as he brings

home the money, Ms Shirley wasn't going to worry about it. Since she married Clarence, she has never had to work. Clarence has given her everything she ever wanted, including a brand new Deuce and Quarter. Sometimes she welcomed another woman, so Clarence wouldn't bother her so much.

Ms Shirley was bored; she cooked a big meal, and had nobody to eat with her. She was waiting to hear from Patricia. Usually they'd talk sometime during the day, but today, she hadn't heard a peep out of Pat.

"I guess I'll just go on over there. Lonnie doesn't come home for a few more hours, and Marianne is working late tonight. I don't know why she won't answer her phone. I sure hate to wake her up if she's sleep. I want her to eat some of these greens I cooked . . . Pat Pat (knock knock knock) Pat, girl wake up. Get your butt up and open this door. I got some greens for you." Ms. Shirley, went around the back to see if the back door was opened only to find that is was securely locked too. She had known for years where they kept a spare key.

"Patricia, it's me. I got some greens for you . . .open this door girl." (Bam . . .bam) Ms Shirley continued to talk to herself; she was reaching under the backstairs for the extra set of keys that's stashed behind the second step.

"Oh shit, Patricia, . . .dang, I hope I don't touch no worms up under here. . .If you don't open this door Pat, I got to come in. I know you're not sleeping this damn hard, where you don't hear me knocking on this door like this. (Knock . . . knock) Pat, it's me, Shirley. I brought you some greens, girl."

Ms Shirley opened the back door and continued to walk though the kitchen, she went down the hallway headed toward Patricia's room. Shirley continued looking, she opened the bathroom door, poked her head inside, while giving an excuse for coming in the house.

"You didn't open the door, so I had to come on in and check on you."

41

Pat laid still. She hadn't acknowledged Shirley was in the house, yet.

"Patricia, are you alright?" Shirley sat the plate of greens on the highboy dresser, then moved closer. "Pat, girl, what's wrong with you? Didn't you hear me calling you?" She started shaking Pat. "Wake up, wake up sweetheart." Shirley continued to shake Pat, softly at first, then she starting shaking her harder and harder, but it wasn't a hint of life in Patricia Robinson.

"Patricia . . . Patricia, baby, are you okay? Wake up for Ms. Shirley. Oh My God. Patricia, sweetheart, can you hear me. Oh my goodness. AAAAHHH! Help . . . Help! Help me Lord! Oh Jesus."

Ms. Shirley was in high gear. She immediately dialed zero for the operator.

"Hello, this is the operator. What's your emergency?"

"Operator, Operator, We need the ambulance, I've got an emergency. Send the ambulance to 2117 Vine Street. Hurry, please hurry. I don't know if she's breathing. I have a pregnant woman here that's not breathing. I don't know if she's alive. Lord, I need some help. I need help right now. Oh Lordy. Please hurry."

"Ma'am, there's an ambulance on the way. What's the name of the patient?"

"Her name is Patricia Robinson."

"Are you a member of the family?"

"No ma'am, I'm not. I'm her next door neighbor. She's pregnant and I just came by to check on her. I found her like this, like she was just sleeping in bed. She didn't answer, so I came on in the house. I just found her like this. Lordy, Lordy . . . she's pregnant."

Just then there was a knock on the door. Ms. Shirley opened the door and motioned the men from the ambulance to come in and go to the first room on the right. They worked on

42

Patricia, giving her mouth to mouth, resuscitation, listening for a heartbeat, feeling for her pulse, before transporting her to Kansas City Memorial Hospital.

The men from the ambulance seemed focused and weren't paying much attention to Ms. Shirley or the crowd of onlookers that grew in front of the house. Everybody stood like statues on the lawn, watching and whispering with each other. Trying to figure out what was happening with their beloved neighbor. You could hear some of the talk . . . questions about her health . . . the fact that she was pregnant. She was too sickly to carry the baby. The medical team carefully carted Patricia Robinson into the ambulance. Ms. Shirley watched closely, making sure they weren't covering her head with the sheet that was draped over her body.

Razz heard the news about Patricia. People were coming in, eyes wet full of tears, summing up different accounts of what happened but all accounts ended the same.

"Mr. Charlie, hey man, this is Razz. Isn't that Pat Robinsons' little girl working for you, waiting tables?"

"Yeah man, What about her?

"Is she there tonight?"

"Yeah man, why you asking about little Marianne? She's been working for me a while now. Why you ask?"

"I didn't know if you've heard or not, but there's some kind of emergency over at her place. It's a mess over there. The ambulance and the police are all over the place. Send her on home, man. She still lives in Ms. Maxine's old house, don't she?"

"Yeah, that's the place. You say something is going on over there?"

"Man, you better take her on home. I heard it wasn't good. That's Lonnie Evans's old lady. I just sent somebody downtown to get him. It's bad, man. I think they took Pat over to Kansas Memorial. Charlie, I heard she didn't make it. It's just rumors, man, but that's what I heard."

Uncle Charlie hung up the phone. He was rubbing his forehead trying to figure out the best way to break it to Marianne, at least, he wanted her calm until they got to the hospital. Marianne and her momma are so close.

"Rosie, honey, get your purse. We're gonna close shop. That was Razz on the phone. He said, they rushed Pat Robinson to the hospital, said she was at Kansas City Memorial. Get Dee and Marianne, tell them to get in the car."

"Why . . . what's wrong, Charlie. I hope everything's alright with her and that baby. Did he say what was wrong? Is the baby alright?"

Uncle Charlie could barely speak. His voice quivered. "Rosie, they said she didn't make it."

Chapter 4

In a dreamlike state, Marianne floated toward the hospital room. It wasn't real. She couldn't drum up the right feelings, it wasn't real. But somehow Marianne knew that this was it. The most dreadful experience she'll ever face in her life.

"How much farther?" she whispered to Uncle Charlie.

The whole atmosphere of the hospital felt dreary. All the nurses were dressed in white, wearing their white nurse hats. They looked serious. The hospital smelled like disinfectant.

Uncle Charlie asked one of the nurses, again, where was Patricia Robinson. A nurse pointed them to the right room. Marianne looked around hoping to find a good sign, there wasn't any. The nurses conveniently looked off, trying to appear busy, not wanting to give any signals to the family before the doctor had a chance to talk with them. Was she ever going to get to the room? Finally, the last room in the corridor showed the name Patricia M. Robinson.

Marianne was shocked when she saw the severity of the situation. Her mother laid there motionless and speechless. She looked swollen. Her skin looked shiny like plastic. Machines and tubes were connected everywhere. She looked at the monitor and saw what she only heard about. It was a flat line. But her mother was breathing, her chest moved up and down. Why was there a flat line beeping on the monitor? This was the first time her mother didn't acknowledge her or make some sort of gesture that she was there, in her presence.

"Momma . . . Momma. Can you hear me?" Marianne couldn't believe what she was seeing. "Uncle Charlie, what's wrong with my momma. Look at her! Look at my momma. What happened to her?" Without waiting for an answer, Marianne screamed, "Mommmmmmmmmmmma, Mommmmm!

Marianne was devastated. She couldn't believe it, she couldn't talk. She looked for help. Her eyes were silently pleading for help. She needed a miracle. Marianne and her mother weren't the church type. They believed in treating people right, doing good. She believed in God, but they never asked for anything. Where to start? What would she say? How do you ask for help? Now she needed Him to bring her back? She needed to pray hard. Before this night, she never even talked to God.

"Oh God, help me please. I don't know what to do." Marianne finally whimpered.

Uncle Charlie held Marianne up, keeping her from collapsing to the floor. She couldn't walk without his help. Seeing her mother hooked up with tubes and monitors that only revealed a flat line. But, the machines continued to pump, as if there was a sign of hope. A nurse stopped when she heard the crying and commotion, she stood outside the room and listened intently, just in case she was needed. The nurse listened to Marianne begging, crying and praying.

"This poor child!" She couldn't take it any longer. The nurse slowly entered the room. "She's gone. That's your mother?" The nurse nodded and didn't wait for an answer. "Honey, I'm so sorry but she's gone. Dr. Clark is here, he'll be in to talk with you."

Dr. Clark eyes were blood red and moist when he entered the hospital room. He couldn't look at Marianne without breaking down himself. Lying there, dead, was his friend since high school. He thought about Patricia Robinson such a beautiful, classy person. All her life she was nice and sweet, now she's gone. When they were young, he was a little sweet on Patricia, himself; but that was before everything happened.

"Dr. Clark, she's moving. She's going to be alright isn't she? I saw her move. You saw her move Uncle Charlie, didn't you?" Dee was pleading for her friend that wasn't able speak; Dee said what everybody else was thinking.

46

"Sweetheart, let the doctor talk." Ms. Rosie finally spoke through quiet tears.

"Marianne, I want you to understand that your mother is dead. The movement is just the body's nerves that haven't closed down yet . . . and that'll soon end. She has no brain activity so she's not alive, sweetheart. You understand?" Dr. Clark didn't wait on an answer. "We're keeping her body artificially supported until after the surgery. She went into a diabetic coma and just slipped away. I'm hoping the baby didn't suffer any damage. I feel we got to her in time to save the baby. The baby's receiving oxygen and water. I heard a strong heartbeat. I believe the baby will be just fine, and there's every indication that it'll be healthy. After the delivery, I'll pronounce her dead . . . so now, I'll give you some time to spend with your mother." Dr. Clark looked at Uncle Charlie. "Let me know when I can come get her."

Uncle Charlie, Ms. Rosie and Dee left the room to give Marianne some privacy. Dee was crying hard. Marianne couldn't believe what just happened.

"Mom, what is happening? What happened to you? I thought you were doing better. This is crazy. How did you just die like that . . . I need you. What am I gonna do now? Please don't leave me. Not now, momma. You were doing so good. I don't know what happened."

Marianne started crying hysterically. Her head lying on her mother's chest. "You're leaving me momma, what am I going to do without you? Who's going to take care of me? Why God is this happening to my momma? I should have been there for you, momma. I should have stayed home. You were sick and you needed me, I wasn't there. I didn't know. You needed me and I didn't know. Oh momma, I'm sorry. I'm so sorry."

Then Marianne heard her mother's voice. "Marianne, take care of your brother."

Marianne's heart stopped. Her mouth dropped opened but nothing came out. She held her head up to look again at her mother to see that nothing had changed. Patricia Robinson still laid motionless, with machines pushing her chest in and out.

Marianne whispered, "Mom, what was that? Was that you? Did you say something?" Not waiting on an answer, she laid back on her mother's chest, almost crawling in bed with Patricia. "I heard you, momma . . . I heard you. Okay momma, I love you, momma. I'll take care of him. I promise."

Although Marianne clearly heard her mother's voice, she still couldn't believe what she heard. She looked at Patricia's motionless body . . . machines continued doing its job of pumping her chest up and down.

"What was that? Momma was that you, for real?" Marianne questioned her mind or sanity . . . was it real? Did she really hear her mother's voice? Marianne's tears came to a halt as she watched her mother . . . waiting to hear from her again. Hoping to hear from her . . . just one more time.

Lonnie came running down the hall. His eyes were wild and furious. He stopped before entering the room. Lonnie grabbed his head. "No . . . no . . . no." He made a quick turn, as if he needed more time before entering Patricia's room, then he came back and saw her. Lonnie was almost screaming.

"What in the world . . . Patricia? What the hell happened to you? Oh My God!" Lonnie was in shock when he saw the severity of the situation. "Aaaaawh baby, naw naw, baby". Lonnie stopped in front of the bed and stomped every word. "DON'T . . . LEAVE . . . ME!" He growled between his teeth. "Baby, I had plans for us. Aaaawh Pat, . . . sweetheart." Lonnie grabbed Pat, picking her up from the bed, disregarding all the tubes that were connected to Patricia's body. "I don't want to live without you. Oh God, please, not this. . . .come back to me, baby. NO . . . NO!" Lonnie fell in the chair and cried uncontrollably. He didn't care about

48

anything anymore. His love, his life, the only woman to ever care anything for him, the one that truly loved him, unconditionally, was gone forever, and he was sure real love would never come his way again.

Marianne watched Lonnie for a while. She wanted to jump on his head and beat and beat Lonnie Evans. She wanted to scream at him to get out of the room. She blamed him for getting her mother pregnant; the pregnancy that killed her. She wanted to beat Lonnie's head into the floor.

She thought to herself, "Look at him . . . just look at him. He finally got his way. He took my mother from me. I hate his guts. I wish he would die." She couldn't take it anymore, seeing him crying over her, touching her. "It's his fault." Marianne said good bye to her mother then quietly left the room.

It wasn't long before the aides came to wheel Patricia's body into surgery. Marianne couldn't help but think about what she heard. It was real. She heard her mother's voice. "Marianne, take care of your brother."

Time seem to stand still, no feelings of anticipation for the baby, no kind of joy or worry. They waited without thought. It wasn't long before Dr. Clark came to tell them about the baby that was just delivered.

"Everything seems to be good. The baby looks healthy, nothing's missing."

Lonnie asked with little interest, "So what is it?"

Before the doctor could answer, Marianne spoke up, "It's a boy, and his name is Patrick."

Uncle Charlie decided not to question Marianne. How did she know that?

"We'll want to keep the baby, . . .uh, Patrick, here for a few days for observation, but everything looks normal." Dr. Clark gave Marianne a little hug, then walked away. Silently Dr. Clark made peace and prayed for Patricia Robinson

49

"Goodbye Pat, darling. You always were a good person. I'm gonna miss you. There was a time when I wanted you myself. Say hi to Maxine up there . . . Poor Marianne, what's she gonna do without her mother? I'll check on her and make sure she and Patrick are alright. I can't believe you're gone. Well at least we were able to save the baby . . . Lord, I tried to get her to take better care of herself. She wouldn't listen. Now she's with you Lord."

"Dr. Clark, Dr. Clark, can we see him. Can we see the baby?" Dee was running to catch him before he made it to the elevator.

"Sure, I'll have a nurse come get you when he's ready."

Marianne sat down with Uncle Charlie. She didn't want to see little Patrick. It's his fault. She was mad. She didn't know who she was more angry with; Lonnie for getting her momma pregnant or Lil Patrick, her baby brother. She didn't care for either one of them.

Uncle Charlie rocked Marianne as they sat quietly. He had his arms around her in a reassuring way. He wanted to give her a little security. He wanted to talk with her. Of course, this wasn't the time or place. But he decided he would help Marianne. She and little Patrick could live with him and Rosie.

Lonnie didn't say anything to anybody when he left the hospital.

It was a clear, beautiful summer night, with a cool breeze. The sky was sparkling. The parking lot was empty, so Lonnie talked to himself.

"I had plans for us, girl. I bought you a ring. I think you would have liked this. What am I going to do with it? How in the world am I ever going to find someone like you? I'm old. Hell, when I was young, I never had anybody like you. Patricia, girl . . . I love you. Can you hear me, baby?" Lonnie repeated it a little louder, "I love you, Pat . . . I wanted to take care of you. I would have made you happy. All I ever wanted

50

in life was you." Then he whispered, "Now you're gone. How in the hell you gonna leave me like that."

As he continued walking outside, he looked around for his car. He noticed a young family rushing toward the emergency room. He thought to himself, "I hope they're alright," then he continued walking along the sidewalk, toward his car, he finally said what he didn't want to admit.

"I don't want to see the little motherfucker. I don't care if I never see his fucking ass. He took my Patricia from me. We didn't need no damn baby." Lonnie kicked at the air, got in the car, then raced to Razz's to get drunk.

"Man, she's gone. Can you believe that shit? Just like that." Lonnie wiped his eyes. "You never know do you? You never know how long you got with somebody, you never know. Razz, man . . . I loved her. She didn't know about my plans. I wanted to surprise her . . . I have a ring, you saw it. I showed it to you, didn't I? Damnit, we were almost there. Life's not fair. Man, just when you think you got everything figured out, you get hit with a curve ball, that'll make everything that you've been working for worthless man. It'll make everything worthless."

Lonnie pulled out the big diamond ring he was going to give his bride- to- be. "What am I going to do with this now? Yeah, I was going to surprise my baby." Lonnie smiled just thinking how happy Pat would have been. "You know Razz, I was going to be a good husband. I wish I would have married her. She was mine." Lonnie was hitting his chest. "Mine! She was my wife."

"Here, Lonnie, have a drink on me."

"Thanks man."

Razz poured Lonnie a big glass of scotch, then moved to the other customers. Lonnie, wanted to drink in peace. Lots of the regular gamblers were there, whispering. Razz was just telling them how Lonnie bought the ring and had wedding

51

arrangements all planned. Everybody understood.

Every now and then when his glass was getting low, somebody would send the waitress over with another glass of straight scotch and a big glass of ice water. Lonnie decided to move to the darkest corner of the club so he could finish getting drunk. It was never this hard to get drunk before. So he drank and drank all night long.

* * * * *

Marianne, Dee, Ms. Rosie and Uncle Charlie were visiting little Patrick. Marianne watched her little brother, trying to stir up some kind of affection for him, but there was none. He was just another baby.

"He's a cute little fella." Ms. Rosie was in love at first sight. Lil Patrick was a sandy golden baby, with sandy curly hair that's the same color as his skin. He had one dimple on his right cheek, just like Patricia's. His eyes were wide open. He was looking around, cooing, sporting that dimple.

Ms. Rosie couldn't keep the excitement from her voice. "Look at him, Charlie. He's looking around smiling at us. Oh Charlie, like he knows us or something. Hi Lil Patrick. Hi little fellow . . . oh my goodness. He's laughing. Oh he's a smart boy."

"He looks just like your mother, Marianne, only he's light skinned. He sure is cute huh, Aunt Rosie. He's sooo cute." Dee confirmed Ms Rosie's thoughts.

Marianne wondered where, what, and how were they going to live. All she knew was they were going to be alright, she would take care of Patrick. She'll never forget her mother's voice, telling her to take care of her brother. Marianne swore in her heart that she would honor her mother's wishes. Somehow.

The funeral came so fast. Thankfully Ms. Shirley was available, and she stepped right up without a second's thought.

The program had a beautiful picture of Patricia Robinson's portrait. She looked like a movie star; her shoulders

52

were out with white mink draped around her arms and chest. It looked like a painting. The funeral service was held at the corner church. Rev. Williams was the presiding minister over the ceremony. Lonnie asked that we use Rev. Williams. In fact, he was adamant about using him. Marianne didn't mind. She didn't know one preacher from another.

Ms. Shirley had been our neighbor for over thirty years. She remembered my mom when she was in elementary school. Come to find out, she remembers when I was born. She must know my father, I never found out about him, or his side of the family. There's not a picture or anything. I understood not to ask, it didn't keep me from wondering or hoping that my father would come. Now that my mother is gone, he would somehow find compassion and want me with him. I daydreamed of seeing him. Somebody would introduce us . . . then tell me "This is your daddy." Then he would come to my rescue. But nothing happened.

Everybody was there. The whole block showed up. For some reason, it was a bigger funeral than my grandmother's funeral. The school workers and teachers gave tribute to my mom. I thought that was nice. There was so much food that it fed the whole neighborhood all week long before the funeral services ever started. Everybody came by with their condolences, then they fixed them a plate of food.

Patrick was dressed in a white laced gown. Ms. Shirley had been keeping him, taking care of Patrick since we brought him home. It's funny, Patrick didn't make a sound through the whole service. I thought he would cry at some point, but he didn't. Every time I looked his way, his little eyes were glued at me. He looked sad, like I felt. Whenever he wasn't smiling, he looked like Lonnie. Whenever he laughed or cooed, he looked like my mother, then my heart would melt seeing his little dimple like my momma's. What are we going to do?

My mother had an insurance policy that paid for

everything. I had money left over. Uncle Charlie handled paying the bills for the funeral and he talked with the insurance people for me. He told me we would talk about our future once everything settled down. So I didn't worry about the money, our house, or Lonnie. I was so hurt, I couldn't.

Lonnie looked sick. He was smaller than normal. I felt sorry for him. Lonnie looked more broke down than usual. Dang Lonnie.

"Little girl, you alright?"

"Yeah."

"Take care of your brother. I'm leaving town." Lonnie took Marianne hand and put a little box that contained a diamond ring in her hand, securing her fingers around the box so hard, that it hurt. "I think she would want you to have this. Nobody deserves my baby's ring but her. I can't bare to think somebody else having it. I know I didn't give her much, but I had plans for Patricia. I wanted to ask you if you thought she would like this ring, but I was afraid you wouldn't want me to marry your mother, so I didn't say anything. Hey, Marianne, I can't take this. I can't stay. If you ever need anything. Call this number."

"What? What do you mean. Where are you going?"

Lonnie never answered the question. He walked away. He didn't attend the burial.

"Where's he going. He's not going to the grave site." Ms Rosie was asking, me or Uncle Charlie, anybody that would answer. Nobody did.

Chapter 5

Uncle Charlie and Ms Rosie were disappointed when me and Patrick didn't move in with them. They took for granted we would move in their house and be the children and family that they always wanted.

"Now Marianne, I think it would be better for you to stay here. Rosie and I can watch the baby while you to go to school. There ain't no reason why you should let this opportunity slip by you, girl. You need to think about it. Hell, my Rosie loves that baby. I can make sure you get your education. You'll get a good education; you'll go to the best college. I'll make sure of it. Baby, these days, girls have to get an education just like boys. We can rent those rooms out and put that money in some kind of savings for you and Patrick. Me and Rose don't need anything, we don't have any children, you've always been like family to us. Me and your grandma were good friends, I watched your momma grow up, then you, we'll be happy to have you staying here with us." Ms. Rosie was in tears when I declined their offer.

"Uncle Charlie, I don't want to live in your house. I want to live in my house. I want to stay in my own room. My grandma left me that room. I can't leave my house. Me and Patrick can sleep in my room together. It's so big. I can rent the rooms out again. Before Lonnie moved in and started messing with my momma, we used to have good renters. Then he made them all leave. They'll come back. We were all family when grandma was alive."

"Baby, you're not thinking straight. How you gonna run a rent house? Do you know what kind of people rent places like that? I'm not saying this place is bad or anything. It's a nice place, but you got all kinds of upkeep, and bills, sometimes people don't have money to pay their rent. You gonna have all kinds of problems. Hell, you might have to put somebody out on the street. You think that's easy, well, it ain't."

"Can I keep my job here at the restaurant?"

"Yes, baby, sure you can. But there's all kinds of bills and problems that come from taking care of property. There's taxes that got to be paid, can you handle that? I'm just trying to make you understand."

"I understand, Uncle Charlie . . . I want to stay in my room. I can't leave my house." Marianne started to cry. This was her home. She had already lost everything else and leaving her house was the last straw. "I just want to stay in my own room. Me and Patrick will be okay." Hot tears streamed down her young cheeks, but determination and strength reflected through her eyes.

"I'll tell you what, you and Patrick stay there. Give it a try, see what it's like. We'll get you some renter's again. Yeah, we're gonna make sure you get some decent folks in there. You don't want none of those crazy guys from Vietnam staying here. They're coming back from the war crazy as hell. They're on heroin and everything else. Naw . . .naw . . . we're gonna stay away from them. If you need anything, just let me know. Me and Rosie will be here, if you need us. All you got to do is let me know. We'll take care of it. Okay . . . Okay?"

Marianne nodded and tried to smile.

"Girl, you're a hard one . . . just like you're grandma, Maxine."

Uncle Charlie was fast on the job of getting renters at Maxine's old house. A rent sign was up before Marianne made it to work that day. "Man, he works fast." She was so glad to have a job. She and Patrick were going to receive a social security check every month. She never knew about that, but Ms. Shirley was on top of getting everything started. The checks weren't that much, but it helped. With the renters ready to move in, and her job at Uncle Charlie's Que House, Marianne felt safe. Things were going to be alright.

56

Ms. Shirley and Ms. Rosie fussed over Patrick sooooo much . . . Oh my God, he couldn't let out a good sniffle without one of them running to his rescue. Ms. Rosie decided to teach Marianne how to make her famous potato salad, macaroni and cheese, and cole slaw. She taught her to bake cakes. Marianne was eager to do it just like Ms. Rosie. If Ms. Rosie was going to stay at Marianne's house taking care of Patrick, then Marianne was definitely going to pull her weight at the restaurant. She gave Marianne her famous sweet potato pie recipe too. Ms. Rosie didn't mind.

"Ms. Rosie, you make the best sweet potato pie in the world. Everybody says it."

Ms Rosie just smiled. She knew exactly what everybody said about her sweet potato pie. In fact Ms. Rosie was surprised nobody ever tried making it before. She just mixed a pecan pie and a sweet potato pie together. The pecan topping and the sweet potato filling were a natural together. Over the holidays, Ms. Rosie made over a hundred of her specialty pies.

Before he knew it, Uncle Charlie was explaining to Marianne how he needed to have all restaurant receipts together in numerical order, when the utilities bills were due and she was told about ordering supplies. He was shocked that she grasped the concepts of checks and balances so fast. Surprisingly, he felt comfortable knowing she had all the information and was taking notes. She was a natural and he was satisfied.

* * * * *

It was almost time for Dee to go back to Texas. Dee had already decided she was going to stay in Kansas. She was used to getting her way with Aunt Rosie and Uncle Charlie.

"If Marianne can live by herself, then I know I can live with her. She ain't grown either. Uncle Charlie will do anything Aunt Rosie says and Aunt Rosie will do anything I ask". Dee worked everything out. Everything out.

"Uncle Charlie, I'm gonna stay here and go to school, I'm not ready to leave. I want to stay here with Marianne and help take care of Patrick. I can work and babysit too. Anyway, Texas is sooooo bad. The teachers beat you, the kids are always fighting, I can't go there. They're mean to me Uncle Charlie. They think cause I'm half Mexican, I'm not supposed to be treated right." Dee started to cry. "All those white people treat me bad. The colored girls jump on me and the Mexicans say that I ain't one of them. So I'm gonna stay here where I belong. I want to stay here, Uncle Charlie. I can go to school with Marianne. I can work here. I promise to get good grades and be a good girl. I'll work hard, Uncle Charlie."

"Baby, now, your mother isn't going to let you stay here. Who's going to help her with your little sister and brother?"

"Uncle Charlie, my mother don't care. She sleeps all day, she won't know I'm missing."

"Dee, don't say that about your mother. You know better. She tries hard. She's my wife's niece, and I'm sure she loves you very much and cares about what you do. You ought to be ashamed of yourself saying something like that 'bout your momma."

"I'm telling the truth, Uncle Charlie. She thinks her boyfriend likes me anyway. She'll be glad to get rid of me. Uncle Charlie, I've never told anybody, but her boyfriend, Buddy tried to kiss me. I had to fight him. I'm scared he will make me do other things . . . if I go back there to Texas, ain't no telling what might happen to me. My mother don't believe me so I can't tell her about Buddy. She believes him and not me."

Dee was squinting and batting her eyes, finally a tear slipped out. She grabbed Uncle Charlie's hand and held it to her face. "Uncle Charlie, I can stay with Marianne at her house." Dee's accent got very thick. "I can help you around here. You'll be surprised how good I can help." Dee stood up

58

and moved closer to Uncle Charlie. She continued to hold his hand then moved it across her breast. She was looking deep into Uncle Charlie's eyes and continued to hold his hand over her breast.

"Sit down, sit down Uncle Charlie. Let me show you something." Dee forced Uncle Charlie into the chair and began to sit in his lap. Uncle Charlie had his hands at her waist not allowing her to completely rest in his lap, but she was forcing and turning her hips, so that she finally got in the position where she could feel her butt between his legs . . . she could feel his penis move. He was right where she wanted him to be.

"Ummmm Uncle Charlie, I like what that feels like."

"Naw . . . naw . . . naaawh!" Uncle Charlie forced Dee over, shifting her, but she didn't get up.

"Uncle Charlie, my mother is a little jealous of me. She brings all those guys over all the time, then she gets jealous cause they look at me. Do you think I'm pretty?"

"What? Wait a minute. What'd you say?"

"Do you think I'm pretty? They say I'm very pretty." Dee's voice was low and her accent very heavy.

"I think you're a little girl. You're a little fast girl."

"You'll be surprised what a little girl like me can do. I can make you very happy. I can help you out better than anybody." Dee wiggled, arched her back, then motioned her butt harder in a circular motion while in Uncle Charlie's lap.

"Dee, let me tell you something." Uncle Charlie grabbed a tender spot on Dee's inner thigh then began to twist and pinch her hard. He wanted to make sure he left a bruise where she would remember their conversation.

"You are my wife's grandniece, you are sixteen years old. There's nothing I need from you. Do you understand? If we ever have this conversation again, I will never allow you to come back here. Do you understand, little girl. Next year, you stay in Texas." Uncle Charlie gave Dee a hard push, she landed on the floor. He slapped her upside the head. "Girl, I ought to whip you. That's what you need, a good whipping. You ought to be ashamed of yourself, as much as your Aunt Rosie loves you. You go home tomorrow. I don't want to look at you."

* * * * *

I was lucky to get two of our old renters back. Mr. Jeffrey White and Pali Tyson shared a room together. I gave them Lonnie's old room, so they're upstairs next to me and Patrick. Mr. White is a doorman at the Amador Hotel. He's a really good looking guy. I think a lot of women hate Mr. White because he'd rather be with Pali then one of them women. Mr. White is tall, dark and handsome. He speaks perfect English and loves to show off his beautiful teeth when he pronounces each syllable. His clothes are tailored, fitting him perfectly. He keeps his fingernails manicured and his hair is never out of place. The shoeshine man, Blackie Nelson, has a stand inside the hotel where Mr. White gets a shine every day and Mr. White is very picky about his shoes.

The white folk at the Amador Hotel loves Mr. White. He has a big reputation when it comes to hotel business, because he knows all the good clean white women. The white women tip him good too for giving them a good recommendation. I heard he takes care of all the special needs too. He said sometimes those folk like strange stuff. All the high dollar white girls that come to the Amador have to be approved by Mr. White. No colored girls are approved unless they are maids or cooks. Mr. White said that was fine by him. Mr. White makes a lot of money off those working girls.

Pali is a cook. He wears his white uniforms and his chef hats. He loves running the kitchen at the Amador. Very seldom have I seen Pali out of his uniform. Then he wears slacks and turtlenecks. His shirts and pants are the exact color, too. It must have taken a lot of time finding exact colors like that. His hair is in a conk, but you never see it, cause he keeps a scarf tied

60

around it.

Pali is more sensitive than Mr. White. When that movie, "Imitation of Life" came out; Pali must have cried a week straight. Pali and Mr. White have lived together close to twenty years. They've worked together even longer. They lived here when my grandma Maxine was alive. Lonnie made sure he got rid of them first.

My grandma loved Mr. White and Pali. She never let anybody talk about them in our house. She always said they're money is green just like everybody else's and they were on time with rent. They were a big help in keeping everything clean too.

Once grandma died, people started mistreating Pali and Mr. White. They couldn't leave the house, except to go to work. Finally they moved into a room at the Amador. Thankfully, it's under new management and now they can't stay there any longer. I was sure glad when Mr. White called. He was right on time. I'm happy to have them back with me. It's like my family is coming home.

Billy Joe Washington moved in downstairs. He moved into my mother's old room. He was a really good guy, like a big teddy bear. Billy Joe is always smiling. He's a gambler that just came home from Vietnam. He doesn't try to be flashy. Most of time, he wears bell bottom jeans and a white cotton shirt that must have been starched with cement.

He smells good. I love the way Billy Joe smells. That's that Old Spice cologne that he splashes everywhere. I was glad he moved in. We were protected. Nobody was going to break in, or talk bad . . . noooo, no! Not with Billy Joe living in the house. He wasn't crazy at all, he was fun. Billy Joe wanted to eat a different meal every day, so he bought lots of groceries. Between Ms. Shirley, Pali and Rosie, we always had a good meal cooked.

Clarence, Ms Shirley's husband comes over to our

house for dinner. He teased that Patrick had taken his wife from him. I think Clarence loves Patrick just like everybody else. I'd come home from work to find Clarence and Patrick in the recliner chair knocked out. Clarence would be snoring, Patrick flopped in his lap, fast asleep with the TV blasting. Ms. Shirley would say, "Leave'em alone. Let'em sleep."

Then Darlene Anderson grabbed the last room that was downstairs next to Billy. It worked out good because we couldn't hear them when they came home from Razz's, and Darlene had protection getting off work so late at night.

She was pretty . . . she was very pretty. Darlene was a waitress at Razz's. She went to school to be a nurse during the day and worked at night at the club. She was always telling me not to get stuck on no boys, get your education, girl.

"When it all comes down to it, Marianne, you got to have your own money. Soon as a man start spending money on you, he thinks he owns you and can tell you what to do. My nanna always told me,

"If you don't like the man, leave his money alone."

I want my own money. Girl, these guys will tell you anything to get in your pants. Don't let em. They'll pay you, if you let'em . . . will give you all their damn money, if they want it bad enough. Keep your panties on, girl. Then when the right one comes, you'll be ready."

"How old are you, Darlene?" I always wondered because she barely looked older than me.

"I'm 20. Why you asked?"

"I don't know. You look so young, but you act old."

Darlene couldn't help but smile. "That's because where I come from, in New York, a girl grows up fast. I just had a good grandma that told me the right things to do. She told me about men. Girl, it's a cold world. People will use you up. So as long as you got your own, then nobody can take advantage of you. Always have your own. You're a smart girl, you'll be

62

alright."

Marianne thought about Darlene. She watched her work hard, getting off work early in the morning, then going to school. If she was lucky, she got about five hours of sleep. Every day, Darlene worked.

I got $75 per month for each room. Mr. White and Pali paid $125 per month, since it was two of them, they needed to pay more. Plus, Pali stayed in the bathroom longer than anybody in the world. Oh, they wanted to complain, said it wasn't fair, but I just told them Uncle Charlie was making the rules. It wasn't fair for two of them to pay what everybody else paid.

With my social security check and working for Uncle Charlie, I had plenty of money for me and Patrick. I decided to put my brother's checks into a savings account. If we ever needed it, for an emergency or something, then it'll be there. If nothing else, Lil Patrick would have some money saved when he's older.

I got a little white Comet to drive around with the insurance money that was left from the funeral expense. I was glad that my mom had the chance to teach me to drive before she died. It was fun . . . her teaching me to drive.

Summer break had come and gone. All my friends were back in school. I tried to stay in school, but it was hard. I was now working full time at the restaurant. Uncle Charlie finally stopped talking about me going to school, or staying in school or talking about college. He was just trying to be concerned about my future. But I can't worry about that. I have Patrick to think about. So Uncle Charlie lets me work all day. I cook the side dishes, cakes, and pies. I make the deposits to the bank. Uncle Charlie was very happy to have me working with him.

Uncle Charlie's Rib House was the after school hangout. I became somewhat of a celebrity. The other kids thought it was cool that I wasn't going to school, and that I had so much control over the restaurant. They thought I was lucky to have renters at my house, so they wanted to hang out with me. I really didn't mind, but I didn't have much time to visit. The after school crowd was tiresome, we were slinging hamburgers and fries, left and right. I didn't have any time to visit or be a kid with them. I watched as some did their homework, while they enjoyed their after school get-together and music. I missed going to dances and the Prom.

Fridays are really busy. It starts early on Fridays. The jukebox was playing, some of the kids would dance in the corner. It was okay, as long as they weren't in the way of other customers. In fact, I liked watching them dance. They told me about everybody in school. Who was pregnant, who was thrown out of school for fighting. Their new classes; and what teacher was low down. I sure missed going to school, but I couldn't think about it.

I was making a good living. Uncle Charlie said I was doing good as anybody. He's been making sure I knew everything about the business. I even started writing checks to pay Victor and Calvin. I even write out my own check. I would never cheat Uncle Charlie, he's been so good to me and Patrick. I couldn't do anything to hurt him or Aunt Rosie. Shoot, Uncle Charlie wants me to take over the restaurant one day.

* * * * *

Lil Patrick is growing so fast. Seems like just yesterday when we brought him home from the hospital. Dr. Clark has been keeping an eye on Patrick's sugar levels; he personally comes by the house with his testing supplies. Poor Patrick gets stuck at least once a month. Dr. Clark said Patrick is a high risk for the disease and we need to be watching it closely.

I guess I've grown to love Lil Patrick. He seems so helpless. I couldn't let anything happen to the little fella. When he smiles, it's like my mom just entered the room, he look so much like momma. I love him. I was so angry with Patrick for so long. Somehow watching him grow and seeing my mother's smile through him, has turned it all around. Now, I love Patrick so much.

Plus, Patrick goes crazy when I come home from work. He jumps up and down, he squeals loud. Yeah, he's loud like Lonnie. And grins so hard, he's a little charmer. He does his little jig dance for me. That little guy knows how to throw his charm on, with his smart self. It's his way of flirting. He'll roll his eyes, then his head, then start laughing, throwing the charm at me hard. Now, how that little boy know how to do that? His little arms reaching for me, and man can he scream if I don't get him fast enough. He squeals.

"Hey boy, what cha doing? What cha doing? Where's your little doggy."

Clarence brought Patrick a big furry stuffed puppy that Patrick wrestles with every day. Patrick can pull up on the coffee table now. So we have to move all the glass trinkets from his reach. He crawls around so fast that we have to close all the doors so he'll stay in the living room. That boy is fast and he's growing even faster.

I guess I'm lucky to have so many people in our lives. I was a little confused at first, cause Lonnie left us. It seems to me he would have been the main person to stay and make sure we were alright. But he just left. I hadn't heard anything from him since. He gave me a telephone number, just in case I ever needed anything, but I haven't. So he can stay gone.

Chapter 6

I was now use to my routine. I get up around 6 a.m. and get dressed; then I wait for Ms. Shirley or Ms. Rosie to come over to take care of Patrick. I get to the restaurant, open the blinds and windows then start my routine. The place smells after a long night of work, man . . . I got to air it out, get rid of all the stale smoke from cigarettes and ashtrays. Plus, I need some light; you know, let the sun shine in. When it's fresh inside, I can start work.

I check the supplies early, in case I need to make a rush order with the bread man or order some soda pops; you can't run out of drinks. I told Uncle Charlie we should sell Kool-Aid and forget about soda pops, but he said he'd rather have cold cokes for his customers.

I make sure the restroom, floors and tables are presentable. Then I start the macaroni and cheese, potato salad, coleslaw, and baked beans, I make them fresh.

Uncle Charlie is there way early, waaaay before me, checking the meats and checking his famous barbeque sauce. He'll make the sauce at least once a week. He'll take half a dozen slabs of ribs, two full briskets and at least a dozen chickens outside to the smokehouse. We usually have plenty of meats already cooked from the night before. Uncle Charlie will put the leftover meat in the heater for quick lunchtime meals. The meat that Uncle Charlie puts on this morning will be ready for the lunch and the afternoon crowd. By then, Victor and Calvin will be here. They'll come around 10:00 and start the evening cooking. Everything was routine.

On Sundays we're closed. That's my shopping day. I spend that day with Patrick. I feel so sorry for him. He'll never know his mother. He'll never know how beautiful she was, and how much she loved us. I take all my tips and go to the shopping center to spend on me and my little brother. We're always getting stopped about Patrick. Everybody loves this kid.

"You really got a cute little boy. Look Doris, look at his eyes." Two ladies were walking next to us and decided to make small talk.

"He's my little brother." Nosey old ladies, they just wanted to know if this was my baby. I know I look too young to have a baby. I look a lot younger than my seventeen years. Anyway, Patrick loves the attention.

"He's really cute. How old is he?"

"He just turned 16 months. He's growing so fast." Patrick was eating up the attention. Somehow he knows when he's the center of attraction and he plays it to the letter. Patrick started pattycaking and squealing. "Maarianne!" Patrick pointed at me. "Maaarianne."

"You sure take good care of him. Where's your parents?"

Man she's nosey. "My mom died giving birth to Patrick, it's just me and him."

"Is that right?"

"How old are you?"

"I'm nineteen." I lied. Man, I got to be careful; they could try and take Patrick from me. There was something in the lady's eyes when I told her that my mom died. Her face lit up. Daaanng!.

"So, you're probably taking some classes somewhere, what school are you attending?"

"Ma'am, I got to go." I was irritated. "My Uncle is waiting for me." I hurried out of the shopping center. I couldn't believe those ladies. I didn't feel good about them at all. They made me feel scared.

I mostly bought clothes for Patrick, but I bought me an outfit to wear to the Natalie Cole concert next Saturday. Everybody's going to be there. Me and a few friends that hang out at the restaurant are all going together. We're going to dress alike, we're wearing white bellbottoms and a black halter top, with a flowered headband, big earrings and we all got the same platform shoes. Our shoes are black with rhinestones all over them. Man, we're going to be sharp. They say that the radio station is hosting a party after the concert and there's going to be a James Brown dance contest. The winner will get 100 bucks. I think second place will get 50 dollars and the third place is getting 25 dollars. My friends, Kim and her boyfriend, Terry Sanders said they were going to enter and win. Kim just might do it.

Kimberly Renee Boyd is my new best friend. She is the oldest of three girls. Her little sisters are very young, like me and Patrick, only her sisters are in school, let's see, ones in the second grade and the other is in kindergarten. Her father and mother both work for the telephone company, in housekeeping. I think she's lucky to have both her parents living with her. I wish I had that. Anyway, they live close to the elementary school that her sisters attend. All her sisters have to do is cross the street to be home. So Kim makes sure they're home and the chores are done before her mom comes home from work. Then she comes to the restaurants with the rest of us.

Her boyfriend, Terry Sanders, is big. You talk about opposites, they are. They've been going together for a couple of years now, that girl can do the James Brown better than anybody. And she's so good that it made her very popular. When she walks in the room with Terry, everybody gets ready for her to dance.

She doesn't look like the type either. She's about 5'6", and wears these thick cat framed, pink glasses. She's a light skinned girl, and her afro is big and pretty. Kim is really smart too. Kim said she was going to move away from Kansas City as soon as she graduates. She said she wanted to be an attorney or be a school teacher. One time she said that she was joining the Peace Corps. She's really smart. I think Kim will do something good with her life.

Now Terry is tall and thin. He is a very smooth, dark chocolate guy. He has the prettiest dark skin that I've ever seen. My mom was dark skinned too, but Terry is a deep dark chocolate brother. And he has pretty white teeth, like my mom, but he doesn't have the dimples. He sings good. Once he was in the school talent show singing a song by the Temptations. Terry sang David Ruffmans' song.

"I know you want to leave me, but I refuse to let you go. If I have to beg and plead for your sympathy, I don't mind, cause you mean that much to me . . . Ain't too proud to beg . . . please don't leave me girl."

Man, if I didn't know he was my best friends' boyfriend, and in their relationship she bosses him around, then I would have screamed my head off, just like everybody else. I think Kim and Terry are the best couple at school. Next year they're going to graduate. That's when I'm supposed to graduate. I don't worry about that anymore. I mean, I don't worry about graduating anymore.

* * * * *

Dee wasn't coming this summer. Uncle Charlie said she had to stay and help her mother out with her little sister and brother. This is the second summer straight that Dee hadn't come up to work since we were little kids. I missed her. But Kim and I have started hanging out more together. I'm telling you, there isn't so much trouble when I'm hanging out with Kim. Dee was always doing something. Or I was always covering her while she sneaked off, somewhere, with some boys. That girrrrl . . . Dee had me nervous.

I wish Kim would work here with me at the restaurant, but she said she was going to Job Corps this summer. She wanted to get a head start with some college courses. Anyway, that didn't stop me from trying to keep my friend around.

"Kim, why don't you work here during the summer?

69

You'll make some money . . . then take your time to check out a few colleges. You can buy yourself some clothes . . . you might even save enough to get a car before you go. Anyway, it's more money than what you'll get at Job Corps. I'll help you find a good college, girl. I promise, I'll help you find a good one . . . close to home." I smiled with that last remark. I could see Kim was thinking about it.

"I don't know, Marianne. I do need a car; it'll help my dad out . . . with money and all. I know mom and dad wouldn't mind if I had a car before I leave for college."

"That's right. You know they'll want you to come home, sometimes. At least be home for the holidays."

"Yeah, cause my daddy can't come get me every time I wanna come home. My poor dad works three jobs. I'll ask my mom and let you know. You're lucky Marianne. You have everything."

"Kim, if you only knew. I'd trade places with you any day."

"You don't know how good you have it. You have a car, a good job, you're running the best restaurant in town, you're making good money and you're only eighteen. Girrrrl you have it made."

"You really think I have it good? You have a mother and a father. I'll trade all this, Kim, to see my mother again. Hell, I don't even know who my father is. I don't have it good. It's just me and Patrick. Some reason they all think I have it made. I wish I felt the same way."

* * * * *

Terry, Kim's boyfriend, works for Rev. Williams at his church, The Redeemer's Baptist Church. He's the maintenance man. Rev. Williams finally got a real church and stopped having church services in his living room, or wherever he was having it. I think my mom was the first person to ever have a funeral there, in the actual building. Anyway, Terry's always

70

trying to get me to come to church.

"Marianne, why don't you come with Kim to church Sunday?"

"Terry, do you know how much I love sleeping in on Sundays? Do you understand that that's my 'sleeping in' day? I love my Sundays. I don't think I can give that up. Plus, it's my time with my baby brother. We don't get to spend enough time together."

"Well, this Sunday, I'll be leading a song. I was hoping my friends would come and hear me tear the church up."

"Aaaah Terry, come on. You gonna make me get up on Sunday. Kim, are you going?" Marianne was looking for any way out.

"Now, you know I'm going. My whole family goes there. What are you talking about?" Kim didn't want to get in it. She was too involved with the rib tips that she was meticulously sucking the meat off the bones.

"Marianne, the whole neighborhood goes to church. You're the only one, around here, that don't go to church." Terry had a rib, putting some of Uncle Charlie's hot sauce on it before he took a bite. "Kim, I'll give you a taste of my cole slaw for a bite of your baked beans." Terry was eyeing Kim's beans.

"No! . . . don't touch my beans. I mean it Terry. He's got a point Marianne. Everybody around here goes to church but you." Kim agreed without looking up from her plate.

"You're kidding me. I'm the only one that don't go? Ya'll are lying. Nobody at my house goes."

They both answered "Yes they do, too."

"I've seen Ms. Rosie and Ms. Shirley both take Patrick with them to church. You're the only one that don't go. Pali was there shouting . . . loooud . . . wasn't he Kim? Tell her . . . tell her."

"You're kidding me. Pali shouts?"

71

"He ain't lying. Pali was shouting. Shoot, he scared me." They all were laughing while Terry started demonstrating Pali's holy ghost shouting methods.

"I hadn't been to church since we buried my momma." Marianne thought about it for a few minutes, she reminisced about that day her mom was laid at the altar. "I guess I do need to go. Man, we're going to be tired. Natalie Cole is here this Saturday and then we got to get up for church."

"Don't let that concert keep you from praising the Lord. You just get your butt on up and go." Terry grabbed Kim and kissed her on her greasy mouth. "We're not letting anything keep us out of church . . . huh baby."

"Dang I guess. Shoot! Ya'll get out of here with all that kissing. Nobody wants to see all that. Gonna run my customer off with that stuff. That looks nasty." Marianne had turned up her nose in disgust.

"Come on baby, let me walk you home. Marianne's mean." Terry pouted .

"Yeah baby, let's go." They both placed they're empty plates on the counter and pretended to be upset, while they began walking toward the door.

"What time you're picking us up Saturday." Kim yelled.

"You need to be here at 6 o'clock. . . . We need to get there before it gets crowded at the stadium."

* * * * *

Saturday evening at 6 p.m., on the dot, Marianne was ready, in her black halter and white bellbottoms. Kim and Terry walked in the restaurant, with their matching black and white outfits. Along for the ride was Reginald Lamont Williams.

"Hey Marianne, you know Pastor Williams' son, Reginald. Reggie this is Marianne Robinson, one of the best people on earth. Ya'll get to know each other. Now, let's go." This was Terry's definition of formally introducing us as we walked toward the car.

"Hi Marianne. You sure look good girl. Turn around let me see you." Reggie got a good lock at Marianne's back end then gave her a wink that made Marianne's stomach jump. "Terry said you wouldn't mind me catching a ride with you guys to the concert."

Marianne blushed, "Naw, I don't mind. We got enough room. He didn't tell you we were wearing matching outfits." They all headed for her white Comet. The windows were down and there was just enough of a breeze that it made a beautiful evening.

"Nope he didn't mention it." Reggie reached in the back seat and punched Terry on the shoulders. "Man, you could have let me in on the plans. I got some black and white."

Terry was into kissing his girl. "Leave us alone, man. Can't you see I'm busy? That's why I brought you along so Marianne wouldn't be bothering me and my baby." Terry directed his attention to Marianne. "Hey girl, can't you keep him busy for a few minutes?"

"Shut up, Terry. Don't talk like that to my friend." Kim ordered Terry before he got out of hand.

"I remember you." Marianne casually mentioned as she drove to the school stadium.

"Yeah, I remember you too. This is the first time we've really met, I saw you at your mother's funeral."

Marianne nodded, "Your dad did a good job for my mom. Tell him thanks for me."

"I can do that." They were quiet for a while, then Reggie decided to make conversation. "How are you doing? You've been alright? I can't imagine how hard it must have been for you, losing your mother. She was so young. And then to pass like that, right before her wedding; that was crazy wasn't it . . . man, I can't imagine how her fiancé must have felt."

"What fiancé, what are you talking about? What

73

wedding?"

"Your mother's wedding. My dad was going to marry them, that guy and your mother was getting married in a few days but she passed away."

"You mean Lonnie."

"I guess that was his name; but I'm sure . . . nawww . . . wait a minute. It was a surprise. That's right. It was going to be a surprise. That Lonnie guy was planning a surprise wedding for your mother. I remember my dad was going to mention it at the funeral, but Lonnie asked him not to say anything."

"This is the first time that I've heard anything about it. I wonder why he didn't tell me? I would have wanted to be in on the surprise. I can't believe it."

"Maybe I shouldn't have said anything. I didn't mean to bring up any sad memories."

"Naaawwwww. That's okay. I'm glad to know. Plus, I like talking about my momma. It's alright. That's probably why you're here so I could know about the wedding plans. But I can't understand why he didn't tell me . . . he was crazy. He got so messed up after my mom died. I used to hate him, but when I saw how hard he took it, I felt a little sorry for Lonnie Evans. I haven't seen or heard from him since. I don't know what to think about him. I don't know if I should even mention him to Patrick. I mean, he hasn't called to see about Little Patrick or nothing."

"Really? You never know about people. You can't tell about folks."

Kim and Terry had stopped their fondling and decided to keep quiet and listen to the conversation in the front seat.

"I guess he didn't want to complicate anything at the funeral, by saying something that nobody knew about. I can understand that."

"It's probably true . . . that he was planning on marrying

74

my mom, because after the funeral he gave me this ring." Marianne held her hand out and flashed the big diamond on her middle finger.

"Whow! That's a nice ring."

"Yeah, it is, isn't it. He told me that he had planned on giving it to momma, but that's all. Then he left town. He didn't even go to the burial. I haven't heard or seen him since. Like I said, he's crazy."

"That is his son, isn't it?"

Marianne nodded her head up and down. "He gave me a telephone number if I ever needed anything, but I don't need anything."

They arrived at the stadium and already there was a line waiting to enter the concert. Reggie took Marianne's hand and held it during the whole event. There was no way he was letting her out of his sight, for that matter. he was proud having her with him. She was the queen around town. Every guy in the neighborhood would have wanted to be in his place right then.

"Look at Marianne and Reggie." Terry was whispering in Kim's ear.

"I know. Reggie's so cute. He's holding on to Marianne for dear life. I'm glad he's tall enough. Marianne never dates."

"She works too much. Reggie works like that too. His father has him so busy that he's too tired for girls. They're a good match. They both are serious."

"He's graduating this year, isn't he?" Kim quizzed so she could give Marianne the information. She knew there was going to be a ton of questions when they were alone.

"He graduated last year, I think he goes to Bishop or Morehouse somewhere like that, I'll ask. I'm surprised he's here tonight. So we're going to skip the party. We got to get him back. I want to keep my job." Terry said laughing.

Marianne and Reggie seemed to gravitate toward each other. It was as if they had known each other a long time. Kim was pleased with the match. Marianne deserved a guy like Reggie.

Natalie Cole was sooooo good. The crowd was going crazy. After the concert, people were trying to get in one of her three limos that drove around the stadium. Natalie's security team carefully got her into a get-away-car. Seeing the exit strategy was as interesting as seeing the concert. It was so much fun. Other people stood around, reminiscing on the nights' event. It was over. It was so good.

Marianne and Reggie were deep in conversation; Kim doubted if they even saw the concert. She was so happy for her friend.

"So Marianne, when can I see you again?"

"You know where to find me. I'm always at the restaurant."

"I don't want to see you like that. I want all your attention. So, answer my question. When can I see you again?"

"I work every day except Sunday's. I basically run the restaurant for Uncle Charlie. So I'm always busy. Uncle Charlie has been there . . . he's really been there for me and Patrick; he's helping me keep my house. He takes care of it. I don't worry about renters. I don't know what I would have done without him. So I don't mind running the restaurant for Uncle Charlie."

"Believe me; he probably appreciates you just as much. I mean, you can't trust people to take care of your business and do it right. He's lucky to have you, Marianne, so don't sell yourself cheap."

"Hey, I had to prove myself. Believe me . . . It wasn't cheap."

"I watch people and I watch my dad. He's always helping people, loaning them money . . . and all they have to do

76

is cut the grass; or something like that.   They won't do it. Believe me, it's hard finding good help."

Now Reggie wanted to change the subject. "Will you come to church Sunday, then after, we can catch a movie or something?"

There was no way Marianne was going to miss church. "That's sounds good. Reggie, what time does church start?"

"Be there at 10:45."

Chapter 7

Before Marianne could make it in the door, her telephone was ringing. "Hello . . . hello . . . Marianne . . . is that you?"

"Yeah it's me. Girl what do you want? It's late."

"Awh now, . . . I know you gonna tell me what ya'll was talking about. I couldn't wait for you to get home so I could call you."

"Oh girl, we didn't talk much, in fact, we didn't talk at all . . . I'm just messing with you. Kim. . . he's nice. I like him. Girrrrl, he asked me when he could see me again. I told him that he knew where he could find me; then he said not at the restaurant." There were loud screams on both telephones. "And he's tall . . . Kim, he's got to be 6'4". Did you see how high my platforms were, and he still was taller than me." There were screams again.

"So, you're going to see him again? You're going to church, huh?"

"You dang right I'm going. I'll be there, on time, sitting on the first row."

"Right on!"

"What time do you usually get there?"

"Marianne, you don't want to go when I go. My daddy gets us there for Sunday School."

"What time is that?

"Around 9 o'clock."

"Naw . . . I'm not getting there for Sunday School. Where do ya'll sit?"

"Up front! I'm just playing. Girl, they'll start shouting up front so I sit in the back."

"I want to sit where I can see Reggie."

"Then you better sit up front. You want me to sit with you? Hey, Marianne, did Terry tell you Reggie plays the piano

78

for the church? I've seen him get happy."

"What! Reggie gets happy? What does he do? Does he shout?"

"Well, he don't shout . . . shout. . . . He's not like Pali, but he'll start playing that piano and singing, girl, he'll tear the church up and everybody'll start shouting. It'll last a long time too."

"Oh man. I don't think I want to see him doing that. Kim, this will be the first time I've gone to church . . . outside of my mom's funeral. I'm kinda scared. What if I get happy or something? I heard it just happens to you, and you can't help it. What if it happens to me? "

"Shut up Marianne, you ain't gonna get happy and shout. But, wait till you see Reggie when he does it." Kim started laughing. "Girrrrrrl . . . Just wait, you'll see what I'm talking about."

On Sunday morning came and Marianne hadn't slept all night.

"Hey Patrick, come here, you want to go to church with me. Come on sweetie, let's get dressed."

It was a pretty morning, bright and the air was clear. Birds were dancing around the windows. Patrick was pointing at the birds, hitting the windows; he was so excited about seeing them flying around the window. "Birds . . . birds . . . see birds."

"Yeah, I see the birds, Patrick. Come get in this water so I can give you a bath." Patrick started running. "Come here boy." They both wrestled and laughed. "Get in this water."

Marianne and Patrick were both dressed in baby blue and white. Marianne had on a matching skirt suit and shoes. Her hair was in two afro puffs and she dabbed herself heavily in Tabu, the perfume she wore for special occasions. It's the only perfume she had left, that belonged to her mother. She looked great and Patrick was cute. She had to make a good impression on Reggie. They were going on a dinner date after the church service. This was the first real date for Marianne and she was so nervous.

When they arrived, the services hadn't started, it was a little early.

"Dang . . . everybody in the neighborhood is here. Hi Ms. Rosie."

"Hey baby, you decided to join us. That's good, that's good. Where are you sitting, Marianne? If you want, you and Patrick can sit with me. Hi Patrick honey . . . no no no, you stay with your sister. Yeaaaah honey, you stay with big sister today, baby."

Marianne laughed at how close to the pulpit Ms. Rosie was sitting. "Ms. Rosie, you must need a whole bunch of preaching to sit that close."

"Hush girl"

"I don't want to sit up front like that. I might get the Holy Ghost or something."

It was Ms. Rosie time to laugh now. "Marianne you ought to be ashamed of yourself talking like that. That's exactly what you need, is the Holy Ghost or something. You came to the right place, I'll tell you that. Didn't she Patrick? She came to the right place, huh baby."

"I was supposed to meet Kim in here, have you seen her?"

"Not yet, she's around, don't worry. Her daddy has them babies here every Sunday."

"Well, let her know that I'm here, I'm going to sit on the other side. I'll see you later, Ms. Rosie."

Reggie spotted Marianne, he gave her the 'I see you're here, eye' . . . then he continued to test the instruments and microphones. Terry didn't wave either.

Marianne felt awkward and wondered where's Kim? She finally found a seat; then continued to make Patrick as comfortable as possible.

"Hello, how are you; my name is Juanita Williams. I'm glad you could make it today. You look so familiar. What is your name?"

"Mom, that's Marianne Robinson that works at Uncle Charlie's Barbeque restaurant." The teenage girl spoke up before Marianne had a chance to say anything.

"Well, very nice to meet you Marianne. You must know my daughter, Rosalyn and these are my twins, Karen and Sharon. Do you know my son, Reggie?" They all were busy, Marianne, Mrs. Williams, and Rosalyn all were wrestling with babies.

"Yes ma'am. Reggie kind of invited me to church today. I'm his guest."

"Oh, is that right. Well I hope you enjoy the service. I have another boy running around here, Joseph. Then the Pastor, Rev. Williams is my husband. Where's your folks?"

"My mother died giving birth to my little brother, Patrick, here."

"Well now, I do remember you. How are you doing? Your mother's funeral was held here, wasn't it? She was a very beautiful woman. And this is your cute little brother. He's gotten big."

"Yes ma'am, he's growing. I can hardly carry him. It's a good thing he's walking." They both laughed a little.

"Yeah, I know what you mean. Well, Marianne, I hope you enjoy the worship service this morning and if there's anything we can do for you, just let me know. We're so happy you can join us today."

"Thank you, ma'am."

Kim walked toward Marianne just as Mrs. William's headed toward her seat. "Hey . . . I see you met our First Lady."

"Yeah, she's nice." Marianne gave Kim a mischievous smile, "That's my future mother-in-law. Where are we gonna

81

sit?"

"Let's just sit here, this is where the choir comes in. You can see Reggie real good from here. What was Mrs. Williams talking about?"

Just then the music started, the choir, in their robes, were marching in step to the song. *"We come this faaarr by faith . . . leaning on the Lord . . . trusting in His holy word, . . . He never faaailled me yet . . . Ohoooo ooohooo ooohoooh . . . can't turn arouuunnnnnd . . . He's never faaailled me yet."*

The minister walked in and motioned for everybody to stand. He continued with a prayer.

"Let the words of my mouth, and the mediation of my heart, be acceptable in Thy sight, oh Lord, You are my strength and my redeemer."

The church service was surprisingly fast. Marianne was pleased that she came and more than happy that Patrick was such a good boy. Again, he wasn't fussy or loud; he was so good.

Reggie and Terry both led songs. Terry was the director of the choir.

"Kim, you never told me Terry was the director of the choir."

"Yeah, he just started doing that. It was too much for Reggie by himself to play, teach the songs, and direct the choir. Terry does good, huh?"

"Yeah, only thing is, he thinks he's dancing up there, or in front of the marching band. Girl, Terry is a mess. Where does he think he's at . . . on stage?"

"I know. That's Terry. So where are you guys going for dinner?"

"I don't know. I was thinking of the new fish bar. I heard they were good. Any place that doesn't sell ribs will be good for me."

"You plan on taking Patrick with you?"

82

"Yeah"

"I'll babysit for you, Marianne."

"Noooo, that's alright. I can take him."

"Marianne, let me babysit for you. You don't need Patrick with you and Reggie on your first date. Girl, what's wrong with you. Can't you enjoy yourself just once? Give me that boy, I'll take him home with me and my little sisters. They'll have a ball with him. Just call when you guys come back, or come by and get him."

"Okay, okay . . . thanks. How do I look?" Reggie walked up behind Marianne and spoke up before Kim could answer.

"You look good, girl. Don't come to church looking like that again. I couldn't concentrate on my music, I was messing up. That crazy Terry wasn't helping. He kept looking at me like I was stupid . . . I blame you for that." Reggie turned to Kim. "Hi Kim, please get your boyfriend. He's back there giving somebody else a head ache."

"I'm not messing with Terry. Me and Patrick are going to my house. We're going to play, huh Patrick. Tell Terry, I'll call him later. My dad is probably in the parking lot, waiting for us to go. Just call Marianne, we're going to my house and eat some chicken, huh Patrick."

Marianne turned to Reggie. "So, where are we going?"

"I was thinking about some fish. They have that new fish house I want to try."

"Me too!"

"Let me tell my parents and I'll meet you out front. Better yet, why don't you go home and I'll come by to get you in about twenty minutes? I just have to make sure my dad is alright. He may need something. I'll check on him, then I'll be there for you, baby. I won't be long. I promise."

"Okay, Reggie." Marianne couldn't hardly put one foot in front of the other as she floated through the church doors.

Once the cool breeze hit her, she snapped back into reality.

"Okay, let me freshen up. I'll go home and brush my teeth again, and put on some more perfume." She decided to change her hair style, those afro puffs were beginning to hurt her head.

After looking at the clock, she realized it had already been an hour. Time was getting away and she started to be a little concerned. Marianne sat in her grandmother's old chair and began to look out her window, waiting for the unfamiliar car to pull up with her new boyfriend. She was so excited.

Marianne waited and waited, Reggie didn't come. She called Kim. "Hello Mrs. Boyd, may I speak with Kim?"

"Yes, just one minute. Kim . . . Kim, telephone. Girl, this little Patrick is something else. He's potty trained. I couldn't believe it." Mrs. Boyd was talking fast before Kim came to the phone.

"Yeah, Patrick was always following me to the bathroom, he wanted to use it, so I got him a potty chair. He's been using his little potty ever since. Patrick won't wet the bed."

"You're kidding."

"No ma'am. He's so smart. I can't believe him."

"He sure is, if you ever want us to keep him, we'd love too. My girls are crazy about him. Well here's Kim."

"Thanks Mrs. Boyd."

"Hi Marianne, ya'll back already. That was quick."

"No girl. He told me to come home and he'd come get me, then he never showed up. Have you heard anything from Terry? Something must have happened. I can't believe he would stand me up like that."

"Naw girl. Reggie's not like that. Something happened. Let me call the church and I'll get back to you."

"Well, I'll be over there in a minute to get Patrick."

Marianne, changed into jeans and a t-shirt. She couldn't

84

remember ever being this disappointed. This was the very first guy that she was excited about, her very first date.

"Was he playing with me? Did he like me? "Was he just being nice to me? . . . He really likes me. I know it. Damn this hurt. I can't wait to hear what happened. I didn't get a phone call or anything."

The phone rang, it was Kim. "Girrrrrrl, you wouldn't believe what happened. I guess while we were having church, somebody broke into the office and stole the safe. Terry said the police are there and they're taking a police report. How can somebody steal from the church? Don't they know that's the house of God?"

"You got to be kidding me?"

"Noooo, Terry is still there too. Reggie asked me to tell you what happened."

"I know it had to be something bad, cause he didn't bother to call me or anything."

"They're too busy answering questions and trying to figure out who had the opportunity to break in, and who even knew about the safe."

"I'm sure we'll hear all about it tomorrow. Hey, I'll be there in a few minutes to get Patrick. I'm so disappointed."

"Don't worry about it, Marianne. He likes you a lot. I can tell. I never see Reggie with anybody. In fact, I think you're the only girl I've seen him talk to around here, but who knows . . .men are something else, you never know what happened before he moved here. Reggie is too fine not to have a girl somewhere."

"You think he might have a girlfriend somewhere else?"

"I don't know Marianne, don't listen to me. It's just that he's so good looking, he's had to have somebody, somewhere."

"You're probably right. Well, I'm getting off this phone. Open the door for me, I'm on my way."

It was approximately 7:45 before the telephone rang.

85

"Hello, Marianne, man . . . we've had some kind of day. You heard what happened? Can you believe that? I just don't know about people. And I'll bet you anything that it was one of those cats that help Terry. He had to strip and wax the floor last week. He hired some cats from the neighborhood. No telling who did this. Then again, it could be one of the regular guys that help with cleaning. It was probably one of them."

"Do you know how much was taken?"

"Girl, they took the whole safe. Can you believe that?"

"From the building?"

"Yeah, that's crazy isn't it? Dad can't make payroll this week. That's what took so long, he was contacting his employees and letting them know that the payroll was taken. I don't know what he's going to do . . . I told him that the people that work for the church will understand. We're going to have dinner at church every night, for everybody, till we get over the loss. At least they won't go hungry. It was probably a few thousand that was taken. Man, my dad is a little worried about everything. He owes for the church building. I try to get him to use the bank and stop using that old safe. I guess he'll think about it now."

Marianne listened and gave a supporting "yeah" every now and then.

"Listen girl, it's still crazy over here. It's not a good time to visit with you. How about tomorrow after you get off work? Can I come by then? Maybe I can get some quality time with you. We can get to know each other . . . with no interruptions. Your brother should be sleep then."

"I can't stay up too late cause I got to open the restaurant in the morning."

"I promise not to stay too long. I just want to get to know you better. I want to know all about you, Marianne. I've never met anybody like you. You are the most together girl I've ever known. You work so hard, and you take care of your little brother. You're so young, and you're organized. You got it together, girl. I want to know you better than anybody else in the whole world. Is that possible?"

"Is that possible . . . I don't know, Reggie. You know I already have a best friend. She may not want to give me up, like that." Marianne was so tickled cause Reggie acted hurt.

"Gosh Marianne! Will you let me be your best friend? "

"Okay, okay. You can be my best friend. Only thing, when you come over, come through the back door. Call me when you get ready to come, so I'll let you in. You, coming over here that late at night, every light in the neighbor will come on. Sooo . . . I'll let you in through the back door."

"Yessar, Miss Marianne. I'll come through the back door. Anything else you want me to do?"

"Noooo, that's it . . . for now."

"Marianne, I'm serious now, I'll be working with my dad, getting our financial picture together, you get some rest and I'll see you tomorrow night."

"Okay Reggie, goodnight and I'll see you later."

Marianne couldn't breathe, she was too excited. "You got a boyfriend, and he is fine." She sang her little song all night long. *"Come see about me, see about your baby, come see about me."* She replayed their conversation over and over. "Man, Kim is gonna just have to get out the way. It's about Reggie right now."

Chapter 8

Darlene was slowly getting dressed. She needed to study for her Psychology test. She had so much to do, but not enough time. Billy Joe wouldn't leave without her and she knew it. She couldn't believe her luck, especially after leaving New York City.

It was just a whim that she ended in Kansas. She caught the first bus out of the city and rode it until that ticket ran out. Then she caught the next bus from there. Darlene continued to ride and ride, finally, she ended up in Kansas City. She didn't know anybody, she didn't have a plan, nobody to meet her once she arrived to wherever she was going, but on the bus, she met a nice man, a gentleman. They talked a while. He said he was headed home from the war.

"How long were you in Nam?"

"Girl, this was my second trip. I first joined the Army. I served four years, spent two years in Nam; then I got out the Army. When I didn't have a job or anywhere to go, I joined the Marines. Of course, they sent me back to Nam, I did another year in the war. Now I'm through, I've had enough of Uncle Sam. After Vietnam, shit, I can make it anywhere in the world. All I got to do is stay out of jail, avoid a bullet, hell, I'm a Vet." They both laughed loud cause Billy Joe was demonstrating a scary face and crazy eyes.

"Billy, I don't have any family that went to war. I know a few guys that went to stay out of jail. They were crazy before they went in the service." Darlene gave a nervous laugh. "I hope they made it out okay . . . I basically stayed to myself. It was just me and my grandma and we took care of each other. In New York, that's the best way to live. Stay to yourself, if you're smart."

"I guess you're going to tell me that you don't have a fella back in New York."

"I don't." Darlene looked like she was lying.

"Either they are out of their minds, or you think I'm out of my mind. Now which is it?"

"There was a guy that I was seeing since high school. That's why I left New York. He wasn't going anywhere so I had to move on. My grandma said I out grew him. We didn't have anything to talk about anymore. I mean, he couldn't talk about nothing but that street life. Everything was about money and drugs. Who was moving in on his money; who's driving a new car. Who's snitching to the police, man, I don't want that life. It's already hard. When he started fighting me, it was really time to skip town. Life is too short." Darlene began to loosen up and explain. Billy Joe listened . . . "He wasn't going to stand by and watch me leave him, or let somebody else date me. He wasn't going to work for them pennies. That's what he calls it, them pennies. Matter of fact, he wasn't going to work, period. There wasn't any choice but for me to leave my town. I couldn't see myself with a future, you know, achieving the American dream. I want a life . . . I want to someday be a nurse. Work in a hospital, taking care of people is all I've ever wanted to do. I think that'll be a good living, don't you?"

"If that's what you want to do, Darlene, just do it."

"Billy, that's easier said than done. I don't think I'm asking for too much. If I can get settled somewhere nice, and get a job, I can work and go to school . . . I can take care of myself, I can do that."

Darlene once loved Randy Howard, but Randy loved the streets too much. He wasn't always like that; when they were young, he would follow her from school, hang out in front of her apartment building until the street lights came on. That was their signal for him to go home. That was a long time ago.

Darlene didn't see any future with Randy. He never finished school. He protected her alright. She felt safe with Randy, but as they got older, Darlene wanted more than the

89

neighborhood bully in her life. She wanted a future, a career, and a real life. She had to leave New York City.

"I understand that. Everybody deserves a fair shot. You're a special lady. There's not many women that would pack up and leave like that. Going to a different city and making your own way is a little scary. You have family here in Kansas?"

Darlene looked lost for the first time. "No, not really. But I'll be alright."

Actually, Darlene didn't have a clue what she would do. Her grandmother gave all she had and she promised to make good of the money, but what next?

"Well, I know a place that rents rooms. The folk that run it are really decent folk. If there's a room available, then you can stay there. Maybe there'll be two rooms, cause I need one too."

"This is what we can do. I'll get a room over there, by the bus station." Darlene pointed to the barely lit hotel with a neon sign flashing . . . Vacancy. "Do you need somewhere for tonight?"

"Naw, baby girl, this is my town."

"Cause, I can get a room with twin beds, if you promise to be nice." Darlene flashed a perfect set of teeth that caught Billy off guard. But he was a man and didn't need no little girl taking care of him.

"If there's a room with your friends, then you can let me know tomorrow. Tonight, I'm going to lie down and sleep in a nice bed."

Just in case, Billy pointed to the hotel that he believed she was talking about. "Okay Darlene, get some rest. What's your last name so I can call you tomorrow?"

"It's Anderson, Darlene Anderson."

"Okay, Ms Anderson, I'll let you know tomorrow, take care and don't be talking to no strangers." Billy laughed and

90

talked to himself . . . "What have I got myself into? She's cute though. She's got that cute little accent too . . . I don't need no extra weight . . . I got to take care of myself . . . Man, I sure hope Ms. Maxine still rents rooms."

* * * * *

The hotel wasn't so bad. It had a little mildew odor. The cigarette burns over the tables and sink weren't pretty, but for the price, Darlene wasn't complaining. She was glad to meet her new friend Billy Joe, that's the best thing that could have happened for her. He seemed to be a good man. Darlene was hoping he'd call her tomorrow.

It had been years since he'd been to this old neighborhood. Billy Joe's closest living relative moved to Topeka, Kansas a long time ago. He couldn't waste any time, Billy need a place to sleep himself. He decided go to Ms. Maxine's house before it got dark. When he arrived at the house, it felt different, but it still looked familiar enough for him to ring the bell.

"Hello, hi, I'm William Joseph Washington. I used to live here, about ten years ago. Is Ms. Maxine around? I was hoping there's a room available."

"Billy . . . Billy Joe. Boy I remember you. This is Ms. Shirley. Remember, I live next door. Come on in here." Ms. Shirley talked and talked to Billy that night. Billy was more than happy to know that there were exactly two rooms ready for rent. "Man, God is good." Billy could finally relax.

She told him everything that had happened while he was gone. Ms. Maxine passed close to eight years ago; then Patricia Robinson's untimely death. She's been babysitting for Marianne over a year now.

Ms Shirley wanted Billy to live there. He was always a good renter. Ms. Maxine called him her adopted son. Billy couldn't believe the news. He really couldn't believe that the little girl that used to play hop scotch in front of the stairs was

91

running the rent house.

Billy got full of red beans and rice, neck bones, and steamed cabbage with Jiffy cornbread while he intently listened to all that had changed while he was gone.

Now it's been close to a year since he's been living with Marianne. Billy felt responsible for his little women. Darlene worked hard at the club. She made her own money and started college. He never met anyone like her, except maybe, Marianne.

Marianne was beautiful, smart, and responsible just like her grandmother. He was proud of Marianne. Man, things sure change fast. All he cared about was his new family. And he wasn't going to let anything happen to any of them that lived there at Ms. Maxine's rent house.

* * * * *

Darlene was finally happy with her life. She loved working for Razz. He was soooo cool. Razz was the kind of guy that came around once in a lifetime. He had a way about him that everybody respected, and if he liked you, he'd do anything for you. Darlene wished he wasn't married.

Darlene especially liked the club. Razz called his club The House That Jack Built, but mostly we just called it Razz's. When you walk in the building the first thing you'll see is the two pool tables on the right side of the bar. They gambled hard on the pool tables; there were pool sharks coming from as far as California and Texas to play at Razz's Club. Then, around the pool tables, were other tables to sit and drink. There were little candles lit on all the tables that gave the club a sexy, soft look. Extended from the walls, Razz built a ledge where most of the barstools were positioned. People could see the pool games, watch the band, or just entertain each other.

On the other side of the bar was a little stage for the band. Of course, there were tables in front of the stage and women that flocked around the bands like you wouldn't believe.

92

There were all kinds that came to Razz's.

Upstairs is where the real gambling went on. There were two tables for dice, then, farther in the back, were the card games. They played Poker, Coon-Can, and Tonk. It was nothing to see a couple of guys betting a hundred bucks a piece, on a Coon-Can game. Every now and then, you could hear a little commotion upstairs, that's when a game got out of hand. Razz kept a man on the door and only members were allowed to gamble upstairs.

If Razz saw anybody cheating in his place, he'd throw them out and it would be a while before they were allowed back into a game. Some people are just lucky. That was Razz, just lucky. He had to be the luckiest man alive, and he acted normal, like a regular guy.

Razz's wife didn't come to the club. I don't blame her, because of all the women that were in love with Razz. I don't know how she puts up with it. I guess she just stays out of his business.

It wasn't long before Darlene realized Razz's pull around town. There was a guy named Fast Eddie that wanted to shoot Billy because he won a big pot on the poker table. Billy Joe wasn't helping the matter; he kept talking trash with a gun pointed at him.

"Fuck that nigga, Razz. He cheated."

"Naw, Eddie, you know I don't allow no cheating at my tables . . . you just lost man. Now put the gun down. Don't bring that bullshit in my place of business."

"Damn that shit, Razz. I'm gonna shoot that nigga. Billy was cheat'n. I know he was cheat'n, you know he was cheat'n and I wanna know why you're taking up for him. But that's alright cause I'm gonna shoot his big black ass. I'll teach his ass to mess with me. I'm gonna blow his damn head off." Fast Eddie was screaming spit mixed with alcohol was.

"Well, Eddie, if you gotta shoot somebody, shoot me."

93

"Razz, I don't want to shoot you, but if you stand in the way of this bullet, then I'll shoot your black ass too."

At that time the gun fired, everybody ducked, and this was the first time Darlene seen Razz pissed off.

"Damit Eddie, look to you. You shooting a gun in my place of business. I can't allow that Eddie. How long have we known each other? Have I ever let anything happen to you in my place? I know your folks. We grew up in the same town; we both from Wewoka, man. How you gonna act in my place of business. I'm not gonna let you shoot one of my customer's. You get the hell out of here."

Then Billy started talking.

"My name is Skitter, better known as the booty beater. I'm raggedy but I'm round here, I was invited why I'm down here."

"Hush Billy! Damnit man, hush!" Razz didn't want Billy to agitate Fast Eddie. That man was ready and willing to shoot a couple of gamblers in there.

"They call me Petey Wheatstraw and I love a good bar room brawl. Razz, I'm not scared of that man, he shoot that gun again, he just better not miss." Big Bill got louder. He was walking around patting his chest; he was performing like he was on a Broadway stage.

"I was born on a pile of butcher's knives. Pierced through the heart by a couple of wives, Got a grave yard disposition. A tombstone mind . . . I ain't lying, I don't mind dyin."

"Billy can't you see, I don't want no trouble in my place. Why don't you just go to my office till Fast Eddie calm down."

"Well, Razz, you ain't gonna take no bullet for me. Naw, not tonight, so I'm gonna stay right here, cause if that nigga shoot that gun again, he better kill my big black ass."

"Eddie, I'll tell you what. Big Bill is dead set on you

94

shooting him. So go on home man, cause you can't shoot one of my customers."

Razz turned looking for Darlene, "Darlene, give Fast Eddie a drink on me and make it to go. Now, Eddie, you go on home and I'll see you some other time. You need to be cool man."

Darlene hurried and made Eddie a real nice drink of Red Label Scotch Whiskey on the rocks. She was shaking it up so he could see the big, nice drink.

"Here you go, Mr. Eddie. Is there anything else I can get you?" With that Darlene gave Eddie one of her dazzling smiles. "Now you be careful with that drink. Don't drive too fast. I want you to make it home safely." Darlene had a way with the customers and Razz was sure glad of that.

"I'll see you later, man." Razz was patting Eddie on his back, walking him to the door. "You get some sleep man, you're too edgy. Man, you was gonna shoot one of my customers, man, you know I don't play that."

"Okay, Razz. I'm sorry. I guess I got carried away a bit. Don't pay me any attention. I'll talk with you later."

"Yeah, be careful out there." Razz didn't show any emotion but he wasn't through with Eddie. Fast Eddie wouldn't be allowed to play in any of Razz's games any more, period.

On the way home, Darlene took her shoe and started beating Billy.

"What's wrong with you? Didn't you see that man with that gun? Are you craaazy, Billy Joe Washington? Are you crazy? Just what am I supposed to do without you?"

"Dang Darlene, that hurts. Stop hitting me with that shoe. Ouch! Hey that was the heel you hit me with."

"What about Marianne and everybody at the house? How are we supposed to feel after somebody's done shot your big black ass? He should have shot you dead." Darlene continued to fuss and beat Billy with her shoe. "I'll tell you what; I wouldn't have shed one tear."

When they arrived at the house, she got out the car, slammed the door, walked into the house and went to bed without another word to Billy Joe Washington.

As she laid in the bed, Darlene began to pray.

"Lord, Jesus, thank you for this night. Thank you for not letting Mr. Eddie shoot Billy right in his big butt. Sometimes these guys are just crazy, they need you in their lives, and I thank you for taking care of that situation. It could have been bad. My friend could have gotten shot, but You looks after these nuts out here, and thank you for that. Thank you for taking care of my grandma too, while I'm gone. Please make a way for me to bring her here with me. I know I shouldn't have left her by herself like that, so help me get her here as soon as possible." Darlene continued to pray and pray till she finally drifted off to sleep.

Chapter 9

Marianne couldn't focus on work, she was too excited, and the day was going by sooooo slow. She kept daydreaming about her plans, tonight, with Reginald Lamont Williams. He's coming to her house; they're going to be in her bedroom, alone, while everybody's at work, or asleep. The only place for them to have any kind of privacy is her bedroom. Marianne started laughing to herself, just thinking about having a man, alone, in her room. And Ms. Shirley, if she were to find out . . . she would throw a fit. Marianne wanted to scream; she was so excited about Reggie.

Reginald Williams is a tall, bright, young man that reminded her of Lonnie, Patrick's daddy. Only Reggie wasn't skinny like Lonnie, Reggie is tall and muscular, his afro is full and a reddish brown color, it hangs over his forehead and connects perfectly to his sideburns. He has a thick mustache; he wears dark sunglasses that go perfectly with his appearance. Reggie is so together and extremely handsome. Marianne really liked the way his clothes fit. His pants showed the muscles in his butt and those bow legs are so fine. She could daydream about him all day long.

Patrick'll be sleep with Ms. Shirley and they're usually downstairs, asleep on the couch, then sometimes, she'll take him to her house. This is Monday night; they'll probably sleep over Ms. Shirley's house. Patrick has his own bed over there. Mainly on weekends is when they stayed with Marianne, Ms Shirley and Clarence, both, stayed there on Friday and Saturday night, while the TV channel blasted the Star Spangled Banner or that loud static noise, until she got home and turned the TV off.

Marianne had it all worked out. She would let him in through the back door; they would walk up the stairs, without awaking anybody. First, she would offer him something to eat. "I'll bring home some smoked brisket." She was planning every detail. Then she decided to be a little different from any other girl he's ever dated.

"I'll run me some bath water then ask him to give me a moment to freshen up." Marianne didn't want the fresh scent of Barbeque with her on their first date. "Naw, that's not cool." Marianne thought about what she would put on. At first she was thinking of shorts and a halter top; then decided not to move too fast. Reggie wouldn't respect her.

Ms. Shirley would probably take Patrick to her house, so she could fix Mr. Clarence's lunch before he goes to work tomorrow morning. That would work out better for Marianne. Then she wouldn't have to sneak up the stairs with Reggie. They could stay right in the living room and visit.

"Naaaaaaw, I want him in my bedroom."

She was thinking about kissing him, what that would be like. His teeth are alright, they're a little crooked, but they're clean. His smile is kind of cute, his front teeth overlapped, crooked, but cute. Marianne had never been alone with a man, not like this. She didn't know what he would expect from her. Marianne was still a virgin and was scared to death, thinking he might try something. Then, again, he's exactly the type of guy she always wanted to give herself to, the type that she would one day marry.

It wasn't long before Terry and Kim arrived at the restaurant. School was out for the summer. They were both disgusted with the robbery at their beloved church. Terry discussed everything he knew about the break in during church service.

"Can you believe that? Some people ain't got a conscious. I'd be scared to death, stealing from the church while people are inside praying and everything. Man, I told Pastor to fire everybody. Ain't that how the old folks did it? They just whip everybody; then you'll know you got the right one." Terry was joking but still meant every word.

"That means firing you too, Terry." Kim wanted Terry to realize what he was saying.

"So what's the Pastor going to do about paying everybody?" Marianne always thought about business.

"The ones that work in the office are okay. The few little janitors, like me, we're alright. People act like they're starving, but they know they got food . . . they'll eat."

"Terry, that's not true. You'd be surprised about people around here, just go to some of their houses." Kim couldn't believe Terry's lack of knowledge of the people in his own neighborhood. She knew how bad people were living.

"Just the other day our next door neighbor, a little girl named Barbara, asked us if we had any leftovers from dinner. Can you believe that? Her father didn't have a job, and she wanted something to eat for her and her little brother. I felt so sorry for Barbara . . . I know it must be hard for her parents. My mom took them a bag of food and told the kids to eat with us until her father gets a job. You'd be surprised, Terry."

"Did her folks send her over to ask ya'll for food?" Marianne was more curious than anything.

"No . . . her folks weren't there. It was just her and her brother at home . . . and they were hungry, Terry." Kim gave Terry a pitiful look. She wanted a reaction from Terry, but didn't get it.

"Well, the Pastor don't have to worry about paying me. I can wait. Now, those cats I hired to do the floors last week, I don't know about them. They're crying harder than anybody. Man, I hate I got involved with them dudes. That one cat, Dennis Harding, you know him, Marianne?"

"Kinda thick, he wears glasses? Yeah, he comes in here." Marianne nodded

"He was telling Pastor that it ain't his problem that he got robbed and he needed his money. Man, how you gonna tell the Pastor something like that, after he gave him a job? That cat didn't show no respect for Rev. Williams. The Pastor just reached in his pocket and gave that fool a twenty dollar bill."

"Reggie said they were going to serve dinners for the church workers, so when are they going to start that?"

"I'm not sure yet. We need to be selling dinners, not giving away free food."

"How many people are working for the church? If it's only ten or so, I can buy dinner one night. I'm sure Uncle Charlie won't mind. I don't think the restaurants' ever gotten robbed . . . knock on wood."

"Ain't that sweeeeet? You gonna buy us dinner one night." Terry mocked Marianne.

"If it ain't too many of ya'll. Let me see. Probably Tuesday, that's our slowest day."

"Marianne, you're alright. I know the Pastor will appreciate it."

"I got to talk with Uncle Charlie first. I can pay for it myself, but I don't want to make arrangements like that and Uncle Charlie don't know anything about it. Aunt Rosie will back me up, it's her church too. I don't think I told her about the church being robbed."

"Girl, you don't have to worry about that. That news spread like wildfire. Everybody was calling before I left the church, Sunday. People came back, standing around, in the way. The police finally asked people to leave. Man, those folks were singing like canaries, who they knew were no good thieves in the neighborhood. Man, it was a circus. The police just told everybody to go home."

"I'll call Uncle Charlie in a minute and let him know what's going on and that I want to buy dinner Tuesday for a few members that won't be getting a paycheck. So how many people are we talking about?"

"It's not that many. It's not like they'll starve. I know Mrs. Rogers, the church secretary, with her big fat ass, won't be looking for food." Kim hit Terry hard on his arm. "The only people that might be having a hard time . . . is me, and I want to eat."

"Shut up Terry. You don't need to eat nothing." Kim is always telling Terry to 'shut up.'

"The other janitor, Steve, I know he'll probably need a little help. He's got all those kids. Rev. Williams will want to come. All of them will come. That's what . . . six, then five, that's twelve with me. Baby, you want to eat with me? That's thirteen with Kim."

"Naw, Kim's gonna help me work. Kim, you can help me serve. So, I'll say, fifteen at the most. I'll let you know when I talk to Uncle Charlie, he'll come in this evening. Maybe we should do it Wednesday night. I might need some extra time."

It was around 9 p.m., before Uncle Charlie came to the restaurant. Marianne felt good about wanting to help the church and she could only hope Uncle Charlie would feel the same. It was getting late too. She planned on being home by 10:30 p.m. Marianne had everything finished. The bank deposit was ready to hand to Uncle Charlie. That's usually the last thing that she did before she left. Tables, restroom and floors were all done.

"Uncle Charlie, you heard about the church getting robbed didn't you?"

"Yeah baby, some people's kids will do anything. I bet it was an inside job. That's why I have to be careful who I hire around here. Now-a-day people are desperate. You just pay attention around here, baby, cause that could have been us. Luckily, nobody got hurt."

"That's true, cause if somebody had walked in on them, no telling what could have happened. But what I wanted to tell you is that, now the Pastor can't pay anybody. He's pretty bad off. He can't make the payment for the new church, either. He can't pay his employees . . . none of them are getting paid. He's

101

in bad shape."

Uncle Charlie didn't know where she was going with the conversation, so he decided to sit down.

"Anyway, I wanted to help. Maybe we can serve dinner one night to the employees."

"Serve dinner to the employees?"

"Yeah, Unck, some of them might be in bad shape. Rev Williams don't have money to pay anybody."

"You mean to tell me, he had all his money in that safe?"

"Yeah. Terry said that his son, Reggie's been trying to get him to use the bank."

"I guess he'll do it now, won't he? So how many people are you talking about?"

"Terry said it's only fifteen, at the most."

"Fifteen, huh?"

"Yes sir. I figure I could pay for fifteen dinners, myself, but I wanted to give you an opportunity to help; just in case you wanted to help too."

"Girl . . . you're just like your grandma. But, I'll tell you what I know about church folk. Once they find out about some free dinners, the whole church will show up."

"Nooooo, it's only going to be the people that work for the church, not the whole church." Marianne was tickled at the thought. Uncle Charlie said the whole church will show up. Wouldn't that be funny?

"I'll tell you what . . . let Rosie call Rev. Williams. Then I'll let you know what we can do."

"Okay Uncle Charlie."

Marianne was in the house exactly fifteen minutes before her phone rang. She let it ring three times before she answered. "Hello . . . oh hiiii, . . . yes I'm home. Yeaaah! . . . I still want you to come over. He's over my neighbors, . . . Ms. Shirley's house. She usually keeps him through the week. On weekends, they'll stay over here, with me. No, I'm not too tired. It's okay. Yeah, just come to the back door. I'll leave it open. How long will you be? Okay, twenty minutes. See you then."

Marianne ran to the restroom, she had to hurry with a bath, get dressed. She wanted to wash her hair, but decided to wait. She found a little sun dress and matching roman sandals that were perfect. Marianne grabbed an afro wig out her closet, earrings, perfume. Then the knock came at the door.

"Reggie, is that you?"

"Yeah"

"It's open. Come in." She still needed time to get dressed.

"Where are you?"

"Up here, I'll be down in a minute."

"You're here by yourself, with the door opened?"

"Nobody's crazy enough to break in on us. Not with Big Billy staying here. If Big Billy ever found out somebody broke in here, it wouldn't be long." Marianne continued to talk loud so Reggie could hear her down stairs.

She was putting lotion on her legs when he came to her door. Knock . . . Knock! "Just one more minute Reggie. I'm getting dressed. I just had to get that smokey smell off me. I'll be down in a minute."

"Can I help you? Can I put the lotion on your back?" Reggie was standing in the doorway, smiling, looking gorgeous. Marianne couldn't refuse him.

"Uh . . . sure. That'll be nice. Thank you." She handed him the lotion that she had mixed with Musk oil. Marianne had on panties and a bra, but didn't feel uncomfortable about her situation. Matter of fact, she felt normal . . . like he's been there . . . doing exactly that . . . a thousand times.

Reggie continued to rub lotion on Marianne's stomach, then legs.

103

"Has anyone every told you how smooth you are? You're really smooth." Reggie was rubbing lotion on Marianne as if she was a delectable desert. He was enjoying every minute. Reggie started taking longer strokes up and down her legs.

"You're beautiful."

He continued with the muscles of her calves; then he started massaging her feet with lotion. Marianne couldn't resist the feeling of closing her eyes. She laid back and let Reggie massage her poor aching feet, then her legs . . . he was up to her thighs again.

"Man, that sure feels good. I've been standing on my feet all day."

"Is that right?" Reggie knew Marianne was talking, but he wasn't listening to a word she was saying. He couldn't take his mind off the young, tender woman that was in the palms of his hands, purring. She's so very beautiful, so very smooth . . . smooth as silk.

"Yes . . . yes, this is, exactly, what I need. Mmmmmmmmmm that feels good."

Before Marianne could say another word, Reggie was lying on top of her, hungrily kissing her everywhere. Marianne spontaneously wrapped her arms around Reggie and was kissing him as if she had done it before. It was natural. But it was actually Marianne's first real tongue kiss.

Reggie whispered in Marianne's ear. "Can I take off my clothes?"

Marianne was shocked. She didn't know what to do. She had never been in a situation like this. But she didn't want to disappoint Reggie. She didn't want to disappoint herself.

She nodded "Yes."

The next morning when Marianne woke up, Reggie was gone. "He's gone. Why did he leave?" She didn't know what to think. Why did he leave without telling her goodbye? Didn't he realize that she was a virgin until last night? Didn't he know that he was the first man she had ever kissed? Marianne kept playing in her mind every scenario that he might think. Should she tell him, does he need to know that last night he took her virginity? Did it matter? She was so confused.

That morning Marianne wanted to sleep in. No one else would be there to open the restaurant. She could have easily called Uncle Charlie, but she didn't like springing surprises like that. He's so reliable. He has never let her down and she wasn't going to let Uncle Charlie down either.

She worked in slow motion. Marianne didn't talk much, only what she needed to say, in as few words as possible. All day she continued through the motions. Everything was so routine that she could do it in her sleep.

Reggie was on the top of her mind. She didn't want to see or speak to anyone else. Marianne was too ashamed to tell Kim that she had gone all the way with Reggie on their first date. Kim would think she's easy. Marianne didn't have anybody to tell her secret to.

It was about 3 p.m., when Uncle Charlie came in to tell Marianne what they would do for the church. Only now, Marianne wasn't as enthusiastic about feeding the church workers anymore. She didn't want to hear about it, she only wanted to hear from Reggie. She needed to talk with him.

"Hey Marianne, Rosie talked with the Reverend last night. They'll eat here next Tuesday. That'll give us time to have everything ready. Rosie was glad to help; she said that was a really nice gesture on your part, to think of the church like that. She's proud of you, just like I am. We'll order some extra chicken, that's what we'll serve everybody, barbeque chicken, baked beans, and coleslaw. We'll have kool-aid to drink and pound cake for desert. Now if anybody wants something different, they'll have to pay for it."

"Okay, Unck, thanks, I know they'll appreciate it."

"Are you okay, sweetheart. I thought you'd be glad to hear about this."

"I am Unck. I'm a little tired today. I couldn't sleep last night."

"You feeling alright? You don't look so good. I'll tell you what. Why don't you go home early today. Just one day off a week will wear anybody down, even a spring chicken like you." Uncle Charlie smiled and kissed Marianne on her forehead. "Go home and get some sleep. You're no good sick and run down."

"Uncle Charlie, that sounds good. Thanks. I'm going home now."

When Marianne got home she was glad to see Darlene getting dressed before heading to the club.

"Hey little sister. I don't get to see you that much. Between the club and work, I barely got time to eat. I got me some of that smoked brisket that was left in the fridge. I hope you don't mind."

"Naw, Darlene. Help yourself, I brought that home for the house. I get tired of all that food up there. When's the last time you talked with Pali and Mr. White? I never see them."

"Them old maids . . . they're locked up in that room upstairs. Girl, you see them more than me. I'm not lying, I hardly have time to wash my butt. It's hard going to school during the day and working at that after hours club all night. It's hard. Then that damn Billy almost got himself shot last night."

"Whaaaat . . . what happened?"

"Oh this guy, you know Fast Eddie? Well, that guy . . . I'm telling you . . . has a 'little man's' complex. We learned about that in my Psychology class. Anyway, he gets mad at Billy cause he lost all his money. You know Billy wouldn't cheat a cheater. Anyway, Fast Eddie had his gun and was gonna shoot Big Bill. Then that fool ass Billy starts agitating

106

him, cracking jokes. I mean Billy was saying all this stuff that rhymes . . . how did he put it? *'I ain't lyin, I don't mind dyin'. My name is Petey Wheatstraw,* all this stuff. It was a mess. People was laughing, and this fool had a gun pointed at Big Bill. I could have killed Billy. I really was scared. They had been drinking, too. You know guns and alcohol don't mix. You'll get killed over money and women faster than anything."

"What happened. How did ya'll get the gun from Fast Eddie?"

"Razz just told him that he couldn't shoot any of his customers. Then he had me fix Eddie a drink. I fixed a big drink for that nut. Razz is so cool. He walked Eddie out the door, then told James, the door man, not to let his ass back upstairs. He can't gamble with Razz anymore."

"Wow! That is scary."

Darlene finally thought about Marianne being home. "What are you doing home this early?"

"I was tired. Uncle Charlie let me off."

"That's good."

"Darlene, can I tell you something? You're like a big sister to me. I don't have anybody to talk with me . . . about my life . . . my personal things . . . you know what I mean?"

"Yeah, baby, I do. It was just me and my grandma. I sure couldn't tell her everything. Well, what is it? You're alright?"

"I'm alright. It's just that I met this guy. I really like him. Anyway, he came here last night."

"Whaaaaaat, you're kidding. Where was Ms. Shirley?"

"She kept Patrick at her house last night. Pali and Mr. White don't come out their room too much. So I had a date."

"What did you guys do here?"

"Well, I was getting dressed then he came in my room."

"He raped you. That nigga raped you, did he?"

"Nooo no no . . . nothing like that."

107

"So did you do it? You didn't have sex, did you?"

"Well, yes, we did?"

"Marianne, I thought you were a virgin or something. I didn't know you been doing it."

"Darlene, I was a virgin. I'm not anymore. What's so bad about it is . . . I don't think he even knows that I was a virgin."

"He knows. Do I know this guy? Who's this guy, where'd he come from? Where's his folks?"

"You probably know him, he's Rev. Williams oldest son, Reginald. We call him Reggie. Darlene, he left without even saying bye. He took my virginity and didn't even tell me 'goodbye,' he didn't ask how I was doing, or anything, he just left. When I woke up this morning, he was gone. He got what he wanted now he's finished with me. I'm embarrassed because, it was my first date and I went all the way with him. Do you think he still likes me?" Marianne eyes filled with tears. She tried hard not to let the tear drop.

"Marianne, he likes you. Are you kidding, girl? Have you looked in a mirror lately? Let me tell you something that my grandma told me about men. Men are hunters. They like to hunt, catch the prey then they'll go for the kill. Last night, Reginald went for the kill. They'll store their treasures in a safe place." Darlene gave Marianne a little wink. "You're his treasure, baby. That's when the two-day rule comes in effect. He won't contact you for two days. He has to recoup, girl. You wore him out." Darlene smiled, but she could tell Marianne was hurt. She wanted to reassure her, and she really didn't want Marianne to feel bad behind some no-good, unappreciative, selfish, piece of dirt, that took that little girl's virginity and didn't have the decency to tell her 'bye.'

Darlene figured Marianne would get over it, in a few days. "Give him two-days before you get worried. Whatever you do, don't contact him. Give him some time and space then

108

let him call you. Trust me, he'll call."

"Okay Darlene. Thanks. Two-day rule."

"That's the two-day rule."

Chapter 10

It was six o'clock Tuesday morning when the phone rang at the Sanders' household.

"Who in the world is calling here this early in the morning?" Mrs. Sanders staggered to the front room where the phone was ringing off the hook. "Hello . . . who is this?"

"Hello . . . Hello, good morning Mrs. Sanders, may I please speak with Terry?"

"Who is this?" She yelled.

"It's Reggie, Rev. William's son."

"Oh Reggie! Just a minute." Mrs. Sanders' voice got a little softer once she realized it was Reggie, he might need something for the Reverend.

"Everything alright at the church? Ya'll find out who broke in there yet?"

"No ma'am, not yet."

"Terry, did you hear me . . . the telephone, boy. Just a minute, it's kind of early for Terry. Let me see if he's up. Terry, Terrrrry . . . get the phone."

"Hello, who is it?"

"Hey man, it's me, Reggie."

"Yeah, what's going on? What you doin' calling me this early in the morning?"

"Terry . . . Man . . . why didn't you tell me 'bout Marianne?"

"Tell you what 'bout Marianne? She's cool with me. Why . . . What's wrong with her?"

"Man, that girl was a virgin."

Terry suddenly woke up. "You got that cherry? . . . You got that cherry? Maaaannn! I can't believe it." Terry was a little mad, irritated, jealous, and proud for his friend. "You lucky dog! How you get Marianne like that? She's a real lady. Every man in town's been trying to luck up on Marianne."

110

"Man, if I would have known she was a virgin, I wouldn't have messed with that girl."

"Ya'll couldn't talk? Why didn't you stop?"

"Are you kidding? Terry . . . it was too late. I couldn't just stop, man. I wish I would have known."

"Well . . . Reggie . . . what you gonna do?"

"I don't know . . . I can't get caught up like this. I'm leaving for college in a month or so. My lady's already there . . . waiting on me. We got plans. We got our whole lives ironed out. I'm not into taking advantage of anybody, especially a good girl like Marianne. I just thought, since she's running a restaurant and a rent house, that she's been doing something. I never would have thought that she was a virgin. Terry, man, I'm engaged. I'm supposed to marry my lady when we graduate, maybe before then."

"What's her name? How long you've been with her, cause you never mentioned that you had a lady to me, man, you never said anything about her."

"It's Vanessa, Vanessa Manson, she's my high school sweetheart. She's at school. We promised each other that we would be faithful while she was away. I love Vanessa, I got caught up."

"Wait a minute, Reggie . . . man, I told you 'bout Marianne, that she wasn't seeing anybody. I told you, man. I've never known Marianne to have a boyfriend. That's why I introduced you to her. She's good, I hate to see her hurt especially with the first guy she's ever dated . . . that I introduced her to . . . I feel bad. So, what you gonna do?"

"I got to let that go, I can't see that girl anymore. I got to explain my situation to her, I hope she understands, I'll take her to dinner somewhere nice and let her know about Vanessa. I wasn't expecting to get involved like that. I really like Marianne."

"Good luck, man. I'm going back to bed. Don't be

111

calling me this early, maaannn."

Almost a week had passed and Marianne hadn't heard a word from Reggie. Kim kept trying to get information from Marianne about their date, but Marianne wasn't budging. There was no way, Marianne would let Kim know what had happened last Monday night between her and Reggie.

"Marianne, have you heard anything from Reggie?"

"No, not since last Monday. Why you ask?"

"Oh, I was just wondering how ya'll's date went. You ain't say'n anything. Did you have fun? What did ya'll end up doing?"

"It was alright. We stayed in, I brought home some brisket; he liked that. We watched TV and ate . . . we talked, that's about all. We didn't do anything special. It wasn't that big of a deal."

"You gonna see him again?"

"I don't know, Kim. Boy, you sure got a long busy nose. What are you and Terry doing these days?"

Kim knew something happened but couldn't get any information from anybody. Terry's been acting more aggressive with her, trying to get her in bed. He knows better than that. My dad would shoot Terry right in his black ass if he had any idea what Terry's been trying to do to her. Nooooo, Kim was too scared of her dad. Something happened with Marianne and Reggie, and Terry knows about it. She decided she would work on Terry. He'll tell her, sooner or later.

"Kim, you know I'm going to need you for the church's dinner tomorrow evening."

"I know, I'll be here. What time are we talking about?"

"Dinner will start at 6:30 p.m., so I'll need you here around 5:30 or 6:00 p.m. Uncle Charlie said the whole church is going to show up." That was the first time Marianne laughed.

"He ain't lying. You know how church people are . . . especially when it comes to free food. Well, we're ready.

112

We're only serving chicken, if anybody wants something different, they'll have to pay for it. "

Marianne was surprised to see Reggie walk in the door, smiling, dressed to a T.

"Hey Marianne, hi Kim."

"Hi Reggie."

"Hi Reggie." Marianne's heart was beating so fast.

"Hey, what are you doing tonight? Can we get together when you get off?"

"I don't know, Reggie. I got a lot to do tomorrow. The church is coming here for dinner."

"I know. That's all they've been talking about, having a fellowship dinner over here."

Kim hurried to cut into the conversation while she had a chance. "Marianne, I'll talk with you later. I got to get home. My little sisters are there by themselves. Now, I keep my next door neighbors' kids too. I'll see you tomorrow, if I don't hear from you . . . I'll be here at 6 o'clock, right? "

Marianne nodded, "Okay, Kim."

"Listen, baby, I know you must think I'm a dog, not calling you. I wanna apologize to you. Can I take you somewhere nice . . . tonight?"

"Reggie, I can't tonight."

"Well, when can I take you out?"

"I don't know Reggie. I'm really busy." Marianne was pissed off that Reggie hadn't called or said anything since their last time together. Her feelings were way too hurt. Just who does he think he is . . . then all of a sudden, he just can walk in here expecting her to jump. No no no, she wasn't that easy.

"Hey, I got something really important to say . . . we need to talk. I'll come over later tonight. around 11:30. If the back door is open, I'll come in." Reggie turned to leave; he walked out the door, without looking back.

At 11:30, on the dot, Reggie was walking in the back

door of the rent house. To his surprise, Pali was in the kitchen fixing a snack for Mr. White.

"Hi Pali. How you doing?"

"Aaaaaaaah Shhiiiiiiiit! Mmmp! Boy! You scared the fire out of me, walking in here, like that. What farm did you come off of? Anybody ever teach you to knock?"

"I'm sorry Pali. I didn't expect you to be down here." Reggie laughed hard, cause Pali screamed, did a dance, and jumped a mile, all at once. His skinny legs were moving.

"I live here, Reggie. What are you doing walking in here, like that? Unannounced!"

"I came to see Marianne. I'll just go upstairs, sorry to disturb you." Reggie wanted to keep his conversation brief with Pali.

"Don't worry about it." Pali settled down and started to laugh hard at himself. He knew he heard something in Marianne room the other night. This just confirmed his suspicions. "Want me to let Marianne know you're here?"

"Naw, that's alright. She knows I'm coming."

Reggie walked through the hallway and up the stairs. He only knocked a couple of times before Marianne invited him in. She was sitting on the bed, still in her work clothes, still beautiful.

"Hi baby. You look tired."

"I am a little. My feet hurt."

Reggie immediately sat next to Marianne, took her shoes off, and began rubbing and massaging the ball of her feet, then the arch, he was taking his time, and it felt so good.

"You don't have to do that."

Reggie ignored Marianne. He continued to work on her, now concentrating on her body. Reggie started kissing Marianne. There was no way she could resist. Her desire to wrap up with Reginald Williams was harder than she ever imagined.

114

"Marianne, you are so beautiful. I can't help myself." Reggie started unbuttoning Marianne's blouse. "You look so gooooood." He was whispering deep in her ear, making goose bumps jump up and down her body. It wasn't long before he had her completely undressed and was lying next to her . . . himself, . . . naked. That's when Marianne surprised Reggie. She took control and began giving Reggie everything that was locked up inside her, that she wanted so much to give, but never had the opportunity. It was okay to do this because for her, he would be the only man that she would ever love.

Reggie wanted to scream and holler, but couldn't because Pali would hear him. So he moaned and groaned, he made unrecognizable sounds from his throat. His hands were waving around uncontrollably . . . what to do with his hands, so he started slapping Marianne's butt, soft at first, then a little harder.

"Hey boy! Stop hitting me like that."

He couldn't do that so he laid back and allowed Marianne to have her way with him. He said a few cuss words, here and there, but for the most part, he took it like a man. He couldn't let Marianne down, so he took all she had to give, until she ultimately gave up. Marianne was out of breath; she then collapsed, still on top of Reggie.

"Your skin next to mine turns me on. It's so dark, and smooth, I'm glowing like a light bulb next to you, lady."

Marianne laughed loud. "You are glowing. I never noticed. Daaanng, Reggie." She was wet with sweat, tired and drained. She had to catch her breathe. They had attacked each other. She was so happy to be there again, lying next to Reggie.

"You're so damned sexy." Reggie continued talking in her ear. He played all over her body, kissing her and rubbing her back and buttocks. Her hair was all over her head. She smelled good with a faint scent of hickory.

"You got pretty hair. It's soft, just like you. Why don't

you wear it down more often and stay out those wigs? Would you do that for me?"

Reggie and Marianne had an animal attraction toward each other. He couldn't resist Marianne Robinson, her Hershey milk chocolate skin was beautiful . . . she looked so good lying next to him. Reggie wanted to keep Marianne, as long as possible, next to him . . . close to him. He desperately needed to talk with her; he had to let her know about his old lady, Vanessa. He didn't want to hurt Marianne; he also wanted to keep her . . . for himself.

Finally, Reggie decided that he wouldn't tell her anything. He would be gone in a month or so . . . why rock the boat. For now, it'll be okay. He'll be gone and Marianne would forget all about him. He hated to admit it, but she'll meet another man.

"Baby, I want you to listen to me. This is serious. Let's not do this again without protection. Get some protection. Get on the pill or something. We can't have any accidents. You're too young and you're waaaay too busy for another baby." Reggie stayed quiet for a moment. He had so much to say, but didn't know where to start.

"Marianne, I admire you, the way you take care of your little brother . . . grown men and women can learn a few things from you. It's amazing. You're so young, so responsible, you have so much going on, and babylove, we don't need any accidents. Shoot, lady, I'll be gone to school in a few days. What I want to say is, let's be careful. No surprises!"

"When are you leaving?"

"In about two months. You'll probably meet some other man while I'm gone. Won't you?" Reggie popped her on the butt again.

"Reggie, I don't want anybody but you. When you met me, did you realize that I was a virgin?"

"Yeah, I found out, a little too late, don't you think?

116

You should have said something. I couldn't believe it. The way you put it on me, Wooooo weeee! and you were a virgin. My . . . my . . . my! How did I get so lucky?"

Reggie got quiet again. "Baby, don't get stuck on me. I don't know how my life will work out. Majoring in music is risky. It's not much money, unless I get real lucky. But that's what I want to do, make music. Hopefully, I'll start a gospel production company. What do you think about that, me making gospel music? I'm gonna work with some big cat's like Rev. Cleveland or Arethea Franklin, somebody like that. I don't know, it's dreamin'."

"Baby, dreams come true."

"Marianne, you got so much going on, I don't want you wasting your time on me. I'm leaving soon. I'll be real busy with everything. I'll have to keep my mind on school and work . . . and getting this company started."

"Is that what you wanted to talk with me about?"

"Yeah, it is."

"I'll get some protection. I'll get an appointment with Dr. Clark. He'll give me some pills."

"Marianne, take care of this . . . okay? Take care of it."

"Okay Reggie."

* * * * *

It was time for the church dinner to begin. Marianne, Uncle Charlie, Ms. Rosie, Kim, Calvin and Victor were ready and in high gear. There was enough smoked chicken to feed an army. Ms. Rosie decided to bake her special pound cake and she had been baking all morning. There were extra ribs, brisket and sides, just in case they needed more.

One by one, members started to float into the restaurant. Ms. Rosie was so happy to have everyone there; it was something that she should have done a long time ago.

"Marianne, baby, it'll be a good idea to set the food out close, so we can get to it. We'll keep it over here." Ms. Rosie

117

pushed three tables together and placed the beans, coleslaw, cake and Kool-Aid on the tables.

"I'll get Kim to serve this table, Ms. Rosie."

"Yeah, baby. That's good. She can do that for us."

"Victor and Calvin got the chickens cut up and ready to go. We can bring that out too."

"Nooo, they can get the chicken first, at the counter. Then, they'll go to the table . . . with Kim. We'll keep them moving all the same direction, it'll be simple."

"Okay, Ms. Rosie."

"Now, baby, I'll need you to take care of the other customers, while this is going on over here."

"Okay, Ms. Rosie."

By this time, Rev Williams and his family walked in the door, everybody was there except Reggie. Marianne was too busy to be concerned. Ms. Rosie greeted Mrs. Williams with a hug and showed them the table where they were to sit. Rev Williams headed straight to Uncle Charlie reaching for his hands. As they were shaking hands, they continued to walk over to a table, away from the rest of his family.

"Uncle Charlie, is that what you want me to call you, sir, Uncle Charlie?"

"Rev, all my friends and family, everybody I know, calls me Uncle Charlie, or just Charlie. My given name is Charles Jackson."

"Well Uncle Charlie, I want to formally thank you for inviting us here. It's a wonderful act of kindness on your part. It's examples like this that makes a community stronger. It shows leadership and guidance during difficult times. Your business stepped up and now showing your strong presence. I'll never forget this kindness you've shown me and my family. Thank you."

"Rev, I'm happy to help. So, do you have an idea who broke in the church?"

"I have an idea, but I'm not positive. I'm sure about one thing; I won't leave myself vulnerable like this again. Uncle Charlie, I've been a fool. I haven't contacted banks around here. I'm still affiliated with my bank in St. Louis. I should have been better with the church's business. What bank do you use around here?"

"There's a local bank on 3rd and Main. We've used that bank for years. It's a little bank, they've served us well. I haven't had any problems with them. Talk with Harold Akins, let him know I referred you."

Suddenly the restaurant was full of people. All at once members of The Redeemer's Baptist Church flocked in the restaurant's booths. It was busy, noisy, and full of life. People were greeting and hugging, as if they hadn't seen each other in months. Other people decided to stop and eat, seeing all the hustle and bustle, they wanted to know what was going on.

Rev Williams stood up to make an announcement.

"Good evening, everybody. Let me welcome you to our Fellowship dinner here at Uncle Charlie's. First, I'd like to thank Uncle Charlie for opening his doors and showing such goodwill during these trying times. Thank you, sir, on behalf of The Redeemers Baptist Church, we thank you." Rev Williams continued speaking to his church members and everybody else that was present and wanting to be a part of this evening.

"I hadn't had a chance to discuss much with Uncle Charlie, but I feel this is a start of a good thing. Maybe we can celebrate our Fellowship dinner here on an annual basis. I'd like to show our gratitude to Mr. Charles Jackson and his lovely wife, Ms. Rosie by supporting this establishment every year, around the same time. Amen? Amen?" Rev Williams looked at Uncle Charlie who wiggled in his chair, not knowing what to expect next.

"When someone shows such generosity as has been shown here, today; we need to respond by showing our gratitude. Uncle Charlie, we, the Redeemer church family will show our support to your business. We'll come on a regular basis and buy all yo' ribs. Ain't that right? Amen . . . amen. Now, let's bless the food." Rev Williams raised his hands, bowed his head, "Bless the food, bless the hands that prepared it. Make it work for the good of our bodies, to serve You better. And Lord, I ask for a special blessing on Uncle Charlie and his family. Amen. Now, let's eat."

The dinner was almost over when Reggie finally walked in; his mother and father had eaten and were long gone. That was just perfect. He couldn't risk his folks seeing Marianne and him in the same room. His mother would, immediately, spot their affection for each other. They all know that he was practically engaged to Vanessa Manson.

Rev Williams and Vanessa's father, Mr. Theodore Manson, were fraternity brothers. Besides that, she was Mr. Manson's only girl and his baby. He'd kill somebody over her.

Reggie and Vanessa had known each other in elementary school and had seriously dated since high school. They were both in college.

Reggie had always known that she would, one day, be his wife. Vanessa was beautiful, sweet, and so very smart. She was studying for a Law degree. But Reggie figured once they finished college, they would marry. She would probably teach high school, somewhere. Reggie couldn't see Vanessa doing anything but being the mother of his children. He didn't want her to work. He'd rather her be like his momma, stay home, take care of their kids, be a house wife.

Marianne was tired. Kim and Terry were in the back helping Victor and Calvin clean up. Ms. Rosie had slipped out earlier after the Reverend went home. Uncle Charlie was at a table, counting money. He couldn't believe all the money he'd made, all that food was gone. He thought the whole town must have showed up. Many that came weren't members. They saw all the ruckus and all the cars; so they all stopped and they all ate.

Uncle Charlie was tired but he enjoyed the night. He'd never been around so many church folk in his life. He made so much money; he couldn't believe it, especially considering this was a free meal. All he could do was laugh, scratch his head, and think about his new friend, Reverend Williams.

"Hi Reggie."

"Hi baby." Reggie pulled Marianne to a corner where he was sure they couldn't be seen then he gave Marianne a passionate, wet kiss.

"Mmmmmmmmm, that taste good." She was licking her lips.

Marianne turned Reggie on. He couldn't wait to hold her again. "What are you doing when you get off tonight?"

"Reggie, I got to see Dr. Clark before long. If you come over, you got to promise to be good. You know we've been taking chances?"

"I know . . . I know. Try to get an appointment this week. But I'll come over for a little while. I want to see you. Girrrrrrrrrl! You promise to be good! You know how crazy you get when I come around. You promise to be good if I come over there?" Reggie stuck his tongue in her mouth.

"Oh oh, man, excuse me." Uncle Charlie walked in on Reggie and Marianne playing in a corner. He was kissing her, his hands were on her butt, he was rubbing and squeezing it.

When Marianne opened her eyes, she saw Uncle Charlie watching them, she pushed Reggie away so hard that he tripped over a chair; he tumbled down, barely hitting the floor. Reggie jumped up just as fast. He had a bewildered look when he saw Uncle Charlie standing in front of them.

Uncle Charlie was in total shock. He had never worried about Marianne and some no-good boy. She was too smart for that. She saw her mother with Lonnie Evans all those years.

121

He not providing for them, as she thought he should. Nope, Uncle Charlie never worried about Marianne. Was it time for her to meet a nice young man? He didn't want to face that.

"WHAT'S GOIN' ON BACK HE'AH?" Uncle Charlie was shocked. "Ya'll can't be doing too much work in this corner. Marianne how long before you'll be finished and we can close this place up. You got to come in early in the morning . . . daylight comes fast." He walked back to the front of the restaurant. "Tell that young man you'll see him later."

"Oh, huh, Uncle Charlie, me and Kim will close. I'll be here early. Victor and Calvin are coming early too." Marianne smiled at Reggie, then whispered, "I'll see you tomorrow."

"I'll call you." Reggie gave Marianne the eye. "Take care."

Marianne knew exactly what he meant.

Chapter 11

"Hello. This is Dr. Clark's office, Nurse Helen Watson speaking. How may I help you?"

"Hi, Ms. Helen, how are you? This is Marianne Robinson, I wanna make an appointment."

"Hi baby. Is everything alright? How's that little brother of yours?"

"Everything's fine, Ms. Helen. Patrick's doing good. He's gotten big, and he's talking a lot, we're okay Ms. Helen. But, I wanted to see the doctor for personal reasons."

Ms. Helen knew exactly what that meant. Marianne had some kind of infection. These guys are messing with these little girls, and giving them all these diseases . . . like nobody's business . . . or maybe she needs protection, you won't find her all knocked up. She needs an IUD. That was the best thing to do.

"When you wanna come in baby?"

"Do you think I can see him this week?"

"Sure baby, let's see. How about Thursday morning? You'll need to be here early. I got an opening at 9 a.m., is that a good time, 9 o'clock, Thursday morning?"

"Yes ma'am. I'll be there. Thank you, Ms Helen." Marianne hung up the phone and continued her daily task of opening the restaurant. Victor and Calvin were in the back, smoking meat; they had to cook a whole day's supply of everything. Victor didn't like coming that early, but he didn't like working anyway, so it didn't matter. Victor complained all day.

Marianne was glad to have her doctor's appointment this week. She knew she wouldn't see Reggie. "No . . . not this soon." They just made love, so she wouldn't see him for a couple of days, which was good in a way. It gave her more time to catch up with Patrick and do some window cleaning that she'd had put off for too long.

Lord knows, she hadn't spent enough time with Patrick. He's always asleep when she gets home from work; and in the morning he's asleep before she goes to work . . . sometimes she'll wake him up, just to say hi at night or bye in the mornings. Marianne felt guilty about leaving him so much, thankfully she had her friends. They were more like family, the only family in her life. How could she live without Ms. Shirley and Aunt Rosie being there for Patrick? Even Big Billy and Pali were there helping out with her little brother, they saw him more than she did.

* * * * *

The radio was playing Eddie Kendrick's song, *"Skipping work is on my mind, oh it's such a beautiful day . . ."*

"That DJ ought to be ashamed, playing that song, this early, on this beautiful morning. Dang, it's a pretty morning here, too, Eddie." Darlene sang, *"Skipping work, is on my mind . . . oh it's such a beautiful day . . .* that sure is a pretty song."

Darlene was at the house getting dressed for school. She was thinking about skipping class. It was summer and she wondered what on earth made her take summer classes, as much as she needed a break. Darlene was tired. She worked hard, sometimes all night, really pushing herself to finish college. Well, it was only two classes this summer. They would be over in a few weeks and then she was going to New York to see her grandma.

Something had to be done about that situation. Her grandma was too far away and she promised herself that once she got settled, she would go see her. But that wouldn't do either, because she could only stay a few days, then it would be time to come back home. Darlene wanted her grandmother living with her, in Kansas City.

* * * * *

Billy Joe was sleeping his drunk off when the smell of

pot roast woke him up. He'd usually sleep all morning. He'd get up around 3 p.m., shower in time for dinner, right on time . . . when the food was good and hot. Ms. Shirley was faithful about having something wonderful and ready to eat. There was still spaghetti left over from yesterday, and he'd planned on taking on that responsibility, too. He didn't believe in food spoiling or going bad. That wouldn't be right. Not with all the people starving in the world. Big Billy Joe Washington would handle all leftovers.

Billy rolled around in bed, sleeping all morning, and thinking about the night before. He met a cutie pie named Michelle Parks, and she was meeting him at Razz's place tonight. He'd hit a good lick at the crap table . . . made over 700 hundred bucks. He wore Po Boy out and last night, Po Boy sho wuzz a Poooo boy.

Billy Joe broke Po Boy's confidence. He teased Po Boy all night talking about his white patent-leather shoes, telling him they were Easter shoes. What made Po Boy buy white shoes in the first place? They're janky, bad luck, everybody knew that.

The food smelled so good, he turned on the TV and waited to hear Ms. Shirley call from the kitchen, telling him to come and eat. Life was good . . . good food . . . good women . . . and a pocket full of money, who could ask for more.

* * * * *

Patrick was wrestling and making a fuss cause he was sleepy. Ms. Rosie had bathed and fed him a plate of mashed potatoes and gravy, with a little pot roast cut up real fine. Patrick ate good and it was time for him to let everybody rest. Aunt Rosie wanted to go home; she made a point to be home with her husband by 4 p.m. She was ready to go, and this boy didn't want to take his nap.

"Patrick boy, come here. I don't have time to play with you." She faintly swung the dish towel.

Patrick was running and laughing. He spotted a rolley

125

polley in the window ceil. "Bug! Bug! See bug."

"Yeah I see the bug, now you come on and settle down. I got to go home to my husband."

All of a sudden Patrick bent down and started looking between his legs. He got up, ran around, and again bent down and looked between his legs.

"Boy what are you doing? SHIRLEY!" Ms. Rosie was practically screaming. "Look at this boy . . . You see what he's doing?"

Patrick was there, bent at the waist, looking between his legs, which is the sho-nuff sign that another baby is on the way. It's one of those old wives tales that you can take to the bank.

"Now Rosie, you don't have to worry about that. Patricia is gone . . . so ain't no nuther baby coming 'round here any time soon."

"Yeah, I guess you're right. It's just something. Why is he doing that?" Aunt Rosie grabbed Patrick before he could do it again. "Stop that boy! Get up from there."

"It could be a natural thing that babies do when it's time for a little brother or sister." Ms. Shirley wasn't worried about Patrick was looking between his legs. As far as she knew, Marianne never had a boyfriend and Darlene was too busy to squeeze a man into her schedule. Ms. Shirley wasn't worried at all.

Ms. Rosie began rocking Patrick to sleep. She was leaving and she wanted him sleep long enough to give everybody in the house a break. If he'd take a good nap now, maybe he and his sister could have a little time together, later on, when she gets off work. That poor little baby don't spend enough time with his big sister. Hopefully they can visit before he forgets who she is, altogether.

* * * * *

"Billy . . . Billy, I know you're not still sleep. Get up, everybody in the house is up but you." Darlene was home

126

from school, knocking on Billy's door. "What are you doin' around the first of August?"

"Stop making all that noise. Come in. Do you always got to be so loud and the center of attention, all the time, Darlene? A lady is supposed to be sweet and quiet." Billy made a gesture putting his finger to his lips; then making the 'shusssh' sound.

He was up and moving around, hanging up clothes that were sprawled all over the room. It was time for a good cleaning. Usually Ms. Shirley took care of that, he'd give her a few bucks and she'd clean it like he liked.

"I don't know what I'll be doing then . . . in August . . . That's about two months from now. Why? What's up?"

"I was thinking about going to New York, and getting my grandma. I'm moving her here with me."

"Darlene, sweetheart. I'm not going to New York to do no moving."

"I just thought, maybe you wanna ride with me. It'll be fun. We can make a vacation out of it." Darlene was talking in the sweetest voice she could conjure up.

"Naaaaw, I don't want to ride with you to New York, but thanks for the offer. Be safe." Billy had gotten use to Darlene's beauty and manipulation, so he continued to clean his room while sorting clothes for the laundry mat.

"Anyway, where you gonna put your grandmother? There's not any rooms vacant around here. You can't afford another place, can you?" Billy looked at Darlene, giving her a good warning.

"Don't be bringing your grandma here . . . without a place to put her. That wouldn't be right. You need your own place. Just visit her until you can get your own place, so she can be comfortable."

Darlene sat down, holding her stomach, rocking . . . like Billy just knocked the life out of her. Billy could see he had broken her spirit. She wasn't excited anymore. He was glad that she listened when he talked good old common sense to her.

Big Bill was a little more companionate, he spoke in a softer voice.

"Darlene, you're too quick to do things. Just for once, think things out. Take your time, get you a nice place then bring grandma here. I might ride with you then . . . or give you a couple dollars to help you with your trip, but you got to plan it better than this . . . you can't just go on a whim, and move your grandmother to Kansas City. I bet you haven't even discussed it with her, have you?"

"Big Bill, it's been so long since I've seen her. I worry so much about her, in New York, living all by herself. Nobody's gonna take care of her . . . not like I do. I just don't see how I can leave her again."

"Where you gonna put her, Darlene?"

"She can stay with me in my room. Pali and Mr. White share a room together. Me and my grandma can do the same thing."

"Darlene, that's crazy. What about her things? Where you gonna put all her stuff?"

"I don't know. Shoot that stuff is so old. She has pictures of those two kids, with the big wide eyes, you know what I'm talking about? You know those velvet pictures that was around 20 years ago? Well . . ."

Billy nodding. He laughed "I'd forgotten all about those, she still has one of those pictures?"

"Yeah, she has a couple of them big spoons and forks hanging on the wall too. Maybe she'll leave 'em there. I got to bring her here. I can't leave her in New York."

"Why don't you fly out there? That way you won't spend so much time driving. You can sell her things, use the money to get ya'll a nice place."

"Billy, nobody's gonna buy that stuff. I told you, it's old and raggedy."

"Well, I'll tell you what . . . I'll see you when you get back. I hope ya'll have a safe trip."

Darlene sat in Billy's room not saying anything. She was deep in thought.

"You know what, Billy, I think you're right. I know what I'm going to do. I'm going to fly out there, convince her to come visit me for a little while." She was quiet, still thinking thing through. "My cousins will probably take that stuff. I'll have them send us the family pictures. I have a picture of me and my mother . . . taken when I was a baby, I don't want to lose that, but that other junk can go. My cousin Whitney can stay at grandma's house."

"There you go, making plans before you discuss it with anybody."

Darlene looked at Billy with her pretty smile. She got up, walked to the door to leave Billy's room. Her mind was made up. "I'm gonna fly to New York, get my grandmother, tell her to come visit me for a while . . . then I won't send her back."

"Darlene . . . Darlene! Are you crazy? You can't do people like that."

Darlene wasn't listening to Billy. She headed toward the kitchen. "Damn, I'm hungry. Ms. Shirley, what's that you're cooking? It sure smells good."

* * * * *

It was 7:30 a.m. Thursday morning; Marianne was at the restaurant working fast, getting as much done before her appointment with Dr. Clark. She had decided on getting an IUD. She wondered if Reggie would be able to feel it.

She thought about Reggie, how sweet and thoughtful he was . . . making sure she won't get in trouble. Most of the guys she knew wouldn't give a damn about being safe. He was right, she was waaaaaaay too busy to be getting pregnant, and have a baby running around. One day she would have his baby. When he finished school, they would get married and have a family. Marianne was daydreaming about Reggie, when the phone rang.

"Hello, Uncle Charlie's Que Shop, how may I help you?"

"Hello, Marianne? This is Helen at Dr. Clark's office. There's been an accident in his family. The doctor had to rush out of town. I don't know how long he'll be away, but he won't be able to see you today."

That was not the news Marianne wanted to hear.

"Not today!" This is the day, when she would take care of her and Reggie's personal business. "Is everything alright with Dr. Clark?"

"His baby sister was in a car accident yesterday. A truck ran into her car with her kids and we don't know very much more except . . . she's in a coma. I don't know anything else, I don't know about her kids. I should be hearing from him soon. So pray for 'em."

"Oh that's terrible." Marianne felt a little guilty. "Whow, I hope they're alright. I sure hate to hear that. Gosh, Poor Dr. Clark, I'm so sorry."

"Me too, baby, me too. I've been rescheduling everybody with Dr. Wilson. If you like, I can set an appointment for you, too. I'll just let you know the date and time."

"Ms. Helen, I can do it. You're busy, I can make the appointment. Just give me his number."

"Okay, whatever you like."

Nurse Helen gave Marianne the number for Dr. Wilson's office, but she wasn't able to schedule an appointment as early as she liked.

130

* * * * *

Sunday morning Marianne decided to surprise Reggie by visiting his church. She sat in the same spot, where she could get a good look at her Reggie. He seemed more preoccupied than usual, he didn't give her that 'I see you're here look' that he gave when she visited before. The look that let her know he was paying attention. In fact, Reggie sort of ignored Marianne. She decided it was too soon. They had made love a few days ago. The two day rule was over and he should be glad to see her.

Kim and Terry walked in together. They noticed Marianne at the same time. They didn't seem happy to see her either.

"Man, they don't like my surprise. I should have called before I came here." Marianne thought everybody had gone crazy. She waited for her friends to see what was wrong with everybody.

"Hi Kim, hi Terry."

"Hey Marianne. What made you come to church today?" Terry was speaking while rushing to put on his choir robe.

"I got to sing. I'll talk to you later." The music started, signaling the choir to get in line. Terry got behind everybody, giving last minute instructions as they prepared to march in.

"You decided to leave Patrick home today?"

"Yeah, I thought I'd surprise Reggie, but he's not happy to see me."

"Marianne, girrrrrrrrrl, I hate to tell you this . . . but uh, Reggie has uh . . ."

At that time Mrs. Williams, Reggie's mother walked up with her twin girls in each hand and a pretty friend at her side.

"Hello again, I'm so happy you're here." Mrs. William reached out and gave Marianne a big hug. "Marianne, I just

131

want to tell you personally what a wonderful time we had at the restaurant. They tell me that it was all your idea. You know, it takes a special person to want to do something like that. God Bless you, dear. I get feelings about people and I'm usually right. Continue to do good. God'll bless ya."

"Thank you Mrs. Williams. I was glad to do it." Marianne spoke to Mrs. Williams, but her eyes were glued to the pretty young lady that was with her.

"Let me introduce you to Vanessa. Vanessa Manson, this is Marianne Robinson. She's the one I told you about, that runs the barbeque place . . . wonderful food. I'll take you there while you're here visiting."

Kim flopped down in a seat holding her head down, slowly shaking it.

"Marianne, this is Reginald's fiancée, Vanessa. She's here visiting with Reggie. We're gonna have a wedding one day soon." Mrs. Williams gave Vanessa a motherly smile.

Just then the music started. The choir began marching in step, singing. *"We come this faarr by faaaith. Leaning oooonnn the Looorrrd. Trusting in His Holy word . He never failed me yeeettt. Ohhh oh oh oooh oh oh oh, can't turn arouuuunnnnd. He never faaaillled me yet."*

Reggie began singing, loud and thunderous . . . rocking back and forth, the choir following his every move.

"Nice meeting you." Vanessa gave Marianne a cordial greeting. "We better find us a seat, Mrs. Williams." She then turned to Marianne, "Maybe Reggie'll take me to get some of that good barbeque before we leave for school."

132

Chapter 12

Water was forming in Marianne's eyes. This hurt, but I got to keep my dignity. I'm not going to cry in front of all these people . . . not at this church, not in front of Reggie. Marianne summoned all her strength, determined not to show any signs of pain. Did Kim know about Reggie having a fiancée, this Vanessa girl? Marianne looked at Kim with hurt and anger. Kim knew exactly what she was thinking.

"I didn't know . . . not until this morning. She was introduced to everybody at Sunday school." Kim whispered. "I was going to tell you as soon as church was out. I swear I didn't know."

Marianne started batting her eyes as fast as she could, fighting hard not to drop a tear . . . holding her composure.

"Be strong, be strong." She kept telling her eyes. Thoughts crept in her mind seeing Reggie making love to Vanessa. Why didn't he tell me? Reggie's engaged? He thinks I'm a damn fool.

Kim and Marianne sat together without saying a word. Kim watched her friend. She saw the tears ready to unleash, but not one fell down her perfectly made up face.

"You want to go? Let's just leave." Kim whispered. She wanted to hug her friend. She could see the pain hovering over her body. Daaaannng. Marianne really liked Reggie. They must have been closer than I thought. Terry had never hurt Kim in any way. Kim thought about Terry and their relationship. He better not ever think he could do me like that, if Terry ever played on me, I'll kick his ass.

Just as Marianne and Kim stood up to leave, the Rev. Williams stood up and motioned the congregation to stand with him and he began his prayer.

"Let the words of my mouth, the meditation of my heart,

133

be acceptable in Thy sight. Oh Lord. You are my strength and my Redeemer. Amen, amen. Please, be seated. I'm so glad to be here, in the house of God. Seeing you here, every Sunday, is a good sight for this preacher, and I thank God for you. We have a wonderful God, full of grace and mercy."

"Marianne, maybe we should stay. Rev. Williams always has the right things to say."

Marianne looked at Kim with disbelief. But not wanting to draw any attention to herself, she hurriedly sat down before any more members looked in her direction.

"All those who have your bibles, please turn with me to the book of Romans 1: 19-20. This morning we're going to talk about 'The Love of God.' That's powerful, right there. Amen!

First things first, let's acknowledge the existence of God. We do have a Father in heaven, He's God. Listen to this." Rev. Williams continued to read versus 19 and 20 . . . *20For the invisible things of Him from the creation of the world are clearly seen . . . being understood by the things that are made, even His eternal power and Godhead; so that they are without excuse:"*

"Do you understand what the bible's saying here? We don't have an excuse. Just look at creation, look at the sun and the moon. Look at the earth, where we live. We are witnesses to every new morning. We have to acknowledge God. Praise Him every morning that you open your eyes. Praise Him for each breath you take. And guess what? He loves you. The Father loves you more than anything you can ever imagine."

Rev. Williams had their attention. Marianne had never thought about it like that. She suddenly became aware that she needed to thank God. She got a sense of urgency to praise Him, because she had never thanked Him for taking care of her and Patrick after their mother passed. She had everything she needed and never thanked God. Marianne quietly said a little quickie prayer, thanking God for looking after her and Patrick.

Rev. Williams was getting deep into his sermon.

"Now let's turn over to the fifth chapter of Romans." Rev. Williams had a deep velvety voice. He's a big guy with thick glasses that made him look like a preacher, he walked and talked like a preacher. Marianne continued to check the preacher out, unconsciously grading him.

After thoroughly looking him over, she concluded that he was sincere. Although he was walking back and forth, screaming, sweating and spitting, all over the men that sat in the front seats, she believed what he was saying. She focused back on to the sermon.

"That's real love. The love you can depend on, the love that won't let you down, the love that gave up His only begotten Son, just for you. It's love that wants you, to live forever, with Him in heaven, as a son or daughter of The Most High. There is nothing in heaven or earth that can compare to the love of God. I'm not saying you'll never feel pain. No no no, I'm not saying that, cause it's going to rain on your parade, one day you're gonna hurt. But it's better with Him than without Him. I guarantee you, it's better to know that He's on your side."

Marianne was listening intensely.

"I love my wife. In fact, when we were young, I use to walk ten miles just to see her for one hour, I would have walked twenty. I was sick in love. You may have felt that way, sometime in your life, you may have been lovesick. Brothers and sisters, I have to be honest, one day my wife may leave me, or I could leave her. It's going to hurt more than anything I have ever experience or want to. One day, we'll all have to travel down that road. But if you want to experience eternal love, the love that will never die. Try our God. Give Him a chance in your life. Put your trust in Him. I promise, He'll never leave you or forsake you. Will you try Him?"

Before Marianne could blink, she felt her legs stand up and walk to the front of the church. It was as if she was supposed to go. Tears flowed down Kim's face. Aunt Rosie got up immediately to stand with Marianne. To her surprise, Reggie left the choir stand and stood on the other side of his friend, with tears streaming down his face he interlocked their fingers then their arms, securely holding her close. Kim and Terry followed and stood behind Marianne, they laid their hands on her shoulders.

Rev. Williams was taken back by Reggie's closeness to Marianne. But seeing the other youngsters standing behind her made him proud of the youth in his church. He began to pray.

"Lord, thank you for your daughter, we thank you for the friends that have come to share this time and moment. We ask for favor on her life, we ask that You unleashed the Holy Spirit in her mind and body. Give her strength Lord to stand on Your word, to trust in You and only You. We ask that we become the church family that will continue her growth and knowledge of the love, grace, and mercy that only You can give. Amen. Marianne Robinson, are you willing to accept Jesus the Christ as your Lord and Savoir, that died on the cross as redemption for you as a child of God?"

"Yes, I do."

"Do you want to become a member here, at this church?"

"Yes sir."

"What's your pleasure?"

Reggie responded. "I move that Marianne Robinson become a member of this, the Lord's house."

Another deacon seconded

"What the vote?"

The congregation voted. "Aye"

"The devil has no vote here. Welcome to Redeemers."

136

Reginald looked at Marianne, his eyes told it all. He was guilty. He hugged her then whispered in her ear, "I'm so sorry. I didn't mean for you to find out like this. Can I explain?"

Marianne didn't hesitate. "No Reggie."

Reginald stood looking at Marianne giving her a mental goodbye then turned to stand his mother and Vanessa. He decided to leave early with Vanessa and go back to school.

He lingered tearing down the equipment, checking the microphones and locks. After the recent break in, he had to be careful.

"Reggie, you need some help?" Terry wanted to dodge Kim and Marianne.

"Naw man, I'll do it."

"Let me help you. Look at you. You're feeling like dodo right now. Why your girl come down here, anyway? I thought she was going to summer school?" Terry was trying to comfort his friend as best he could.

"I guess she wanted to surprise me. Then Marianne showing up like that, I've never hurt like this. Man, this hurts." Reginald shook his head disbelieving his mess.

"You hurt? Maannnnn, Marianne was crushed. She had me 'bout to cry, especially when she got up like that."

"She was devastated. Terry I'm going back to school with Vanessa. I can't face Marianne. What am I supposed to say after this?"

"Nothing, she probably won't talk to you."

"I really have feelings for that girl. I feel like . . . I need to leave her alone. I got to let that go."

"When you leaving?"

"We'll get out Tuesday or early Wednesday."

"You gonna see her before you leave?"

"Naw, don't let her stop coming to church."

"Reggie, I don't think you had anything to do with that. I think Marianne was sincere about joining church."

"Every now and then, you'll let me know how she's doing, won't you?"

"Yeah, Marianne's a survivor. If you think she's going to roll over after this, then you didn't know her. She'll be fine, man. You're not going to tell her bye?"

"I can't."

* * * * *

For the rest of the Sunday, Marianne stayed home with Patrick, her mind replaying the day's events. Rev. Williams' sermon was exactly what she needed to hear. It was amazing. It was as if he knew about her situation and was talking directly to her.

She kept seeing Vanessa Manson, Reginald's fiancée, wondering what made Reggie want to marry that girl? Did he really ask her to marry him? She couldn't connect it to reality. Not after everything they'd shared. Did he really love Vanessa? How could he want her after making love to me? It was too much for Marianne to understand.

Then she thought about Rev. Williams. He told her to trust God's love. Marianne decided that day that she would trust God and only God. She thought about the people that she loved the most, they had already left her. Her mother, her father, although she never even met the guy, she still loved him. Her grandmother, Maxine was gone. Now Reggie is gone too. One day Uncle Charlie and Aunt Rosie will die, they'll be gone and leave her and Patrick alone. There's not one person that she could say will always be there. Not one.

She held her little brother. "Baby, I'm going to make sure we're alright. I know Uncle Charlie will try to do everything for us, but what if he can't. What if something happens to him? We'll have to be there for Aunt Rosie, and

Ms. Shirley, and Clarence. One day they'll get old too. We'll have to be ready."

Just then the phone rang and Kim was on the other end hating to break the news, but she felt it necessary to let Marianne know about Reggie's plans.

"Hey girl. I just thought I'd let you know that Reggie's leaving Tuesday or early Wednesday with Vanessa. He decided to go to summer school. Terry said he didn't want to face you again."

"Oh is that right?"

"Marianne, I believe Reggie does care for you. Fiancée or not, he was right by your side in church today. I think you caught him by surprise. He didn't want it to end this way, he probably thought he would leave for school and you would forget about him or something."

"Dang Kim, you sure know a lot about how Reggie was feeling. Too bad you didn't know about his fiancée."

"Yeah, we all were sucker punched with that one. Terry told me all that other stuff. You know they talked after church. He said Reggie just want to leave Kansas City and forget about you."

"Well maybe that's a good idea. I'm tired Kim. I need a nap. I'll talk with you."

Marianne laid down and cried herself to sleep, holding on to Patrick. Every now and then, she'd wake up and ask God. "What now, Lord? What am I supposed to do with my life? Why am I here?" She dozed off again, still crying.

* * * * *

Big Bill was at Razz's with his new girlfriend, having drinks and fun. He had won a few dollars playing cooncan with some of the old timers. He was waiting to see Darlene, she was late; he couldn't remember his little girlfriends name and wanted Darlene to find out before he got in trouble. Darlene knows it, or she'll at least help him out. Big Bill waited and continued to entertain his friend with his jokes and rhymes and toasts.

Twas 1919 on May the 3rd. When the Great Titanic hit a big iceburg. There were 4000 whites on board at the time, and one Nigga by the name of Shine. Shine said, "Capt'n don't you know, there's 40 foot of water on the ballroom flo." The capt'n said "Shine, as sure as this day's gonna pass, if you are lying, I'm gonna kick your po black ass.

About that time the Capt'n wife came on deck, with ruby's on her fingers and diamonds round her neck. She said "Shine Shine save poor me, I will make you richer than a nigga could ever be." Shine said "money is good while it lasts, but Shine has to save his own black ass."

There was loud laughter and every now and then another man would put his addition to the toast, just to let them know that it was more to the story. This time it was Razz that added to the toast.

Then the capt'n daughter jumped up on deck, with titties in her hands and her draws around her neck. She said "Shine Shine save poor me, I'll give you more ussy than any nigga could see. Shine said "ussy on land or ussy at see, you'd better jump your ass in and swim like me."

Again, loud laughter erupted with backslapping agreement around the tables and bar. Razz being the gentlemen that he is, wouldn't say the vulgar words in front of his lady customers. That's why so many women like Razz. He was always considerate of the other person, especially his lady customers.

Just as Bill was getting ready to do another addition to the Shine saga, Darlene walked in the door. "It's about time." Bill whispered under his breathe. "Hey baby, do me a favor, ask Darlene to come over here. Then call Uncle Charlie's and order me something to eat."

"Sure Bill, what you feel like eating?"

"Any thang, it don't matter. Tell Darlene to come here first."

Darlene walked over to Bill, "What's going on, Billy boy?"

"Darlene, what's the lady's name that's sitting with me, the one that told you to come over, what's her name? I forgot it."

"What's it worth to you?"

"Come on now, before she gets back."

"I don't know, what's it worth to you?"

Just then she walked back to the table. "Bill, Uncle Charlie's closed. They didn't answer the phone."

"Michelle, girrrrll, that dress is sure fitting you girl. Where'd you get it?"

"I make my own designs. My sisters and I have a little boutique. We design hats too. Sometimes we order dresses from New York. You should come by the shop. I got some dresses that are cold blooded. Come by some time, I'll give you a deal."

Darlene grabbed a chair from the other table and continued to talk about the dresses at Parks Sisters Dress Shop. She was especially interested in the ones from New York City.

Chapter 13

The summer of 1970 was just about over. Marianne had put the love affair with Reginald Lamont Williams behind her and she was moving on. She had so much to do with work, taking care of Patrick, and a few other things. Uncle Charlie told her to branch out and invest some money. He's been talking a lot about that lately.

"Marianne, I got a meeting at the bank Monday. I need you to come, too. You need to know 'bout these stock and bonds . . . these investments I got for you and Patrick. You need to understand how all this work."

"Okay Uncle Charlie. What kind of stock and bonds?"

"I got some government bonds. A few stocks in the telephone company and GE. But you need experience buying for yourself. Let your money make money, don't let it just sit in the bank when it could be making you a little income."

Uncle Charlie was always teaching and preparing Marianne for the real world. Uncle Charlie taught Marianne how to pay bills, pay taxes and meet payroll. She bought inventory and supplies. She signed all the tickets from the vendors that made deliveries. Marianne even decided to hire two waitresses. She was moving fast and now, she needed room to grow.

"Uncle Charlie, this sauce business is starting to move on up." Marianne did a little dance, then starting singing Curtis Mayfield's song, *Lord have mercy, we're moving on up . . . moving on up.* We need to think about a spot that only makes the sauces. You got all these bottles and supplies taking all my room. We're running over each other around here. If we move the sauces to another building, then we could open up more space at the restaurant. Pretty soon, we'll be big enough to supply the stores and restaurants around here. I know Hickory and Orange Citrus would hit big at the hotels, if we could only supply them, and right now we can't cause we don't have room. Another building would more than pay for itself. What do you think, Uncle Charlie?"

It wasn't a week before Uncle Charlie opened a spot for his famous Kansas City's Gourmet Bar-B-Q sauces. At that point, he hired another three workers. The restaurant was good, the sauce business was exploding, and their money was invested. Patrick was growing like a weed, and her new church was absolutely wonderful. Marianne was definitely moving on with her life.

* * * * *

On Wednesday morning, Aunt Rosie woke up, very early and very disturbed. She had a dream and Aunt Rosie didn't play when it came to certain dreams. She got up, paced the kitchen floor awhile, then made breakfast for Uncle Charlie.

Charlie usually had breakfast on the road. He'd stop at one of the restaurants around town and shoot the bull with the old timers and a few new buddies. But today Rosie was fidgeting around the kitchen, before she realized it, she had ham and eggs, with smothered potatoes, pancakes and hot Louisiana sorghum covering the table, Uncle Charlie wasn't fast enough. The old timers were going to miss him today.

How long had it been since she even remembered a dream . . . years. When she remembered a dream, she could take it to the bank. It was something that was happening, a death or a birth, and she needed to prepare herself right now.

"Hello Shirley, Shirley, honey can we talk? You got time? It's important."

"Okay baby, is everything alright? You and Charlie are alright?"

"Yes Shirley, nothing like that, it's just that . . . I don't know. I'll be over there in a few minutes. I'm waiting on

Charlie to finish his breakfast, then I'll be right there."

"Okay, take it easy Rosie. It can't be that bad."

When Aunt Rosie arrived she didn't waste any time. She went straight to the point.

"Shirley, last night I dreamed about fishes, and guess who's in the dream? It's Marianne. I told you, I told you. When Patrick was bending down, looking between his legs, remember that? Shirley, that's been over two months. That baby was making signs waaay back then . . . Marianne is pregnant."

"Rosie, you can't be serious. You mean to tell me, you're having dreams of fishes and now accusing Marianne of being pregnant. You believe in the tooth fairy? Marianne's not pregnant. That's superstition Rosie. You worry yourself for nothing."

"Shirley, you believe what you want, but I'm telling you here and now, Marianne is pregnant. Everything isn't superstition Shirley, sometime people have dreams. The bible says men will see visions and have dreams. You believe what you want, but I'm telling you, our little girl is pregnant. So you better get ready. You gonna ask her?"

"Oh no Darling! I'm not asking her nothing. You're the one having dreams of fishes. You ask her, yourself."

* * * * *

Sunday morning Marianne planned on attending church. She couldn't believe that she overslept. She slept the whole morning.

"I must have been tired to sleep like this. It's already 10:30. I'll never make it in time for church. Where's Patrick?" Marianne walked downstairs.

"Ms. Shirley, is Patrick with you?" Pali and Mr. White were sitting in the kitchen, having breakfast.

"Is Patrick with Ms. Shirley? I didn't hear her take him

144

this morning."

"Cause, you were knocked out, girly." Pali had a habit of smacking his lips when he talked.

"Mrs. Shirley took Patrick to church with her. You must be really tired? So sugar baby, is it true? Tell me and Mr. White what's happening with you? Is it true?"

"What are you talking about Pali? Is what true?"

"Well, Aunt Rosie's been having dreams of fishes. She thinks you have a little baby growing inside there." Pali pointed at her stomach and turned to Mr. White. "What do you think? Is Marianne PG?"

The realization made Marianne light headed, then dizzy, she was going down. Pali jumped when he heard the hard thump.

"She fainted. Get her, Jeffrey."

Marianne hit the floor before Mr. White could catch her. When Marianne woke up, she was lying on the sofa, and Pali was running around frantic.

"Oh Marianne, I'm sorry. Sweetie, sugar baby, you alright? Is she okay? Honey, speak to me!"

"She'll be okay. She got a little dizzy is all. Marianne, drink this." Mr. White gave Marianne a warm glass of milk. "You drink this down and rest today. Maybe you can see a doctor come Monday morning. Check out these rumors that's running around here." Mr. White flashed his million dollar smile, then continued to feed Marianne the warm milk. "Yeah, that's right, drink it down baby, you'll feel better in a few minutes."

Everybody heard about Marianne's fainting spell. Uncle Charlie left word for her to stay home tomorrow and see a doctor. Deep down, Marianne knew she was pregnant. It was so ironic, because pregnancy never crossed her mind until she heard those words from Pali. And now, she's positive. That

145

feeling of being full . . . it's true. She only had sex three times and that was it. It's so crazy. Pali never should have said that "pregnant" word to her.

Marianne decided not to see a doctor, what's the point? She was already pregnant, she wasn't having any more sex. It would be a long time before she could trust another man. She gave herself to Reginald. She would have done anything for him. Now that that's over, why see a doctor?

Then she thought about having an abortion. Marianne made an appointment. She didn't want a baby. After her mother died having Patrick, she decided not to have kids. She had her brother; she knows exactly what it feels like to have a kid.

In fact, the more Marianne thought about it, the better it sounded. She has a child and a brother. Patrick has a mother and a sister. They didn't need any more babies. Not during this lifetime.

Both, Ms. Shirley and Aunt Rosie were terribly upset with Marianne. Neither one were able to have kids of their own. They couldn't fathom the idea of their little girl having an abortion. Aunt Rosie was so disgusted, she hardly looked at Marianne. Ms. Shirley argued with Marianne constantly, so much that Marianne avoided being around her, all together. The boarding house was never this thick with tension. And Marianne was sick of it.

* * * * *

"I want to tell that girl something. If she only knew what happened with her mother. And Patricia didn't go crazy."

"Shirley, I heard some talk back then, but I never knew exactly what happened." Ms. Rosie finally had to nerve to ask the question that plagued their neighborhood.

"Patricia was beat and raped by one of her teachers. It was bad. She stayed in the hospital almost a month. We didn't

146

think she would ever have any kids, but she ended up pregnant with Marianne. And back then, people were rude, they were mean. That girl couldn't stay in school for being talked about, like it was her fault. She finally left school to raise her baby."

"I never knew that."

"Ms. Maxine took care of that teacher. You talk about beautiful . . . Patricia was a pretty girl back then. She was never the same after that attack. She became withdrawn, quiet as a mouse. She never wanted to draw any attention to herself. Patricia seemed to blame herself for the rape. She had a hard time. It left a scar; she wasn't as cheerful anymore . . . She was always a sweet girl."

"You know, we need to talk with Marianne before she does it. Maybe we can talk some sense into that girl."

* * * * *

Every morning Marianne would throw up before she started the day. Her appointment to end everything was in a couple of days. Marianne couldn't wait for it to be all over, then everything would return to normal. Aunt Rosie and Ms. Shirley would stop treating her so bad.

She noticed her body changing. She's wider around the hips. Marianne was looking in the full bodied mirror, observing her voluptuous breast, pushing them up, standing straight, then looking over her shoulders. She started talking to herself.

"Boy these breast, they're too big, I look like momma. This is exactly how she looked when she was pregnant with Patrick. Maannnn, I look just like her." Marianne continued to enjoy her mother's traits, finally she took a deep breathe, undressed, then went to bed.

* * * * *

Big Bill and Michelle Parks had been seeing each other pretty regularly. She took him home to meet her mother, daughter, and two sisters. It was a house full of woman; nice,

147

churchy women.   Whenever he came to visit they'd immediately started cooking and laughing.   Billy didn't mind entertaining everybody. He had to watch his mouth a bit, make sure nothing too bad came out. He had their attention and loved every minute of it.

Bill really liked his high fashioned queen.   She was funny, pretty, and loved being with Big Bill.   She was careful. Michelle had an eight year old daughter.   She couldn't take chances with men or women.   For some reason, she had a real good feeling about Bill Washington.

Michelle was a stickler for details. Billy teased her.

"Michelle, girl, you're just cheap.   Look at you. Nobody's cheating you, put that receipt down."

"Billy, I have to check everything. We're trying to keep this business going and I got to save every dollar, whenever I find one. My sisters don't handle money like I do, but I can't sew like they can, so we're the Park sisters team, and it works. As long as I keep all the money straight, we'll pay the bills around here, and Billy, it ain't always easy!"

"I know.   You just keep on counting that money."   Bill liked Michelle a lot.

Those sisters loved to fuss over Bill.   He was the only man in their lives.   Big Bill always had a few women fussing over him.   Billy grew up with his mother and Aunt Lois, and even back then; he was the center of their lives. He wanted to be the man and take care of them. They both had cancer, within a year, the two sisters were gone. Bill was seventeen . . . he never had a chance to be the man for his mother and aunt.

That's when he met Ms. Maxine, Marianne's grandmother. He ended up living at the boarding house, then joining the military. He planned on coming home and thanking her. If Ms. Maxine hadn't been there at that specific time in his life, who knows what would have happened to Big Bill.

Now, he's the man and they needed him. Whatever Marianne needed or wanted, he promised he would help her, cause he remembered being young and alone. Bill had a high sense of responsibility and if he accepted you as his family, then he loved and protected you, and there was nothing he wouldn't do for his family.

*   *   *   *   *

Darlene and Michelle hit it off really good. Come to find out, Michelle goes to New York at least once every three months. Darlene planned on joining Michelle on her next trip. It really worked out good because Michelle's sisters were tired of all the traveling. Her sisters, Liz and Nance didn't want anything to do with New York City.

"So, when are you planning on going to New York again?"

"I got to go this month."

"How long do you stay?" Darlene wanted to go. If she didn't stay too long, maybe she could help drive."

"I try to be back within the week. It's not a lot of time. I pick out my dresses; if I'm lucky, I'll meet some new suppliers, that I can trust . . . everybody's so busy there."

"I know it's fast; remember that's my city."

"But, no matter what time it is, day or night, I can get in there, order my inventory, get me a couple days sleep, then I'm back on the road. I won't pick up my dresses until I'm ready to leave. I'm not driving around that city with a van full of clothes so somebody can rob me."

"That's right." Darlene was thinking about Michelle's trip, "Why don't you stay at our place. It isn't the best in the world, but it's clean. You can save that hotel money."

"Oh Darlene, that'll be great. You sure your granny won't mind?"

"Noooo, she'll be glad to have the company. I want to

149

go, I'll check my schedule and see what I can do. I've been trying to get Billy to ride with me to New York, so I can check on my nanna, I want to see about her. Once I'm on my feet, I'm bringing her here with me. I need to find us a place so she'll be comfortable. At first I was gonna kidnap her, but Bill said not to do that, it'd be wrong. If you go there every few months, maybe sometimes I can ride with you."

At the end of September, Darlene and Michelle planned a trip to the Big Apple. After almost two years, Darlene was finally going to see her grandmother. She had to talk her into leaving New York and moving to Kansas. She still thought that the kidnapping idea was the best plan.

* * * * *

Thursday was finally here and time for Marianne to end this pregnancy situation. Although she had morning sickness, and today it was unusually bad, she still felt relieved that it would soon be over. Against Ms. Shirley and Aunt Rosie's wishes, she decided that she didn't want anybody to go with her, it was too personal. Besides, they were crying and they were somehow blaming themselves, it was too much.

Ms. Shirley kept threatening to talk with her, but whenever she sat down for the mighty talk, Ms. Shirley never said anything. Marianne was convinced that she was just stalling, looking for something that might change her mind, but that wasn't going to happen, her mind was made up.

Marianne never confided in her friend Kim. She didn't want to take the chance that she would tell Terry. And if Terry ever found out, she might as well tell the whole church she was pregnant by Reginald Williams, the pastor's son.

When Marianne arrived at the clinic, she was surprised to see so many women in the same predicament, waiting for the procedure. Nobody spoke, smiled, or even looked up from their magazine. She checked in with the receptionist, filled out the necessary papers, than sat down with a magazine of her own.

"Marianne Robinson."

She heard her name being called and immediately got up to follow the nurse behind the closed doors. She was given a gown; then she waited patiently for the doctor to enter. After about 45 minutes of waiting, the nurse reappeared ready to prep her for the procedure.

"How are you doing?"

"Oh, as good as can be expected. How long does this take?"

"Well, before the doctor comes in I'll have to give you a little checkup. I have a few questions you'll need to answer, then we'll be ready. But the actual procedure takes less than an hour. Are you allergic to any medications?"

"No."

"How many prior pregnancies have you had?"

"This is the first."

"When was your last menstrual cycle?"

"It was around the 1st of June."

"Okay, you're cutting it close. But you're not showing at all, you're probably alright." The nurse continued to examine Marianne. She put KY jell over her stomach, then placed the listening device in the middle of all the jelly, moving it around, and around.

"What's that? What's that sound?"

"That's the heartbeat of the fetus."

"That's my baby's heartbeat?"

"Yeah, it's loud isn't it?"

"Oh My God! How can it have a heartbeat?"

"It a strong one, isn't it. The doctor may need to check you more thoroughly, but I'm sure it's alright. A fetus will have a heartbeat within the first month."

Tears clouded Marianne eyes. "I'm sorry, I can't do

this. It has a heartbeat."

When Marianne came home, Ms. Shirley and Aunt Rosie were waiting with Patrick. They were determined not to ask any questions, they would give her the love and care she needed. They couldn't imagine how she must feel.

Ms. Shirley cooked some homemade chicken soup, and was ready to care for their little girl.

"Honey, take it easy. I made some chicken soup for you. Have some then take a nap, get your strength up. I'll get you some crackers to go with it."

"Oh Shirley, that sounds so good. I'm so tired. How's Patrick?" Marianne reached for her little brother, "How you doing sweetheart? You ready to be a big uncle to somebody?"

Shirley jumped on it. "How can he be an uncle now?"

Aunt Rosie had the bowl ready to put soup in it but stopped to hear the conversation. She walked back to the living room so she could understand exactly what Marianne was saying.

"I couldn't do it. It had a heartbeat, and it was louuuud, it was stronger than mine. I couldn't do it."

Mrs. Rosie fell to her knees. "Oh thank God. Oh Lord, thank you. THANK YA! Thank ya."

"I wasn't worried about nothing, I didn't believe she would do it in the first place." Ms. Shirley grabbed the bowl and continued to fix Marianne something to eat. "You better eat all of this good soup, it has plenty of vegetables and vitamins, you're eating for two now."

"Marianne, darling, don't worry. I know you think about your mother. You think she passed because she was pregnant with Patrick. But baby, I'm telling you what God loves, and it's the truth. It was Patricia's time to go. Everybody has a specific time that they're going to live and die. Your mother was doing good. She was taking care of her sugar, checking it, doing everything right, it was just her time to go. Okay. Now you trust me."

"Thank you, Aunt Rosie. I always said I was never having kids. It was really hard on me, momma dying like that. I blamed my brother a long time for momma. I know it was wrong, but I did. I kinda hated Patrick. Then, one day all that hurt and pain went away. I was thankful for you and Ms. Shirley. I was thankful for all of ya'll. I'm so glad I got Patrick. I started loving him so much. You know what, that's when I realized that everything was going to be okay."

"I'll tell you what, me and Clarence will always be there for you, baby. We're glad to have another baby running around here. All these old folks, we need some youth around us. Shoot, me and Clarence lives for Patrick. He loves that baby. It keeps us young." Ms. Shirley laid the soup and crackers down, then grabbed Patrick to feed him, too.

Aunt Rosie kissed Marianne. "See ya honey, I'm going home to my Charlie. That boy wore me out, he wouldn't take a nap."

Chapter 14

Marianne thought about her predicament. Different scenarios were playing in her mind, what if this happens, what about that, every situation being tested.

She never saw herself as the unwedded mother. As much as she loved Redeemers Baptist Church, she couldn't stay there! No way could she attend Redeemers, while having the Pastor's grandchild, swinging on her hips. The thought made her crazy.

Now there's Kim and Terry, that's another issue facing her. They would know Reginald's the father as soon as she started showing, she had to do something about that, but what? She wondered if she could trust Kim, she wanted to tell her, but after some thought, decided not. Kim could end up telling Terry, then her parents. She trusted them all, it's just that, they're members of Redeemers and someway her secret would get out.

She decided to give her friend, Kim, a call.

"Hello, Kim. What have you been doing? We haven't talked in a while."

"Naw, not since you stopped seeing Reggie. Marianne, are you mad at me? After Reggie left, we stopped talking, we haven't spent any time together. We were tight, like sisters."

"Kim, you could have called me. You never call either. I always call you."

"Girl, it's cool. I'm taking summer classes. I'm trying to graduate in four years."

"Are you and Terry going to the same school?"

"Naw, Terry decided to join the Navy. I'm going to miss my baby."

"You got to be kidding me? The Navy! Where did all that come from?"

"Marianne, he's leaving me next week. We're spending as much time together as possible. I decided to go to Langston University in Oklahoma City. I'll leave in two weeks."

"Oh really! Then, I'll have to see you guys soon. Why don't you and Terry come by, and get some barbeque before you go. Kim, you're leaving, Terry's leaving, I guess we're growing up."

"Yeah, we're growing up. I can't promise I'll see you, Marianne, I'm trying to be with Terry as much as possible. We might get married. He asked me . . . I really love 'em, Marianne, I don't know. We might come by."

"Well, if I don't see you before you leave, you take care. Tell your mother hello for me and tell 'big head' to be careful."

"I won't be that far away. Langston is only a five hour drive. I'll see you."

Marianne was relieved that, for now, she could dodge her friends. Who else knew about her affair with Reginald Williams? She played it over and over in her mind, making sure she wasn't missing anybody that could positively say that Reggie's the father of her baby. He would be long gone by the time she's showing. Marianne stopped worrying so much, nobody in the house would say anything. Uncle Charlie or Pali wouldn't breathe a word. Marianne decided to focus more on having a healthy baby. She began to enjoy her pregnancy.

* * * * *

Two years had passed since Dee came to Kansas City. Aunt Rosie was so happy, she loves Dee so much. She's the only niece that spent any time with her and Charlie. The other kids were too young, and they were work, Aunt Rosie and Uncle Charlie were too old to chase after little kids. Plus, Aunt Rosie never got that close with Dee's little sister and brother.

Once, Aunt Rosie and Uncle Charlie talked about adopting Dee. They wanted to give her mother a chance to get her life together; before any of that could happen, her mother was pregnant again. It broke Rosie's heart that she wasn't able to call Dee their daughter. Dee's mother was always willing to let her stay with them as long as she wanted, and she always wanted.

Rosie and Dee were talking long distanced. They talked pretty regularly. She told Aunt Rosie about this guy who wanted to marry her, but she found out he was already married. Now she wants to come to Kansas for a while, to forget all that mess.

"Aunt Rosie, he brought me a diamond ring. Can you believe that? I would have married him too, he has a good job. He's an engineer."

"An engineer! That sounds good."

"Yeah, he works for the highway department, making good money. He even took me with him while he worked out of town."

"You went with him? Dee sweetheart, you shouldn't be going out of town with men you don't really know."

"I know him, Aunt Rosie, Emmanuel Gregory. We've been seeing each other almost a year."

"How did you find out he was married?"

"Well, that's a long story, Aunt Rosie. His wife followed him to my apartment. I mean, I mean, it's was our apartment. We had been living together, on and off for a long time. Anyway, she followed him there, and she came knocking on my door telling him to come outside, then they had a big fight."

"What did you do when they were fighting?"

"I was watching. Then she pulled out a gun. Can you believe that? Aunt Rosie, when I saw that gun, I was soooo scared. I called the police and they took her ass to jail. Manny told me he planned on divorcing her, but he couldn't leave his kids."

"Oh my goodness! They have kids? Dee baby, you got to be careful, people will hurt you over their families. It's some crazy people out there, don't you know that?"

"She don't love him, she cheated on him a couple of times."

"Dee, how do you know that?"

"Manny told me all about her."

"Sweetheart, men will tell you anything."

"He's not lying Auntie. She's the liar. She lied and got him to marry her in the first place. He told me she tricked him and got pregnant, and he didn't want to leave her like that so he married her. Anyway, she said she was going to get me if she ever caught me on the streets. She's one of those crazy Mexicans. I caught her following me around town with a bunch of girls in the car. I was scared Aunt Rosie. Anyway, I thought about coming out there for a while. I just want to forget about him."

"Yeah, baby, you come on out here and let all that mess settle down."

Uncle Charlie wasn't happy to find out Dee was coming there, and Rosie sent her a plane ticket. As far as he was concerned, she could have caught a bus. He never told Rosie about the little trick she played the last time she was there, how Dee tried to seduce him. If his Rosie knew that, it would break her heart. But knowing Rosie, she would just forgive her, so it wasn't any real reason to tell her anything.

When Dee arrived, Uncle Charlie looked at his niece and realized he was still angry with her.

"Look at her; she's a bold little thing." Uncle Charlie mumbled under his breathe. He couldn't figure how she could look him in his eyes as if nothing happened, she didn't blink. He didn't want her staying under the same roof as his wife. It

157

made him uncomfortable, plus he couldn't trust Dee.

"Hi Uncle Charlie. I sure missed you and Aunt Rosie." She grabbed him and gave him a big hug.

"Hey girl, you gonna behave yourself?"

"Yesssssssssss Uncle Charlie, I'll behave." She gave her Aunt Rosie a quick little smirk.

"I don't want no married men looking for you around here. Rosie told me about you messing with that married man. His wife was gonna kick your little ass." Uncle Charlie starting laughing. "You were getting ready to get a Texas style ass whipping. Don't get it started here, Dee. I'll send your little ass home as fast as you got here."

"Now Charlie, why are you acting? We've never had any problems with Dee." Aunt Rosie was embarrassed. She talked in her motherly voice. "Daddy, why are you being so mean to our Dee?"

"Where's Marianne?" Dee wanted to change the subject.

"She's at the restaurant. You get settled in, be at the restaurant in the morning, I want you there when we open . . . that means early, soooo Marianne can talk with you then. There's been some changes since you were here, I got to figure out where I want to put you. Rosie, I'm turning in. When are you coming to bed?"

"I'm going to stay up with Dee a while. I'll be in there, directly."

Dee ended up being a big help for Marianne and Uncle Charlie. Uncle Charlie was surprised that Dee stepped right up, knowing how everything was done. Marianne wasn't so surprised. She tried to tell Uncle Charlie that Dee was a good worker. Marianne didn't know why Uncle Charlie was so mean to Dee. It was so unlike him.

Meanwhile, Marianne was starting to show. Since she

158

accepted her pregnancy, it seems as if her face and nose grew at a faster pace than the rest of her body. She looked swollen. Marianne didn't like it at all.

Ms. Shirley was running around buying clothes again, humming and happy as a lark. She even had Patrick's baby clothes all ready and put up in drawers, waiting for their little fella to come home.

The whole household was happy. The atmosphere was energetic, anticipating the holidays, and the baby. It reminded Marianne of her family. This was the best time of the year. She remembered the Christmas's with her mother. Now, a baby was coming, and they would have another big reason to celebrate.

Marianne's been seeing Dr. Clark on a regular basis now and he said late February or early March is when to expect the new baby . . . still a long time. Dr. Clark asked her who's her baby's father?

"Dr. Clark, I made a mistake last summer. I met a guy and got pregnant. He's a good person and I want to keep him my secret. We have different plans in life and this baby shouldn't be the reason any of his plans change. So I decided to rear my baby myself."

"Marianne, you're talking about the baby's father. His plans are supposed to change."

"It's okay, Doc. We're going to be just fine, cause I'm going to have a nice, fat, healthy baby boy."

"Marianne, you've done an excellent job with your little brother, but having two babies to look after could be too much. You're still a young lady; you should be having a little fun in life. You're working all the time, then coming home to a baby, now another kid is coming. There's another alternative. There's always adoption. I know some good people looking for a nice baby to adopt. I mean some good professional folk that can't have children. It'll make them very happy to have a nice baby like yours. Just think about it."

"Naw Dr. Clark. I'll do just fine. I got a lot of help at the house."

"It's something to think about. When the baby grows up and want to know about its father, what you gonna say? What ya gonna say then?"

"Doc, I was raised without a father. I turned out alright."

"It's a wonder, because what your father did to Patricia was terrible. Ya'll are some strong women up at that house. I'm proud of you and your momma, she should be commended."

"Why? What happened to my mother?" Marianne looked deep in Dr. Clark's eyes, then decided not to corner him. She had to digest what he said, think about it, then decide if she wanted to know. "Dr. Clark, I wanna have a healthy baby. That's what I want."

"Well, Marianne, I thought I could help. I won't mention it again."

The biggest surprise to Marianne was Big Billy Joe Washington. He acted as if he was having a child, in fact, that's just what he wanted Marianne's baby to be his son.

"Marianne, I don't know about your business, but I can see you'll be having that baby pretty soon. I figured as much as your grandmother did for me, I would like to do something for you. Since I haven't seen any man hanging around, trying to claim your baby, I was wondering, well, I thought, maybe, since I got all these benefits from being a vet and I'm a disabled vet, I don't have no kids, or family, or anybody. Matter of fact, with all this medication I'm taking, I probably can't make babies. Well, I'll be happy to put my name down as the father. I got this insurance and if anything ever happens to me, then the baby would get my benefits. When my mother died, we didn't have no insurance, I didn't have no place to stay. Your grandmother, Ms. Maxine, she paid for my mother's funeral. Your grandma did that for me. Then she let me stay here at her house cause I was still in high school, I didn't have no job or money. I joined the service when I graduated. I would like to repay her some kind of way. I know it's something to think about. But I'll be honored to have your baby carry my name."

"Wow Big Bill, You must have practiced that speech because you said it all. That's really nice, and I promise, I'll give it some serious thought. Big Bill, thank you." Marianne gave Bill a bear hug and kissed him on the cheek. She wiped her lipstick off his face, and gave him another hug.

"You're welcome, baby girl; it's the least I can do."

"Why you never told me about my grandma before?"

"I don't know, I guess it never came up."

When Marianne told Uncle Charlie about Big Bill's proposition, he blew the roof.

"I'll be damned. If that baby's gonna have anybody's name on it, it should be mine. Now you know how we feel about you and Patrick. Ya'll are like our own flesh and blood. Hell, me and Rosie practically raised you. How long have you been working at the restaurant, Marianne?"

"A long time, Uncle Charlie."

"You damn right, a long time. Since you were in elementary school, that's how long you've been around me. Now, me and Rosie don't have any kids and ya'll are like our kids, and this Johnny-coma-lately crap with Billy ain't gonna cut it. Boy, I'm telling you. Marianne, I planned on leaving everything to you and Patrick. I got your business in order; you don't need no name from Big Bill."

"Uncle Charlie, he just wanted to help, he told me that my granny took him in when he was in high school; she paid for his mother's funeral, I think he just wanted to repay my granny some kind of way."

"Well, he needs to figure out something else . . . to pay Maxine back."

Marianne laughed. She had no idea that this baby would cause all this commotion and ruckus, it's not even here, yet. It was a lot for her to think about. She knew everybody loved her and Patrick, and they'll love her baby, their intentions were honorable and good, thank God, she had a little time to think.

Since she wasn't able to return to Redeemers Baptist Church, Marianne started attending church with Billy's girlfriend, Michelle and her sisters. First Baptist Church was about a 30 minute drive, closer to downtown. She enjoyed it just as much as Redeemers. Marianne felt better about her life, her future, and believed that someday, she would see her mother and grandmother, again, in heaven.

The pastor at First Baptist Church, Rev. Marshall, was a much younger man than Rev. Williams. He wore more fashionable clothes. In fact, the whole church was a younger congregation. He had a way of explaining more than preaching. That was different. Rev Williams preached hard, this pastor talked hard. He was very friendly, he didn't pry. He didn't mention her condition. It was relaxing. Rev. Marshall had the whole church on their feet dancing every Sunday. Marianne enjoyed First Baptist Church a lot.

* * * * *

Darlene had gone to New York a couple months ago with Michelle. They stayed the week at Darlene's house. She was depressed about leaving her nanna again. She was stressed and nervous about the whole situation. Darlene had forgotten how rough New York City could be, everything in Kansas was much easier and calmer and traffic was slower, she could see a future living in Kansas.

However, Darlene felt as if she had abandoned her

nanna. She decided the next time she rode to New York City, she would bring her nanna back, house or no house.

Darlene made the tough decision to take a break from school and work more. Since Razz stayed opened almost 24 hours a day, she asked if she could work longer hours.

"Girl, I thought you wanted to be a nurse? Don't drop out of school."

"I'm not going to drop out, I'm taking a break."

"That might be your intentions, but sometimes it's hard to get back on track . . . especially after a long break. Don't do that. Stay focused, why you wanna leave school?"

"Razz, I got to make more money, I left my grandmother in New York City. She's living by herself, there's nobody that's looking after her. I got a few cousins, but they'll take advantage of my grandma. I got to get her." Darlene started crying. "When I left her last month, Razz, I felt like it was my last time seeing her. She seemed so helpless. My nanna raised me, my mother died of an overdose when I was two. I don't remember her at all. Anyway, that's who took care of me, now she's old and helpless. I can't leave her again."

"Darlene, I'll tell you what I want you to do. I want you to stay in school, and we'll figure out how to get your grandmother here. Will you do that for Razz?" He gave her a reassuring smile, like it would be alright.

"But Razz, I need a place to take her. I can't bring her to Marianne's. We need our own house or apartment, that's why I need to make more money. It's so I can get us a house. I want to get my nanna a little house where we can have a garden and some flowers in the yard. You know, Razz."

"Yeah baby. I know. Let me look around. I know a few people in town that got some places for rent. We'll get you something, but you got to stay in school. Is that a deal? I'm proud of you, that you're working hard to be a nurse; I want to see you finish. I might want you to do some nursing on me." Razz had a way of rubbing his hands together, like he was washing them in imaginary water. Then he would hold them out for you to grab. That's when he knew he had a deal.

Darlene was happy. She dried her eyes, and flashed her dazzling smile. She couldn't believe how good Razz was being to her. Since she had come to Kansas City, everything had fit in place, like it was planned or something.

First thing, she met Big Bill on the bus, then he introduced her to Marianne and got her a place to live, then she started working for Razz, then she enrolled in school, now she's going to get her nanna. Everything was working out.

"Thank you so much. I promise Razz, I'll get my nursing license and make you very proud. I promise." Before she had a chance to think, she grabbed Razz and kissed him softly on his lips. He smelled fresh and tasted sweet like peppermint. It was brief, but she liked it.

"Okay baby." They laughed a while, hugged hard and enjoyed the moment.

"Shoot, I better go on to class then. I'll see you tonight."

* * * * *

Marianne and Dee were at the restaurant, working and reminiscing about the last time they worked together. It was just after Marianne's mother died, Patrick was born and her life changed dramatically. Marianne couldn't understand why Dee hadn't come back since then.

"Why you hadn't been back? What did you do, Dee? "

"Marianne, it's a long story, I wanted to stay here with you. Uncle Charlie was letting you stay in your own place, like you were grown. I was just as old as you, I wanted to stay too. I didn't want to go back to Texas. My momma's a trip. She makes me babysit two or three days at a time. I have to hussle us food. I couldn't go to school or hangout with my friends. It's really worst than you think. I didn't talk about it to anybody, so I did something really stupid."

"Like what?"

"It's crazy. I can't tell you. It was really stupid."

"Come on Dee, tell me. What did you do?"

"Tell me who's the daddy of your baby?"

"You wouldn't know if I told you."

"I'll tell you what I did, if you tell me, who's your baby's daddy?"

"I can't"

"Then I can't."

Marianne and Dee, both, decided to keep their secrets. They were glad to be reunited, they accepted each other; they had history together. They didn't try to invade the understood pack that they developed with each other. They had a job to do and their futures to work out.

* * * * *

During the holidays and Christmas break, Darlene went to New York to get her grandmother, Nanna. They stayed together at Marianne's house. She's a little lady with a heavy Puerto Rican accent. She loved living at Marianne's house. At home, in New York, she was lonesome. Every now and then one of her grandchildren would come by, but they usually wanted something, or was hungry. They never came without asking for a favor or something to eat.

Here at Marianne's house, she was being spoiled. Big Bill took her shopping for a nice coat and some boots. He loved her cooking so she cooked and cooked for Big Bill.

Ms. Shirley didn't like sharing the kitchen with Nanna. Nanna was too bossy, she took over. Aunt Rosie tried to tell Shirley to relax and let Nanna cook.

"Now Shirley, you calm down. Don't you have a

165

husband to cook for? Darlene and Nanna will be moving in the next month or so. Then you can cook every day, if that's what you want."

"I don't like that old witch running me out the kitchen. I wanted to tell her something, but I didn't. Thank God she'll be gone, cause I couldn't handle her too much longer. I try to be respectful. She ain't that much older than me. I had to bite my tongue a couple times."

They decided that Ms. Shirley would cook during the week and Nanna cooked weekends, Nanna cooked the main meal on Sundays.

Chapter 15

It was an easy delivery. Marianne had a beautiful, brown baby boy with a bright birthmark that splashed down his right thigh, knee and leg. Dr. Clark was just as excited as the rest of the family.

"Girl, you have a big ole boy. We're going to clean him up before we hand him to you. Marianne, he's pretty. I've never seen a baby this good looking right after birth."

"Why don't I hear him? Isn't he supposed to cry?"

"Hold on, mommy." The nurse gave him a little swat then suctioned his nose. "There he is. He's crying now."

"Ohhhhh, a boy. I got a baby boy . . . Aunt Rosie you hear him? Ms. Shirley is he pretty?" Marianne was beaming, sweaty and tired.

Aunt Rosie and Ms. Shirley were still in shock. They had never been in a delivery room. They never witnessed a live birth. They couldn't talk.

"Are ya'll alright? Dr. Clark, check them old hens out, look at them." Marianne was concerned; then she got tickled. "Are ya'll alright?" She wanted to laugh but she couldn't.

They were sick. Her two adoptive mothers were both looking baaaad, with a blank, pale expression that was absolutely hilarious.

"Ummm Rosie, I'm going outside. Stay here, I'll be back."

"Hold on Shirley, I'm going too." They held each other up, as they wobbled their way out the delivery room. "Sweetie, we'll be right back." Rosie whispered and did a little sign language pointing toward the door.

Dr. Clark and the nurse were now laughing hard. Aunt Rosie was visibly sick. The nurse handed her a cold wet towel to pat her face. Ms. Shirley was being as attentive as she could, considering she was sick too. They held on to each other like two drunks; then slowly walked toward the exit doors of the hospital.

"Shirley, I thought I could handle that. Girl, did you see that baby coming out? All that water that gushed out like a faucet."

Ms. Shirley was patting her chest and nodded in agreement. "It was something, wasn't it?" She could only whisper. "Rosie, he was gray. That baby was gray."

"Then that baby came flying out in all that water, oh my goodness. I can't get it out my mind." Aunt Rosie covered her face with the wet towel and her whole body shook.

"Girrrrl, It's a wonder he didn't drown. How did . . . Girrrl, that's why I never had a baby. I don't think I could have done that."

"Naw naw, I couldn't, I couldn't do that, either."

"Rosie, he saw us, that baby saw us. When he came out, he looked dead at us. Did you notice him looking at us?"

"Yeeessssss I did. I thought it was my imagination." They were outside breathing the cool air, getting their bearings together. It was March 10, 1972. Rosie and Shirley had gone through a lot during the past few years, but this was it. Nothing could surpass this. Nothing would ever amount to what they witnessed in that delivery room. They saw a baby come out of little Marianne, it was a miracle.

"Lord, I'm still nervous. Yuck! All that stuff that was on him. It was terrible. I'll never go into another delivery room. That little fellow didn't wanna cry, did he?"

"Nope, not at first. He's going to be smart. I asked Marianne to name him Maxwell, after her grandmother, Maxine."

"I think Charlie wants him to carry our last name. Maxwell Jackson . . . that has a good ring to it. It sounds good,

Shirley."

"It does, doesn't it? Come on girl; let's see how Marianne's doing. You're alright now?"

By the time Aunt Rosie and Ms. Shirley got back to Marianne's room, she was taking a nap with her baby sleeping in a little glass container next to her. It was hard for them to leave, but they decided to go on home and give Marianne and her little boy a chance to rest.

Everybody at the house was there, eagerly waiting for all the details about the baby. The anticipation was too much for Nanna, she stayed busy. Nanna started cleaning and cleaning, she worked hard cleaning windows and floor boards, the house smelt of pine cleaner, ammonia, and moth balls. It was squeaky clean, it looked uninhabited. Everything was immaculate.

Pali and Mr. White quietly waited. They wanted to be excited but didn't quite know how, or what to do. Sometimes Jeffrey White felt guilty living at the boarding house with everybody. He knew about the gossip. People talked about him and Pali living at the house with little Patrick, as if, somehow, they couldn't contain themselves around a little boy. It hurts. It was so silly how people acted. They wanted to protect Marianne, but on the other hand, she was their family and they couldn't control what other people said. People can be cruel. They'll say stupid things. Mr. White decided him and Pali would move into their own place. Maybe they'll have their own boarding house for gay people like them. But for now, they couldn't worry about other people. That's their problem.

Darlene wanted to be at the hospital except she couldn't afford to take off work. She had a plan that would put her in a house within two months. Darlene stayed on course, she didn't, even a little, deviate from her plan. Marianne having a baby was an exception, she would have taken off; but there were

169

already too many people around. Darlene stayed long enough to hear everything was alright, once she got word that everything was fine, she ran out the house to go to work at Razz's.

* * * * *

Razz was there waiting for Darlene. He had a surprise for her.

"Darlene, I want you to go over on Posey Ave, look at that house with the rent sign up; here's the keys," Razz handed Darlene a set of keys. "See if it's something you would like for you and Nanna."

"Are you kidding? Anything is good, Razz. I'd like anything you get. Can I go now?"

"You better go now. It's getting late, you wanna be able to see. I don't think the lights are on over there."

Darlene ran to her car to check out the house on Posey Ave. She could almost touch her dreams. She wanted a little house, with a little garden, for her and Nanna. She would be a nurse in a couple of years. What more could she ask for?

* * * * *

When Aunt Rosie and Ms. Shirley made it to the house they were hit by the strong cleaning scent of ammonia and Nanna was still working around the house. Their eyes were burning from the fumes.

"Pali what's going on?" Shirley looked at Pali.

Pali looked off. He wasn't getting in the middle of this. "Jeffrey, lets go to the hospital to see Marianne. She can have visitors, can't she?"

"Nanna, what's going on? What did you do? Honey, is that mothballs you got in here. We got to get those up, the baby can't be inhaling mothballs. It'll kill him. It's burning my eyes. Where's Patrick? Is he inhaling all these fumes."

Before Aunt Rosie could say another word, Nanna

170

started rolling out profanity. Everybody stopped in their tracks. They couldn't make out exactly what she was saying, but every third word or so was hard core cussing and they knew that.

Mrs. Shirley looked at Aunt Rosie with one of those 'I told you so looks.'

Nanna was crying. She stomped to her room, slammed the door, then continued with her profanity from inside her room.

"Come on Shirley, let's open some doors and windows. That lady must be crazy. Where's Patrick?"

"He's in Bill's room." Jeffrey grabbed his jacket. "How's Marianne and the baby?"

"Jeffrey, I've never seen anything like it in my life. Everybody's fine, except maybe me and Shirley. I'm telling you, it scared me to death, seeing that baby come out . . . It was terrible."

"What's the little guy's name?" Pali quizzed Shirley and Rosie. "Who does he look like? How's my sugarplum? Is Marianne's doing okay?"

Jeffrey and Pali were standing at the door, ready to head for the hospital.

Shirley had a broom, sweeping as many mothballs as she could fine.

"How did ya'll let that old crazy lady throw all these mothballs around like that? Pali, you and Jeffrey need to help me get this stuff up before Marianne comes home. I know it must have been burning poor Patrick's eyes, bless his heart. Why didn't ya'll stop Nanna from putting all that stuff down. Where'd she get it anyway?"

"She was only trying to help, Shirley. Big Bill took Patrick to his room. They were asleep last time I looked."

"They probably passed out. You can't mix cleaners like that."

Mr. White chuckled then continued as if she hadn't made that remark. "Patrick sure sleeps rough. When I looked in on them, he was half way lying across Billy's head. I hope he doesn't crawl all over the baby like that. Patrick's going to have to grow up. He won't be the baby around here anymore." Jeffrey was summing up Patrick's new life. "He's going to grow up real quick now."

"Patrick's always going to be my baby." Shirley pouted.

"So what did she name him?" Pali still hadn't gotten an answer.

"I think she's going to name him Maxwell Jackson, after Ms. Maxine and Charlie." Aunt Rosie stopped Ms. Shirley from saying anything else, she didn't want Shirley to jinks them.

"Shirley, you don't know that. That's just the name me and Ms. Shirley thought of, we never even asked her about it."

"I did. I told Marianne to name the baby Maxwell, after Ms. Maxine, a long time ago."

"Well, she was sleep when we were going to ask her about his name. I hope she'll name him Maxwell." Rosie continued to find mothballs and fuss with disbelief that Nanna would put so many down, especially when a newborn baby was coming home in the next couple of days.

When Jeffrey and Pali got to the hospital, Marianne was nursing her baby.

"Ooops! We'll come back."

"It's alright. He's finished. Come in."

Pali rushed to Marianne. "Girl, how are you doing? Let me see that baby. Girl, he's precious. Look Jeffrey, he's as sweet as he can be. Ms. Rosie said you're naming him Maxwell Jackson. I like that name. It sounds real important. He's going to be an important man around here, Marianne."

172

"Wait a minute. What did you say? I'm not naming him Maxwell. His name is Jackson, we're gonna call him Jacks for short. Jackson Williams Robinson. Huh baby. Your name is Jackson Williams Robinson."

"Oh Marianne. I like that even better. You like it Jeffrey? Ohhh, I just love it. Little Jackie Robinson, when you coming home so everybody can spoil you?"

"How's Patrick doing?"

"He's fine, girl, Big Bill got him. They're sticking together like glue. What made you name him Jackson. Let me see, that's three last names, he's got three last names, Jeffrey."

"Well Jackson for Uncle Charlie, Williams for Big Bill and my family name, Robinson, that's everybody. Billy wanted Jacks to be his namesake, he don't have any family so he wanted Jacks to carry his name, well so did Uncle Charlie, and I wanted him to have my family name. Now he's got everybody's name and I love it." Marianne was in love.

* * * * *

Marianne was finally home with her baby. Patrick and the rest of the family had adapted to the newborn in the house. It was as if Jacks had been there all the time. Patrick was little Jacks protector. He wanted to feed him, change his diapers and pick him up. That just about drove Aunt Rosie to the crazy house, having to watch every move Patrick made toward Jacks. She was a nervous wreck because Patrick was determined to pick him up and carry him off somewhere. Aunt Rosie was Jacks grandmother in every way. There's nothing she wouldn't do for that baby. She especially loved watching him sleep. He was such a good baby.

"Look at him Shirley, isn't that the sweetest thing you ever seen in your life."

"Yeah, can you believe we watched him come into this world. Little fellow, I hope he'll be alright. He's gonna have to

173

grow up, and Lord knows what's waiting for him out there in this world."

"He'll be alright. He's a smart boy, he's been here before."

"Now Rosie, there you go with that superstitious stuff."

"I'll never forget the way he looked at us Shirley, he already knew us."

"Stop it Rosie!"

* * * * *

Darlene finally moved with her grandmother over on Posey Ave. They were happy with the house. In fact, it was more than they had expected. It was a two bedroom house with a huge kitchen, a little dining area, it had a little bathroom, but that was okay. How much could they do in the bathroom anyway? The surprise was the sunroom. To the back of the kitchen was a glass sunroom with little areas around the glass walls for plants. Darlene had never seen anything like it. The center was big enough for a table and two chairs. The way the sun shined through, the brightness of it all, made you feel special. Darlene couldn't wait for the winter, just to see how it would look when it snowed, cause glass windows were all over . . . the top was glass, the walls were glass, it's going to be beautiful this winter. It didn't have a door leading to the outside, you had to come through the kitchen. It was like something in a magazine. It was perfect for growing a nice garden, some tomatoes and peppers, or planting flowers. They could easily sit there during the summer months for breakfast or lunch or all day. It was so cute. Darlene loved her little house.

Every Sunday Darlene and Nanna would have dinner at the boarding house. It was expected, the family get together. Ms. Shirley was glad to have her kitchen back. Clarence, her husband, had gotten used to eating at the boarding house. In fact, he enjoyed all the company. For so long it had been just him and Shirley, he welcomed all the people and all the excitement that came along with it.

\   Dee moved into Darlene's old room.   She always wanted to live in the boarding house with Marianne. They were so close.   Marianne understood Dee.   She understood that somewhere down the road, Dee had been sexually molested. She had been sexually abused a lot. Dee learned to use her body to get what she wanted and to manipulate men as much as she could. In fact, it came natural to her.

Dee proved to be a big asset to the sauce business. She had a natural knack for business, just like Marianne. Dee didn't take any bull from her buyers.   She had a way of smiling, smirking, and teasing to get the business and prices that Uncle Charlie wanted.   Dee even had Aunt Rosie develop signature sauces for some of the main restaurant chains and buyers. The sauce business was booming.   Uncle Charlie's face was cartooned on every bottle that left the building. If you saw Uncle Charlie's face on the jar, you knew it was good sauce. He became a household icon around Kansas City.

Although Dee handled the sauce business and she was important in Uncle Charlie's Famous Sauces; Uncle Charlie was really glad she was out from under his roof. Uncle Charlie thought there was something really wrong with Dee because she did it again. She tried to seduce him.

"Listen to me Dee, you need help girl. You are like a daughter to me. I'm an old man, hell, I'm your Uncle Charlie. Why on earth are you acting like that? I don't want you baby, not that way. I want you to get some help. You need one of those head doctors. I don't understand. You're just crazy.

"Uncle Charlie, why don't you like me?"   Dee was crying hard.

"Dee, can't a person like you without having sex with you? It's not always about sex, baby. It's about being a family

175

and caring about each other, like your Aunt Rosie, she truly loves you. Do you want to have sex with her? The way your Aunt Rosie loves you, is the way I love you. Dee, that's not sexual. Do you understand? I want you to see a doctor about this. You have a lot to offer, but you got to get over this thing. You don't have to have sex to feel good about yourself. Men don't make you important, you make you important. Hell, if you're trying to get approval from me, then you'll never be worth a dime. "

"I just want you, Uncle Charlie. Why don't you like me?"

"Did you hear anything I just said? What do you want from me . . . some validation that you're a good person. You're a good person, Dee. Now, I said it."

Dee walked over to Uncle Charlie again, this time she touched his private areas. He naturally became a little excited. Uncle Charlie pushed her away, she stumbled but he stopped her from falling. He was disgusted with Dee and with himself because his body responded, he was sexually aroused.

"You're sick. What happened to you? How did you get this way?"

"I told you. I told you a long time ago, I tried to let you and Aunt Rosie know what was happening to me. All those men my mother used to be with, they all wanted me more than her. I wanted to stay with you but you didn't let me. My mom was even jealous cause they paid more attention to me. She stayed drunk. They'd get her drunk on purpose, then have sex with me. All the time."

Uncle Charlie wiped the tears from his eyes. "What happened to your little sister and brother?"

"They had a daddy. I didn't."

"Well, I'm getting you some help. You're seeing a doctor. Dee, we're going to have to talk with Rosie about this.

176

She needs to know about your problem. I can't have you making passes at me every time she turns her back."

"Please don't. I promise to be good. I'll get help, but please don't tell Aunt Rosie." Dee gave Uncle Charlie a little smile and started walking toward him. "What she doesn't know, won't hurt her." Dee's Mexican accent was getting heavier. "Let's keep this our secret, Uncle Charlie. You don't understand how I feel about you. Aunt Rosie can't find out." Dee was close enough to Uncle Charlie to make him a little nervous, she touched his chest, then she grabbed his hands. "Feel my heart, Uncle Charlie, my heart is beating so hard." She placed his hand over her chest. "It's pounding, isn't it?" She made sure his hands brushed across her breast.

Uncle Charlie didn't know what to do about Dee. He rode around in his truck thinking about the little girl that came every summer to visit him and Rosie. Uncle Charlie was never the failure, he was never the one that squandered on his responsibilities. He was Uncle Charlie, the one that everybody counted on, but here is this little girl, that stayed with him so much of her life, who needed a father figure and he let her down. The most vulnerable person in his life, he hated her. All he saw was a fast dishonest little girl that happened to be his wife's niece and he didn't want anything to do with her.

She's sick, and he has to help her. It was partly his fault that she had been abused at such a young age. He had no idea what was happening to Dee. He just thought she didn't want to babysit her little sister and brother.

Then there were a couple of years that he didn't allow Dee to come to Kansas. What did that girl go through, what did she have to do, just to survive? Uncle Charlie continued to wipe his tears using an old work rag he kept in his truck. He decided not to tell Rosie. But she had to get away from him. That's when she moved in with Marianne at the boarding house.

Chapter 16

Jacks was now two years old. Marianne was working at the restaurant, checking everything, making sure the supplies were good, the food was good, and the customers were happy. She always had a huge crowd, especially during lunchtime. So she wanted to get in and out, without causing too much distraction. So many people wanted to talk with her, they asked about the sauces, even food critics scouted around to catch her coming or going.

They had previously extended and upgraded the restaurant. It was twice as big as before, and now was more of a tourist attraction. Marianne was proud, but not as proud as Uncle Charlie. He called Marianne and Dee his 'A Team.' He recognized their hard work and because of them, they were listed in the state's travel brochures as a place to go for delicious Kansas City style barbeque.

Marianne was talking with Victor about the smoke house out back of the building, she wanted to remodel it or add a smaller compartment so they could include smoked seafood on their menu. Victor was concerned about the smell getting on the other meats. They were deep in conversation, detailing how they could provide smoked shrimp and salmon, when he noticed a lady playing with Jacks.

"Who's that lady talking with Jacks? That lady took your baby to her table, look at her. I better get Jacks, Marianne." Victor walked closer to the lady, getting ready to politely take him from her, when he recognized who she was. He walked back to Marianne. "Oh, it's alright. That's Mrs. Williams, the pastor's wife. She's just playing with him."

Marianne's heart stopped. She was glad to see her playing with her grandson, but on the other hand, she didn't want to cause any family troubles. Marianne watched them for a few minutes. Jacks had on summer shorts and Mrs. Williams was examining the birthmark on his little ashy leg. She gave him a hug then began a game of patty cakes. After about a minute, Mrs. Williams took a napkin from the table and dabbed her eyes. This was too much, Marianne walked over to them.

"Hello Mrs. Williams, it's been a long time since I've seen you." She leaned over and gave her a slight little hug, then sat across the table from them.

"Yes it has, Marianne. The last time we spoke was nearly three years ago, at the church, you stopped coming after that, but I haven't stopped getting this barbeque. This place has really grown. Redeemer's has grown a lot too."

"I started attending another church."

"Well, as long as you're going, that's all that matters. Is this your baby?"

"Yes ma'am."

"He's a cutie. How old is he?"

"He turned two in March." Marianne watched as she calculated the months in her mind. Marianne thought to herself, She knows.

"That's interesting. You know Marianne, I want to talk with you when we have more time to visit. I can see you're busy and I have an appointment that I can't miss. Can we get together a little later this afternoon?"

"This afternoon? I don't know about this afternoon, I have a few errands today, I won't be free until late this evening, some other day might be better. What is it you want to talk about?"

"Can I be honest with you?"

"Yes ma'am, I'd appreciate that."

"Well, Marianne, this may sound abrupt, but I don't know any other way to say it . . . I can recognize my grandchild.

179

He feels like one of my babies. Were you going to keep this secret forever?"

"I don't know. Mrs. Williams I made a mistake and I didn't want any problems for Reginald. I didn't know what I was going to do, but we've are fine. We're doing real good."

"Something's you can't hide. The truth is always waiting for the right time to show up. My Goodness! This is very complicated. I can come back around 7 p.m."

"That'll be fine."

"So what's his name?"

"Jackson"

"Jackson what?"

Marianne had never been honest with herself, about the real reason she put Williams as Jackson's middle name. She wanted something to remind her of who he was, Reginald Williams' son. Now she was going to face this decision head on.

"Mrs. Williams, I named him Jackson Williams Robinson. We call him Jacks for short."

"Oh Marianne, how long did you think you could keep this a secret? I'll be back."

* * * * *

After Mrs. Williams' appointment with the Kansas Coalition of Preachers Wives she stopped by the church to talk with her husband. But Rev. Williams wasn't taking the news very well, his anger shocked her. He made it clear under no circumstances did he want to discuss anything about a grand baby by Marianne Robinson, the girl at the barbeque joint. In fact, he forbade his wife to talk with Marianne again about the subject.

Reginald and his wife, Vanessa were expecting their first child and Rev. Williams didn't want anything to spoil this time for his daughter-in-law, or the family. As far as he was concerned, these fast women will say anything. They'll do anything if they think they can get some kind of money or child support. Reginald had worked hard to build his music company, and he has an exciting future in gospel music. In fact, there hadn't been many record companies that produced gospel on his level. They had invested a lot of time and energy in the company and he wasn't letting anybody mess this up for his son, Reginald.

* * * * *

It was now 8 p.m., and Marianne decided not to wait any longer. She could only imagine what happened. She was sure Mrs. Williams told the Reverend about Jackson, but she wasn't sure if Reginald knows.

Mrs. Williams didn't come back, she didn't call or anything. The news must have been awful for them. Marianne's got sick to her stomach, not knowing what happened was terrible. Mrs. Williams wasn't the type to make frivolous plans, especially when it had to do with something as delicate as her newly discovered grand baby.

It had been a few weeks since she had talked with Mrs. Williams, and it took a long time for Marianne to get over it. She never mentioned to anybody what happened at the restaurant, it hurt. As far as she was concerned, it probably was better to forget the whole incident. One thing for sure, Jacks wasn't responsible, and she wasn't letting anybody mistreat her baby.

She never wanted anything from the Williams. She was successful and what reason would she need to discuss it any further? Patrick and Jacks had a family, more than enough people in their lives, and more than enough men that loved them. There was Uncle Charlie, Big Bill, Clarence, Razz, then Victor and Calvin. She couldn't leave out Mr. White and Pali, although they were different, they were around and loved her

181

boys.

There were plenty of women that played the grandmother role, too. Mrs. Juanita Williams wouldn't be missed. There's Ms. Shirley and Aunt Rosie. Then Dee and Darlene are their aunts and that's what they called themselves too, their aunts. On top of that Nanna was always there, if they needed a great grandmother. Marianne thought she was lucky to have so many people that she loved in her life. Who needs the Williams?

* * * * *

Dee had been working on a contract and was on the phone talking with buyers of a national food chain when the mailman rang the doorbell to deliver a certified letter addressed to Marianne Robinson stamped 'Personal and Confidential'. She signed for the letter and placed it on the dining table, away from the other mail, making sure Marianne wouldn't miss it whenever she came home.

It was the boy's day out and Marianne took them for a long day of playing at the amusement park. She tried to do something with them every week, they were little kids and Marianne wanted them to have good memories of being little plus they could have some quality time with her instead of always having to share her with so many people. She felt bad because she worked so much and so many long hours; Marianne made a point to take them where that they could play, and they played hard today.

Once they were home, Marianne headed straight for the mail.

"What's this?" She opened the letter and it was a letter from Mrs. Williams.

Dear Marianne,
I'm sorry I couldn't meet you as we had planned.

Something came up and please forgive me, it wasn't intentional. I wanted to show you something. This is a picture of my father sitting on a porch in California. Jackson favors my father. Look at the birthmark on his right leg. It's almost a carbon copy of little Jackson's birthmark. Not only did he have the birth mark, so did my grandfather. That's how I recognized Jackson. It's a striking resemblance, isn't it?

My father was a minister and so was my grandfather. My father's name was Rev. Marcus Masters. My grandfather's name was Rev. Elmer D Masters. They were great men. They traveled throughout Mexico, Haiti, and hundreds of other town and villages as missionaries. Your son has a great legacy. His forefathers were great men.

I won't be contacting you concerning Jackson anymore. My husband has poor understanding, I don't agree with him, but he is my husband and I want to keep the peace in my marriage.

Reginald and his wife are expecting their first child. I'm told it will be a girl. He's living in Atlanta and he has a production company called Sounds For Life. Reginald's looking at a very handsome future in the music business. I just thought you should know.

It's good to know your family's history, I hope one day you will tell your son about us. I pray and trust that we will be united together as a family. I want that so much, I'm sorry I can't be a part of his life right now. He seems to be a wonderful child. If he's anything like my

father and grandfather, then he will have a special gift.
You'll recognize it. I'm sure I'm missing a treasure of
memories. I'll pray for you and Jackson. May God
continue to keep you in his care.

Always,

Julia Williams.

PS: Please tell Reginald about Jackson.

Marianne sat down and read the letter again and again.
She looked at the picture over and over. Jackson looks like his
great grandfather. He's just like him. She looked at the
birthmark on the picture, almost exact. Boy if Aunt Rosie was
to see this picture, she'd swear it was Jacks . . . all grown up.
She says that Jacks has been here before. She says he's an old
soul.

Just then Ms. Shirley walked in the door. She was
struggling with groceries.

"Honey, help me put this food up. I got some ice cream
for my fellows." Ms. Shirley stopped because Marianne wasn't
answering.

Marianne sat in the chair without looking up. She held
the letter reading it again.

"What's the matter, sweetie, are you alright?"

"Ms. Shirley who's my father? I'd like to get a straight
answer. All my life I felt like I'm not supposed to ask, but I
want to know and I want you to tell me, who is he? What
happened to my mother . . . that everybody in town knows, but
me?"

Ms. Shirley sat next to Marianne, she let out a big sigh,
turned to look at Marianne dead in her eyes, then asked

"Honey, what are you reading, who sent you that letter?"

Marianne ignored her questions then proceeded with her
inquiry. "One day when I was pregnant with Jacks, I was in Dr.

184

Clark's office, and he said something. He said something happened to my mother, and it was terrible. I didn't press the issue. I was scared to ask. Nobody around here wants to talk about it, but I need to know where I come from. It's only right. I want Jackson to know about his folks. All my life I felt like part of me was missing, so I thought maybe I was too young to know everything. I'm old enough, now. I want you to tell me this big secret about my father. You were around Ms. Shirley and you know. What is it about my father that nobody talks about?"

"Oh Marianne, this is hard. Baby . . how am I going to tell you this?"

"Just say it, Ms. Shirley. Please."

"Your father's name is George Hill. He was a math and science teacher at Paseo High, where your mother went. She was a sophomore, only 14 when it happened. Anyway, he used to have her stay after school, saying she was helping him on this and that, some science projects or something. He was a well-liked teacher. Good looking as hell! He'd ask Ms. Maxine if Patricia could stay after school, and by him being a teacher, Ms. Maxine trusted him. He did alright for a while. He made sure she was safely home; he'd walk her to the door, and deliver her right to Ms. Maxine. Well, I guess he had some crush on Patricia. She was such a beautiful girl, outgoing and smart. She would laugh and make everybody laugh with her. So beautiful; anyway it was a Friday night, the school was having a basketball game, so there was a lot of noise. Nobody heard your mother's screams for help. Well, George Hill raped your mother, he raped her pretty bad. We were told she would never have any children, but she ended up pregnant with you." Ms. Shirley hugged Marianne. "It's hard telling you something like that. Family secrets can destroy a person but you don't have to let something bad destroy your family. Patricia loved you. In

185

fact, you were the joy of her and Ms. Maxine's life. It's something how things work out, something so tragic and terrible ended up being the joy of their lives. God is so good."

"What happened to the teacher?"

"Ms. Maxine got hold of him before the police did. Back then it was a lot of street girls that stayed at your house. Ms. Maxine protected them from pimps and husbands. Men would beat them girls back then, so they hid out at the house. Well, they got a hold of George for Ms. Maxine and put something in his drink, drugged him up, knocked him out. I think it was eye drops. That stuff would knock you out, they changed it now, but back then, it would knock you out. Anyway, they got him in a hotel room, tied him up and Ms. Maxine cut off his balls."

"Whaaat, did you say?"

"She said the only reason she didn't kill his ass is because he didn't kill Patricia. You know, he knew he would be caught and probably put in prison. It was crazy. He brought her home to your grandmother and he took off. He stayed gone a while. Maxine found his ass. He was hiding out in one of those country towns around here. Yeah, she castrated that fool. Anyway, she handed him his balls and told him if she ever saw him again, she would kill him. We never heard from him after that."

"My grandmother cut off his balls?"

"Yep, she sure did! Then gave 'em to him. Man, when that story got around town, nobody messed with Ms. Maxine. She sho' got a name for herself after that."

"I guess! . . . So, I have a father that's a rapist. He raped my mother. What kind of man would do that? Thank you Ms. Shirley. I see why it was such a secret."

"Marianne, sometimes these guys dream up stuff in their heads and they believe it. He thought Patricia liked him too.

He had a crush on your mother, she was so pretty. After that, she dropped out of school and raised you. Patricia never was the same, she stayed to herself, quiet as a mouse. Patricia, bless her heart, was never the same."

Shirley decided to go home and stay with her husband tonight. It's been a while since she paid any attention to him. But today, she's the one who needed comforting. She wanted to curl up under Clarence and forget about everything.

Shirley felt bad. Marianne came to her for some answers. She asked Shirley to be honest, but she couldn't. She could never tell Marianne what her father really did to her sweet young mother.

It was a damn shame what that man did to Patricia. How he beat Patricia and left her outside in the cold, barely recognizable, like a piece of trash. He thought she was dead. Patricia stayed in the hospital fighting for her life over a month. Patricia wouldn't go outside after that, she never went back to that school.

How could she tell her that Ms. Maxine had her father, tied up in Pali and Mr. Whites room, bleeding like a pig, begging for his life. Ms. Maxine was something else. Marianne caught her off guard. Ms. Maxine said the only reason she spared that bastards life is because God spared Patricia.

Chapter 17

Time flies. People and circumstances are constantly changing. And that's good, who wants to be in a decade stand still? Who wants to exist around the same old, same old, without any movement; just a mediocre, run of the mill, vapor of life? Who wants that?

That's not the case at the boarding house. If walls could talk. Those old stories that would be told over the years were challenging to believe. The people that came and then left the skeletons of the past, but you know the old saying, 'what doesn't kill us . . . makes us stronger.' And you live on; if you're lucky.

A lot of living had been going on at the boarding house. Most was good. Big Bill got married. He and Michelle decided they weren't getting any younger, so they might as well do the right thing and tie the knot, or jump the broom.

Michelle was getting tired of Bill's old jokes anyway. He had to choose. She was tired of everybody at that boarding house. Anytime Darlene broke a fingernail, Bill was running to her rescue. So she put her foot down. Either Bill was going to be the man she and her daughter needed or she was moving on, before it was too late for her to find a man.

Michelle needed a partner that she could talk to about her business. She needed Big Bill and she wasn't sharing him any longer. Why should every woman at the boarding house benefit from her work; she was the one sleeping with Big Bill, not Marianne, Dee and Darlene.

* * * * *

After about five years working as a nurse at the hospital, Darlene began working at the nursing home where she put Nanna. There was no way she could continue at the hospital, work those long, excruciating hours; then come home to care

188

for her grandmother. So she placed Nanna at Solomon's Rock Nursing Home.

Darlene would pitch such a fit at that place, that they gave her a job. They figured out a way to get Darlene to shut up. Plus she was the nurse that they desperately needed. Now she's the director of the nursing home. Darlene loves her job; she has more time to spend with Razz.

Yes, Darlene and Razz became very close after his wife left. He was her confidant, her friend and her lover. It came so natural for her to make love to him. He was that stability that she needed. She could always trust his advice when it came to making important decisions. Darlene had never met anyone like Razz. Everybody respected him, and it was a deserving respect. He was everybody's mentor, like the neighborhood godfather. Darlene loved watching Razz wiggle through tough situations.

Then at night, when she walked through the doors at the club, Razz would act like she was the most wonderful thing on the planet. He'd be so glad to see Darlene. Razz was proud of Darlene too. He remembered how hard she worked getting ahead. How dedicated she was in getting her grandmother out of New York City. Over the years, watching Darlene grow into the women she is now, made Razz want to beat his chest. He knew he had a lot to do with her success.

*****

Pali and Mr. White finally retired. It was a long stretch working at the Amador Hotel. They gave them a retirement party comparable to an affair in Hollywood. People flew in from all parts of the country. You would never think so many famous people cared for the distinctive couple. Then they moved to Florida. Every year Marianne got a Christmas card from Pali asking her to come out to Florida for a visit. He really loves it. He says Miami is the retirement paradise. Marianne didn't write, but she called her friends regularly, promising them a surprise visit.

* * * * *

After the situation with Dee and Clarence, Marianne asked Dee to move out. She couldn't have Dee living under same roof after what happened. Clarence had been slipping in the back door at the boarding house and getting in Dee's bed. It was a bad situation. Clarence was there, naked as a jaybird and dead as a doorknob. Poor thang had a heart attack. They say if you live by the gun, then you'll die by the gun. I guess his gun finally killed his ass.

Ms. Shirley never found out what actually happened. Marianne has so many ways like her grandmother, Maxine. She has a way of handling situations, too.

That night Dee called Marianne, frantic. She was whispering.

"Hey Marianne, come down stairs. It's an emergency, hurry up and be quiet."

"Dee, what time is it? Girl, I got to get up in the morning, I don't have time for this bullshit. Don't be calling me this time of night." Marianne hung the phone up and turned over. She drifted back to sleep, she was tired and snoring.

Suddenly, there were quick, little tappings at her bedroom door.

"Marianne, Marianne, get up. Girl, you got to help me. It's Clarence, something happened to him." Whenever Dee got excited her accent got very heavy, this time she was barely speaking English.

"Something like what?"

"I don't know, but he's not breatthing. Aye yai yai!"

"Where is he? Call the ambulance."

Marianne jumped to her feet, put on a robe and followed Dee downstairs, making sure she didn't wake the boys that were

190

asleep in the room next to her. She entered Dee's room to find Clarence naked, appearing to be sleep, with a pleasant look on his face. She knew immediately Clarence was gone.

"Oooh Damnit Dee, what did you do?"

"Nothiiing! I swear. We were just fuckking. He's always in my room. I do nothiing."

"What do you mean, you didn't do anything? Dee, he's dead. Lock the damn door and don't let anybody come in here. Stay here with him, till I come back. My Lord, what are we going to do?"

Marianne immediately called Darlene.

"Darlene, I got an emergency. You need to get here quick. When you come, park down the street and walk up here. We can't wake Ms. Shirley. Girl, it's bad."

"What happened, Marianne?" Darlene spoke distinctively and precise.

"It's Clarence, he was messing with Dee and died."

"I told Dee she was playing with fire. Oooooooo . . . Ms. Shirley is gonna kick her ass."

"Somebody needs to do something. She needs a good ass whipping, Clarence is in her bed. It must have been a heart attack."

"Are you sure he's dead?"

"That's why I'm calling you . . . Yeah, I'm sure. He's dead Darlene. Girl, what am I going to do? I can't let Shirley see him, not like this. Dee's like a daughter to Ms. Shirley."

"I'm on my way, I'm gonna call Razz. He'll know what to do."

"Please don't wake Ms. Shirley."

"I won't."

After Darlene explained the situation to Razz, he had his boys come over to get Clarence. Uncle Charlie helped Darlene and Marianne clean him up. They got him dressed, then Razz's boys carried him next door, placed Clarence on the porch, as if he died there, trying to get in his house. Only thing wrong, Ms. Shirley was watching.

Clarence had a nice funeral and he left his wife financially secure, as always, looking after his beautiful bride. Ms. Shirley never told anyone that she saw Razz, Uncle Charlie and three other men carrying Clarence home that night. Her husband died of natural causes. She figured he was out somewhere, doing something he had no business doing, she appreciated Razz and Charlie bringing him home. They were trying to protect her, that's why they secretly laid him on the porch for her to find. The circumstances surrounding his death didn't matter, it couldn't change the facts that Clarence was gone and there wasn't anything else to say.

Thank God for her family at the boarding house. Thank God for Aunt Rosie and Uncle Charlie. Ms. Shirley was able to move on with her life. She continued to take care of Jackson and Patrick. They kept her busy and kept her mind off the love of her life. She missed her husband. Time never replaced the emptiness she felt after Clarence died.

* * * * *

Patrick was now twelve years old and Jackson would be ten in a couple of months. They went everywhere together, best friends, uncle and nephew, closer than brothers. There were a few other kids on the block that hung out with them, all best friends, riding bikes together, catching the bus through the city and going to the movies. They even did homework together.

In the summertime, the community center was the hangout. They'd go early enough to swim all day, later they played pool and ping pong. Marianne was busy but stayed involved with the kids. She always wanted to know what her boys were doing and who they were hanging out with. But basically, the gang was a good set of kids.

192

There was Zetty, Raven, and J Rock, they were the older set of kids. Zetty was the oldest, he'll be fourteen his next birthday. Raven and J Rock were both twelve, the same age as Patrick. Tia Mae, Blue Baby, and Jacks were the younger crew.

Jacks liked Blue Baby's mother, Angie. She was pretty, very pretty. You could say, Jacks had a crush on his friend's mom. All the boys in the neighborhood had a crush on Angie. She didn't act like the other mothers. She acted young. She played with all the guys. Jacks would never admit it, but the reason they all kept Blue Baby around was because his momma's so fine.

Tia Mae being the younger girl of the group had to keep up. Tia was a cute little girl, but she was one of the guys. They all were best friends. Tia's mom didn't play. Tia would get in trouble every day for staying out too late. Marianne would step in and take her home, or she'd call Tia's mother to let her know she was with them so Tia wouldn't get a whipping.

Marianne got mad a few times at Tia. She didn't condone her disobeying her mom. Every time Marianne had to take Tia home, she had to listen to her momma fuss. Marianne would tell Jacks afterwards,

"I'M NOT DOING IT AGAIN. IF SHE'S SUPPOSED TO BE HOME, THEN SHE NEEDS TO BE HOME. IT'S MAKING ME LOOK BAD. THAT'S A LITTLE GIRL AND HER MOTHER IS RIGHT. SHE AIN'T GOT NO BUSINESS STAYING OUT LATE WITH YOU BOYS. DON'T ASK ME TO TAKE HER HOME AGAIN, JACKS. I'M NOT PLAYING."

"Mom, we were just playing the Atari game. We didn't know it was that late."

"JACKS, I DON'T CARE. If she stays out again, I'm not taking her home."

Next week, Marianne was calling Tia's mother letting

her know she was over at the house and she was having dinner, she'll bring her home. She wasn't doing anything but playing video games with the other kids. On and on, same thing again.

Marianne gave them all jobs. She felt that there was always something they could do around the restaurant, so why not let the kids make a little money. Zetty and Patrick made bar-b-que deliveries, Jackson, J Rock and the other boys kept the building clean, cutting the yard and cleaning the restrooms. Raven and Tia bus the tables. It was a way to keep money in their pockets and teach the kids to work. One thing for sure, the parents appreciated what Marianne was doing. She didn't have them working too late and they all knew what their children were doing, making some money and staying out of trouble.

Jackson was so mature, way past his ten years. He had plain old common sense that was hard to find in boys his age. He was the one that kept the older kids from doing something stupid.

One day these guys that lived around the block wanted Patrick, J Rock, and Zetty to help them in a fight, saying they had to protect their neighborhood women. It was a fight over some girl. Jacks just told them plain and simple.

"We don't have a problem with those cats, if you have a problem, then you fight them. We ain't got a problem."

If Patrick, Zetty and J Rock had been by themselves, without Jackson, they would have gone to fight without knowing why. Just be fighting. That could have started trouble for years. That's when Marianne gets mad at Patrick, when he does things without thinking. She has to make him take Jackson just for reasons like that, because Jacks is going to use his common sense.

Marianne dreaded Patrick getting older. Patrick is good looking. He looks like his mother, Patricia, but he's built just like his daddy, Lonnie, tall and slim. Marianne had to buy clothes every couple of months because he out grew everything so fast. One thing for sure, Patrick was going to be tall, very tall. He had eyes that change colors. They change when he's happy or mad, they even change when the weather change. That boy will change his clothes to match his eye color.

Ms. Shirley calls him her pretty boy. Not only does Marianne have to worry about these young girls, she has to worry about old ladies chasing after him; them thinking he has money doesn't help. Ever since he was a little boy, she has had to keep an eye on Patrick. Marianne has her hands full.

She'll never forget the time at the grocery store when a man asked if she needed help. Marianne didn't think anything about it, so she let the man hold Patrick while she put the food in the car, and that guy started walking off. Marianne grabbed a bag of potatoes and hit him over his head. Potatoes went one way and Patrick went the other. Thankfully, a security police was close enough to see what was happening and they arrested the man.

Marianne enjoys her boys. She enjoys all the kids that hang out and work at the restaurant. Zetty and Patrick do pretty good delivering barbeque, especially on weekends when folk didn't want to cook. Mostly, it was the same people that they made deliveries for, and Razz had them delivering until she closed at night. It was alright because she can watch them ride their bikes all the way to Razz's club, then home.

* * * * *

Marianne was lonely. Her kids were great, her customers and friends are alright, but she wanted a man to feel and touch, she wanted to lay down at night with more than her pillow. There was no way in a million years, she would have thought that she would be a single parent. When she was a girl, she had everything figured out. She would go to the military, travel, have a career, but nothing worked out the way she planned. She often laughed at herself. Although her life wasn't what she planned, she wouldn't change a thing, except having a little time for a man friend.

Whenever her boys get a little older she's going to date again, but now, they're too young and she's too busy. Too busy for a man, too busy for some affection, or love; she'll wait. She just hoped and prayed that the wait would be worth it.

Ms. Shirley was everybody's everything. She cooked, cleaned, wiped tears, told old stories of good old times; she was their granny. The boys loved their Ms. Shirley. She always had their dinner ready, cooked them pies and cakes, and she was funnnny.

* * * * *

One day Jackson was walking with Blue Baby and Tia on their way to the arcade when he had to stop walking. He stopped in his tracks. Jacks couldn't see. Everything went black. He waited, waiting for his sight to come back. All he could do was stop and hold his hands out, trying to feel what was happening. He fell down, it was almost like he was knocked down, but nothing touched him. Then there was a blast, so loud that he grabbed his ears and screamed. In the blast was a bright light that flashed almost at the same time. Somehow through the darkness, he saw the light. He looked horrified; he patted the ground, hoping to get his bearings together.

Immediately, a car stopped, it was Juanita Williams. She jumped out, ran to the sidewalk, and cradled Jackson.

"Jackson, Jackson, sweetheart, are you alright? What's wrong, baby? What happened to him?"

"We were walking, then he started acting like this. He fell down and then you drove up." Tia was trying to explain to this stranger that was yelling at her, like it was her fault.

"I can't see. Tia what's happening?" Jackson never felt

196

fear before. He was so scared that he literally shook. His teeth were chattering like he was in freezing cold weather, but it was summer time.

"Jacks, Jacks, what happened, you alright, man?" Blue got down on the ground with Jacks, so he could get closer. He started shaking his friend's leg. "You gonna be alright? Man, tell me what's happening to you?"

"Jackson, this is granny, I mean, uummm . . . this is Juanita Williams, I'll stay with you till your mother comes." She turned to Blue, "Run get Marianne. I'll stay here with Jackson."

Jacks continued to feel around the ground, trembling. "I can't see. I can't see."

Juanita Williams tried to keep him still, she rocked and cradled Jacks. Right at that time, Ms. Shirley came running down the street with Blue Baby.

"Where is he?"

Jacks was getting up. It was over, he was a little shaken but he seemed to be alright.

"Baby what happened? What's wrong?"

Jacks couldn't describe what had happened. "I don't know, all of a sudden I couldn't see. Ms. Shirley, I was just walking then I couldn't see. I was scared Ms. Shirley, I was so scared."

"Let's get you home, I'll call your momma. Thanks Mrs. Williams for helping. Where did you come from?"

"I was driving down the street when I saw little Jackson in trouble. Of course I stopped to see if I could help." Without anyone noticing, Juanita Williams slid a twenty dollar bill in his jeans pocket.

"Thank you, ma'am. I'll get him to his momma."

"Why don't I drive you home? It's a little walk, but please, let me drive you."

Actually, Juanita Williams purposely drives down the streets where she knows Jackson, her grandson, walks and plays. She just wants to see him every now and then. Marianne never told Reginald about Jackson, but that wasn't going to keep her from looking at her first grandchild, every now and then.

After Dr. Clark checked Jackson out, he seemed to be fine. The doctor ran test for diabetes that's prevalent in his family, but that was all normal. Dr. Clark said he couldn't find anything that could have been wrong with Jackson but to keep an eye on him for any further signs. He thought he might have gotten too hot or excited, but he seemed to be fine.

It wasn't long before Marianne began to relax. Jacks seemed to be alright, he was back to his old self. Jackson made her and Ms. Shirley stop babying him so much. He reminded them that he was getting older and they needed to act like it. Marianne had to let go, after all, she didn't want to smother the boy.

Chapter 18

Zetty and Patrick were out on the town with a few girls. Patrick had just bought his first car, a little green mustang. They all rode together, packed deep, and had left the movies. All the girls wanted to talk to Patrick, but Patrick barely said a word. He was quiet. Zetty, on the other hand, was the one that entertained the girls, but for some reason, Patrick's silence was more intriguing.

Actually, Patrick was afraid of girls. Patrick was a junior in high school and never had a real girlfriend. They were always talking to him, he was a lot of fun, but he didn't want anybody to know his secret; that he never had sex. It never really happened. He kissed and got close a few times. He felt like he had sex, but he would always have an accident, then it was over. It was embarrassing; he would have to jump up and the girls always knew. It was so embarrassing that it was better for Patrick not to get close to girls period.

Now Zetty was always there to help. He knew that his friend was a virgin. The way he played and talked with the fellows, he should be the same way with girls, but he wasn't. Sometimes, Patrick would break out in a sweat talking with a girl. Zetty tried and tried to get Patrick a date with a woman that was more experienced, that might get him to loosen up a bit, and show him a few things, but he never opened up to the much older women friends of Zetts. Sooner or later, the meetings would die off with nothing ever accomplished. Zett teased that he's gonna be a virgin all his life.

Zetty had a secret stash, an older woman that he had deep feelings for; she teaches him everywhere it feels good to girls, so now he knows. She made him promise not to tell anybody about their affair. He's been seeing this woman for six months already. Zetty debated sharing her with his best friend

199

but she wouldn't go for it.

"Hey Patrick, I got a friend I want you to meet."

"Man, why are you always trying to get me some old lady stuff. One of these days, you gonna get me something I can't get rid of . . . man, when I meet the right woman, I'll do it. Stop trying to set me up. Set your own self up."

"Okay . . . okay, but when you find out about this one, don't say I didn't try to introduce you to her."

"Who is it?"

"Man I ain't telling you shit."

"I don't care. That's you, all the time bragging 'bout some woman. What makes you think I want your leftovers, anyway . . . I bet you ain't doing nothing, just talking noise. You know people that brag all the time ain't doing nothing, Zett."

"Just for that, I'm gonna make your sorry ass wait. I ain't telling you nothing . . . with your sorry ass."

Patrick threw him an imaginary punch. "Boy, see that, you better be glad that didn't connect. I woulda knocked you out, with that one."

* * * * *

Jacks and Tia were now freshmen in high school, they were taking their time walking home and looking for Blue. They hadn't seen him all day. They were just about home when they saw two men walking toward them. The men were smiling like they were happy to see them. They stopped and continued to smile. Somehow, Jacks felt as if he knew them, too, from somewhere . . . but where? And for some reason, he was happy to see them, too.

"Hello Jacks . . . hi Tia."

Tia was stunned that the two strangers called them by name. "Who are you? Where ya'll know me from?"

They didn't answer, still smiling, they waved for a

200

couple of seconds, then turned to walk away.

"Hey stop!" Jacks smiled, "Wait!" He wanted to talk with them, waving his hand hoping for them to stop. He started toward the two strangers, he felt like they were his old friends, but they were walking away.

"Who are those men, Jacks? Do you know them?" Tia was wondering about their whole attitude.

"I don't know, I thought maybe you knew'em. They probably come to the restaurant or something."

"You don't remember seeing them before?"

Jacks looked back to see where they were going but they were gone. "Where did those cats go? Did you see where they went?"

"Now, that's weird. They're gone, Jacks."

Just then Blue Baby caught up with them. "Hey what's going on. Where ya'll been? I had two tests in Ms. Adkinson's class. I was there all day."

"Did you see two guys walking by you? They should have passed you. Did you see them?"

"There wasn't anybody that way. I just came from there, I didn't see anybody."

"Jack's that's really weird, cause we saw them. Where did they go?"

"Oh well, I'm not going to sweat over it."

"What if they were angels, Jacks?"

"Right! Tia you been watching too many movies."

"Soooo, where'd they go? They .. are . . . gone!"

"If they were angels, then we must be special. Think about that!"

* * * * *

Jacks hadn't had a blackening spell in a while. Sometimes it happens a lot, like in the same year; then it wouldn't happen for a year or two. It's starting to change, too.

201

He might see words, but he'll wake up before he can read it. He wanted to know what the words were saying, what the black outs were about. One day it'll make sense. So he decided not to worry . . . it was mostly the same, a big blast, with a bright flash in the dark; then when it was over, he'd feel sad.

The last time it happened he was with Patrick, they were delivering dinners together. Patrick knows what to do whenever it happens; he'll sit and wait with Jacks until it's over. They made a pact with each other not to tell Marianne because she'd worry too much. Anyway, there wasn't a thing anybody could do about it, Jacks always returned to his old self, as if nothing happened.

He tried, once, to talk to Uncle Charlie about it, but Uncle Charlie went to sleep without him getting an answer. Jacks covered him up then walked home still wondering what it all meant. It wouldn't mean so much to Jacks, but lately, he's been having a lot of things happen. Somehow he knew when people were lying. It's like a joke because it's plain as day when someone's lying. He sometimes can feel what other people are feeling, like when they're worried or happy. Sometimes he feels when they're in pain, too.

He confided in Patrick that he knows about people, just to see if it was unusual. Patrick just listened in awe, waiting to see what else he could do. Now Jacks sees colors around folk.

Patrick now asks Jackson to feel people out before making a decision about anything. Jacks would be right on time too, about everybody.

Patrick knew he had something good. He started taking Jackson gambling at Razz's. They would beg Razz for hours to let them in a game. At first it was a little game of Tonk; then it was Cooncan, and they were winning. Jackson knew when those old cats were bluffing or cheating. He knew automatically when someone hit a lick; he'd immediately fold his hand.

202

Patrick would follow. All Jacks had to do was look at Patrick and Patrick knew exactly what move to make. Patrick and Jackson had a little rhyme that they'd say when one of them made a sting.

"Jacks and Patty, just got happy. Two peas in a pot, ready for the next Hot Shot . . . at Razz's." Then they would do their signature hand shake, sit down, and get ready to play again. The old cats would shake their heads, and grumble about beginner's luck.

Old Razz told them to stop teasing when they win, it wasn't cool and it makes enemies.

"Just be cool. Let your game do your talking. These cats don't like being disrespected. And stop saying that thing about beating my Hot Shots, these are my customers. So knock it off."

But Jackson had a mouth. He'd win then say something slick; it only made the old cats laugh. Patrick was the quiet one.

Razz told Jackson to stay focused on school and a career, but Jackson was beating some big time gamblers. It's hard to talk sense to a boy when he's making that kind of money, and at sixteen! Anyway, Razz couldn't help it if grown ass men wanted to lose money to a little sixteen year old Ace like Jackson; who was he to stop'em.

The fact of the matter was; Razz liked watching his little homies take that money. He kept his side bets going and was getting a house cut too. That was it. Razz loved it. It didn't matter whose kids they were, they had to learn the ropes and he was just the one to teach 'em.

Only thing about it, Razz wasn't letting them stay out late, they had to leave his place at midnight. Marianne wasn't getting on him about her boys. Whenever she called, he'd tell her they left, or . . . I'll send'em on.

If Razz ever found out that they were messing up in

203

school, or cheating in his place of business, then he would ban them out, just like anybody else. He never had to threaten them about anything, cause they were pretty good boys, never did anything wrong. Jackson was a straight A student, and Patrick was graduating this year. They were good kids.

* * * * *

Dee ended up moving back with Uncle Charlie and Aunt Rosie. They were older and needed Dee there with them. She didn't have children and she finally stopped trying to seduce Uncle Charlie; he was now, finally, like a father to her. It was a long time getting her to that point and it took a whole lot of counseling.

Uncle Charlie told her to get help or he was letting her go . . . for good! She couldn't continue to be around him and his wife. Clarence was the last straw. When Uncle Charlie gave her the look, she knew he was serious. He didn't like being deceptive to his wife, and he felt like he had lied to Rosie and Shirley by not being truthful about Dee or Clarence's death. It was Uncle Charlie's last dance with Dee.

All her life she was sexually abused. He understood that sex was just like breathing air to her, now she's addicted to it. Dee would go out and pick up guys on the streets, at clubs, the grocery stores; she even used her workers if there wasn't anybody else.

It was hard for her. Dee had to stop having sex all together. It was real hard. Her therapist said that she had to focus on having a trusting relationship. She was thankful that, this time, Uncle Charlie didn't give up on her before she tried to do better. This was all the family she had and she didn't want to lose them, too.

Dee hadn't seen her mother, sister or brother in years. Every now and then, she'd get a letter letting her know about a newborn niece or nephew, and that was all.

Dee wanted to be normal. She knew she had a problem. It was more of a problem for everybody else then it was for her, but she loved Marianne, Uncle Charlie, and everybody. She didn't like the fact that they watched her around the boys. So it was important for her to get help, because she loved them so much.

Uncle Charlie appreciated Dee, her being there for him and his wife. His Rosie had slight Alzheimer's and Arthritis had Charlie permanently bent over. They were now deep in their golden years. Dee was there! She kept Uncle Charlie's Sauces going strong.

He decided to leave the sauce business, the recipe patents, and his house to Dee, the child that he let down so many years ago. Maybe this could somehow make up for his short sightedness and Dee could become a fulfilled woman, maybe have a husband and family one day. She deserved better. She had suffered enough.

He left the restaurants to Marianne. There were three different locations in the Kansas City area. As long as the restaurants, groceries, and hotels are in business, then Marianne and Dee would be alright. Uncle Charlie could rest, if he wanted too.

* * * * *

Tia had a boyfriend. She had to stop hanging out with Jackson so much because her boyfriend got real jealous. She was too busy anyway, working at the restaurant; going to school, singing in the choir, and being with Stevie Brooks took all her time.

From the beginning, Stevie was too possessive. The first time he met Tia, he watched her like she was his property. He had a little aqua blue hatchback car, the front passenger seat was gone, but it was comfortable, it had character. He was her personal driver and body guard. He took Tia everywhere she had to go. Her mother, Brenda, thought it was nice. She was a little relieved that her boyfriend was so reliable and conscientious. He made sure she was home on time, work on time, church, everywhere she had to go, there he was to take her. Tia liked it too, at first; then he started getting too bossy.

"Where were you, Tia? You know I was coming to get you, why you so late, and got me waiting on your ass? What were you doing?"

"Damn Steven, I can't go to the bathroom and take a shit without you wanting to follow me in there. What have YOU been doing? You always talking about me, you must be guilty about something," Tia rolled her eyes, had her hands on her hips, shaking her head with each word.

"You know what, Tia. You're gonna make me knock you out."

"IIIII wish you would!!! You want to hit me, don't you? DON'T YOU? Tia started yelling. "WHY YOU ALWAYS TALKING ABOUT DOING SOMETHING TO ME, STEVIE? IF YOU FEEL LIKE YOU GOT TO DO SOMETHING TO ME, THEN WE NEED TO STOP ALL THIS CAUSE YOU AIN'T MY DADDY AND I AIN'T TAKING NO WHIPPING FROM YOUR SORRY ASS."

Stevie grabbed Tia and started choking her. "You know what, Girrrlll, if I didn't love you, . . .Tia . . . watch your mouth. You better start acting like you know who I am around here, raising your voice at me . . . I'll kick your ass . . . keep on Tia."

"I'm going to tell my momma, Stevie. You can't be putting your hands on me." Tia couldn't talk, tears were dropping on her blouse like rain.

Tia never told her mother about Stevie's fighting, but she told Stevie that she wasn't allowed to see him anymore. She lied.

Tia was sixteen years old, this was her first boyfriend,

and he was overbearing. She couldn't do anything, he was too jealous. She wanted to tell her mother but was afraid. So she thought to teach Stevie a lesson; she would break up with him if he didn't stop hitting her.

Brenda, Tia's mom, started asking about Stevie. She was so used to him being around the house and taking Tia where she needed to go. Stevie was convenient, and it was a nice break for her.

"Soooo, where's Stevie? I sure like that boy. He got some damn good sense. You can't find a boy these days that'll walk you to the door, come in and talk like he got some sense. Naaawww, not these days."

"Momma, Stevie's too possessive. He's getting where he thinks he's my daddy or something."

"Girl, that's how all boys are about their girlfriends. I just feel better about you being somewhere with him, I know he's going to take care of my baby."

"Well, right now, he's got a job that keeps him busy. He had to give me a break."

"That's alright; you can do some things yourself. Tell him hello for me."

Tia shook her head and debated whether she should let her mother know what was happening in her relationship with her first boyfriend.

* * * * *

It was a cool October night. They had just finished working at the restaurant, and were on their way to Razz's to make their nightly delivery of leftover food for the club. It was dark. Jackson and Patrick were riding listening to music, when Jackson saw the two men from a few years back. It was the same two men that spoke to him and Tia when they were walking home from school. Jacks remembered that they called them by name. What were they doing in this neighborhood, this time of night?

"Hey, hold up Patrick. I want to talk to these cats. Pull over. Hurry up."

Jackson jumped out the car and ran to the two men before they would leave. Only thing, they were waiting on Jackson.

"Hello Jackson. I'm Josias and this is Uri."

They greeted Jackson and seemed happy as they spoke with Jacks. "Soon it'll be your season." Uri spoke, with his finger pointed at nothing in particular, "You'll know what it means."

The man named Josias looked in Jackson eyes, holding his shoulders with a firm grip. "A lot is expected from a man that has been given so many gifts."

"What are you taking 'bout? Oh, you talking about . . . "

"How's Tia? Let her know you saw us, and keep an eye on Patrick. Help him regain what he lost."

The two men walked off. They looked back once and smiled. Jackson waved, then walked back to the car where Patrick was listening to some old tapes.

"What was that all about?"

"I don't know. I saw those cats a couple years ago. I just wanted to know who they were. They seem to know me."

"Did you find out?"

"Sorta."

"Well, Jacks, ya'll were talking. What were you talking about?"

"I think they were talking about my blackouts, but I don't know for sure, they said something about my season is coming. They said I was going to know what it means."

"Man, I don't know about that, Jacks. It sounds weird. Where did you first meet them again?"

"They told me to keep an eye on you, Patty and to help

you find what you lost. Have you lost something?"

"Yeah, the other day, I lost a million dollars!" Patrick turned the music up then drove home telling Jackson about everything he lost . . . in his dreams.

Chapter 19

Jackson impatiently waited for Tia to let her know about the two men. He hoped that ignorant Stevie wouldn't be hovering over her. She couldn't say a word to Jacks anymore without her boyfriend mean mugging him. He belongs to one of the local gangs that's trying to get a reputation. But Tia is his home girl; she works for his mother. That man ought to understand. He'll see her at work, but Jackson was anxious to tell her about last night.

Jackson didn't see Tia all morning. He went through the cafeteria but she wasn't there. He asked a couple of girls if they saw her, everybody pointed in different directions, finally he gave up; he'd see her later tonight at the restaurant.

Patrick was on his way to get some Mexican food when he saw her.

"Hey Tia, let's get lunch."

"Where you going?"

"To get some chicken tacos. What do you want?"

"I'll take tacos. You buying me lunch, Patty?"

"Yeah, get in. I got to find Jackson. He wanted to talk with you about something. Oh there he is . . . Hey Jacks, over here! Get in."

Jackson looked at Patrick. "Where'd you find her? I've been looking all over for this girl."

"Patrick's buying me lunch; more than you do, Jacks."

"This girl never brings any money. Why you so tight Tia? Spend some of that money you making. You got all those old men giving you their whole paychecks in tips. Have you seen her tips, man?"

"Yeah and it's going in my savings. My momma don't have money like Marianne."

"Girl hush, with your tight self." Patrick sped off in his

210

mustang. "What time you have to be back, Tia?"

"At 12:30, then I don't have a class till 1:45, then I'm out after that."

Jackson turned to Tia, looking serious. "Girl, guess what? Remember those men we saw a couple years ago, I saw them again last night. They said to tell you hello."

"What men?"

"You remember the men that knew our names and when we looked back they were gone."

"Yeah . . . yeah. I remember something like that."

"You said they were angels, Tia. You can't remember that? Girl, what's wrong with you?"

"I remember, damn Jacks . . . It was a couple years ago."

"They told me to tell you hello. They remembered you again. I thought it was something. They were smiling like they did last time."

"What else they say?"

"That everything is going to make sense pretty soon. I think they're talking about my blackouts. Tia, it was weird. They wanted me to make sure I tell you hello for them. You know what? I do think they are angels or something. They were real cool. I felt like I know'em from somewhere."

Patrick, Jacks and Tia got out the car and went toward the window to order their lunch, when a car pulled up, with a loud, sudden stop making the skrerrrr! The door opened, two boys jumped out.

"Oh shit! I'm not in the mood for this stupid shit."

"What's wrong with your man, Tia? You better let that cat go. He's crazy."

It was Stevie Brooks and he grabbed Tia and threw her in the back seat of a low ride, old school car. Jackson and Patrick didn't know what to do. They were more surprised than anything.

Tia looked at Jackson through the back window and did a little sign language and lip movement. "It's okay. I'll see you later."

They watched as Stevie sped off with Tia.

"Man, you think we should call the police or something?" Jacks laughed but was worried.

"I don't know. That Stevie's a fool. What does he think? She works for us. That's a damn fool she's messing with."

"When she gets to work tonight, I'm gonna have a long talk with that girl. He don't act right."

* * * * *

Zetty was now in a full blown relationship with this older woman. It has been a while now. Patrick told him he needs to let her go, that she was sucking up his youth. Zetty didn't go to any of the school dances; he didn't date any other girls his age. It's like he's married to this old woman. Zetty won't tell him who this woman is, either . . . but he says he's in love.

This older woman has been nurturing Zetty for a long time, it's been three years and he belongs to her. He hated having to sneak in and out her house. Then at night, he crawls out his bedroom window and runs to her house, so he can feel her next to him, just to get a good night sleep. There was no other way for them to spend time together. If his mother found out, even if his friends found out, it would be a mess.

As long as her son never finds out about their relationship, it's okay. He's the only thing that really matters. Zett knew it too, they were almost the same age, it would be over if her son ever found out.

But she was his woman. He knew everything about that woman, how to treat her, how to make love to her, they were soul mates. When her son goes to college, it'll be okay, that's

212

just one more year.

Zett decided not to go to college. He would get a job around town, maybe work as a mechanic since he was good with cars. She didn't want him to leave her. She has a good paying job and a nice house; she says not to worry about money . . . so it'll be okay in a couple years. But for now, things are a little hard.

Zett laughed just thinking about all his buddies finding out about his woman. He wanted to tell Patrick, it would be a relief, but she made him swear not to tell.

Zett wondered what he would do once she gets old, if he'll still feel the same for her. He finally had to stop thinking about it, when that time comes, then he'll worry about it, but for now, he loved her too much.

Angie wouldn't think about getting older. She wrote it off as, no relationship is perfect. She tried to break it off one time, but Zetty cried, then she cried. It was too hard. They decided to keep their relationship as long as possible.

* * * * *

When Patrick and Jacks got to work, they talked with Marianne about Tia. They wanted to know if they should get involved.

"Mom, this cat is fighting her. I got a bad feeling about this man."

"Have you asked her about it?"

"Naww, not really. But I know he's fighting Tia."

"You know what, baby. You can talk with Tia, but you can't make her leave that boy. Sometimes when these hormones get involved, it's best to get out the way and let them grow out of love or lust, whichever it is. But if I were you, I'd talk with her; make sure it's not something we need to be concerned about. She's kind of young to be having a boyfriend beating on her."

213

"I wonder why she's so late for work?"

"If she don't come in, I'll call her momma and see what's going on."

Just then Tia walked in the door, you could see she had been crying. There was a scar or bruise that looked like finger prints across her face.

Marianne went to the window to see if Stevie was still outside. "Baby, you don't have to take no whipping from that fool. I promise you he won't come around here with that mess. Matter of fact, he bet not come back around here. Tia, I'm going to talk with your mother. Does she know that he's fighting you? You're too young for this. Girl, get rid of him now. Come here; let me look at your face."

"It's not too bad, Jacks."

"He's still outside. He's gonna wait till you get off work? Let me go outside and talk to this brother."

Jackson was fed up with Stevie Brooks. He couldn't think of anything Tia would do that deserve him hitting her like that. He must have hit her pretty hard to leave his hand print on her tender little face. Jacks went outside to where Stevie was parked in front of the building.

"Hey man, what is it with you? You know Tia is like my little sister, what is it that you got to hit her. Man, you're gonna see her with me and Patty a lot, man, she works for us. If you ever put your hands on her again, then you gonna have to deal with me. That's a promise Steve. Don't do it again."

Jackson didn't wait for an answer; he walked back into the building. Marianne was watching through the windows, prepared to call the police. There were a few customers ready and willing to jump in if need be.

"Marianne, I'm sorry. I shouldn't have come over here like this. I didn't know where to go. My mother can't see my face like this. She'll make me quit Stevie. He said he was

214

sorry. I didn't have anywhere else to go."

Marianne couldn't believe what she was hearing from her little Tia. She was worried about seeing him again.

"Tia, baby, you might be too young to be in such a serious relationship. You're sixteen, you're beautiful . . . and you're not thinking about yourself. Sometimes we need to grow up a bit before we get too involved. In a couple of years, you won't think twice about Stevie, so don't get too hung up. Okay? You need to be thinking about college and a career, not about some boy kicking your ass if you talk with your friends. You understand what I'm trying to tell you?"

"Yes ma'am. Look at him, Ms. Marianne. He's still outside, he's sorry. If he ever hits me again, then I'll leave him, I promise."

"Okay, let's put some ice on it, maybe it'll go down before you go home this evening."

"Marianne, I was hoping I can stay here. If my mom sees this, then she's going to be mad. I don't want her mad. Will you call her and let her know that I'm staying here tonight, or for the weekend."

"Oh Tia, I think you mom needs to know. You can stay, but I'm telling Brenda about Stevie hitting you."

Marianne asked her friend, Det. Byron Combs to talk with Stevie. Byron had rank and influence with the Kansas City Police Dept. He was one of the few blacks to make Detective. He had the entire police department coming to the restaurant for discount rib dinners and they had their special occasions catered by Marianne and Dee. So she was thankful for Det. Combs.

Marianne thought about dating him once, but didn't because she caught him eyeing Dee a couple times. There was no way she would take the chance on dating Byron and then have him sneak around with Dee. That thought made her think twice about all men.

But she decided to have a talk with Byron about Tia. Besides, she didn't want any trouble between her boys and that Stevie Brooks gang.

"If I have any trouble with Stevie, you'll be putting the cuffs on me."

"Yeah, I'll take care of it, I know his folks. His dad is a good guy, he works hard. I don't know what happens with these young men around here. Little Stevie don't have a record, he's never been in trouble. I'll talk with him."

"To tell the truth, I even felt sorry for him." Marianne couldn't understand. "That boy stayed outside the building looking pitiful for hours. I finally went out there and told him to go home, that Tia was staying the night with us. He left alright, said he was sorry for what he did to Tia. They need to slow it down is all."

"I'll have a talk with his folks." The Det. repeated.

* * * * *

It was late, Patrick was riding around town. He made a delivery and was on his way back to the restaurant when he saw a girl that he recognized from school. Her name was Sherry Tucker. She reminded him of the pictures of his mother. Only thing wrong, she had one leg longer than the other.

"She's really pretty." Patrick discussed with himself as he watched her limping down the street. "Where is she going?" He rode in his car at a distance behind her. She went inside a little homemade convenient store that was a house, then she came out with a pack of cigarettes. She opened the pack and started smoking and walking back toward the direction she had come.

Patrick got out his car and was turned away from her, so she didn't pay any attention to him as she passed by. Before he could think clearly, Patrick attacked her from behind and dragged her behind some deserted houses. Patrick turned her head to the ground as he proceeded to snatch her dress up and pull her panties down.

"Don't scream, don't say nothing. I'm not going to hurt you, just be still."

Sherry was terrified, too terrified to do anything. She didn't fight or move, she was completely still waiting for it to be over. It was over pretty quick.

"Don't move until I tell you. If I see you get up or move, then I'll kill you. You understand me. Don't move."

"Okay, okay, I won't."

Patrick was up zipping his pants, trying to put in perspective what he had just done. Did he really just rape a girl? What was he thinking? Patrick sat down against the wall trying to think.

Sherry turned her head and got a good look at the man that just assaulted and raped her.

"Didn't I tell you not to move?" Patrick hit her with his fist and knocked her unconscious. What was he going to do now? She saw him. He was certain that she recognized him from school and the restaurant. He had to think.

Patrick left Sherry unconscious and rode to get Zetty. He was speeding; he couldn't get there fast enough. What was he going to do? When he got to Zetty's house, he went to the back and knocked on his bedroom window.

Zetty was in his room, playing a video game, waiting for his folks to go to sleep before he left for the night . . . then he heard the knock on his window. Zett moved the curtains to see Patty looking like he just saw a ghost.

"What's wrong with you?"

Patrick climbed in the window and confided to Zett everything that he had done.

"Patty this is serious. You can go to jail. You think she's still behind the house?"

"Man, I don't know. I hit her pretty hard. Zetty, I'm going to jail aren't I? I don't know what happened. I was just watching her, then I wanted her. I told her not to look but she looked anyway, then I hit her. Man, what am I going to do?"

"We have to get rid of her."

"How? You think we can give her some money and she leave town or something? I got a little savings that I'll give her. I'll give it all to her, if she don't tell."

"Naw man, we're going to do something else. Let's go before she wakes up."

Patrick and Zetty drove in silence to the place where he left Sherry still knocked out.

"Come on man, watch the streets for anybody coming and we'll put her in the trunk."

"Put her in the trunk? For what?"

"Patty, we got to get rid of her. We're going to throw her somewhere; where she won't come back."

"She won't fit in my trunk."

"Put her in the back seat. Well, you better ride back there with her, just in case she wakes up."

Patrick and Zetty rode till they were out of town, in the Kansas mountains. Zetty was looking for a place to dispose of her body. He pulled over and walked close to an edge of a cliff, then came back to the car.

"I found a place we can throw her. Is she still breathing?"

"Hell yeah, she's breathing. Man, I ain't gonna kill this girl. I can't do it."

"You gonna have to, or go to jail for rape. She saw you, she can identify you."

They picked up Sherry and was taking her to the place to throw her body over when she started waking up.

"What are you doing? Where did you take me?" When

218

Sherry saw what was happening, she began to cry. "Patrick I won't tell. I promise, I won't tell. I always liked you but I didn't think anybody would like me because of my leg. I promise I won't say anything. Don't let him hurt me Patrick." Sherry was crying hysterically. "Don't . . . please don't."

Sherry was wiggling and struggling trying to get loose from their grips. Zetty hit her hard, making her stop fighting.

"Don't hit her, Zett. It's not her fault. She wants to live."

"Patty you can't believe her. As soon as she gets back she's going to call the police."

"No I won't. I'll stay with you . . . I'll stay with you. I promise, I promise. I always liked you Patrick, you never looked at me before. I'll do anything you ask, if you don't hurt me. PLLEEEAASE let me live."

"Zetty, I can't do something like this. I can't kill this girl because I did something wrong. I'm not doing it. If she calls the police, it's okay. I'm not killing her."

Patrick and Zetty rode back to Kansas City without much to say. Sherry rode in the back not wanting to breathe to loud. Patrick dropped Zetty back at his house and headed back to Sherry's block.

"Patrick, Zetty was wrong, I won't ever tell. I'll never say anything, if you promise to be my boyfriend."

"What are you saying? You'll forgive me for what I did to you. I was about to take your life so I wouldn't go to jail, you're willing to forgive me for all that, if I be with you?"

Sherry nodded, yes.

"Where's your folks? They're going to be worried about you?"

"I'll call them and let them know that I'm alright. They're probably drunk by now."

Patrick drove to his house and took Sherry to his room.

219

Chapter 20

Jackson's been anticipating the promise the two men made to him. They said soon it'll all make sense. His life was going to make sense . . . the dreams, the blackouts, his abilities to see things or see through things like lies or even truths; that Patty, his mom and others can't see.

Jackson was excited and happy at the thought that he would know more about himself. He tried to imagine his future, who or what he'd be, once he finished high school . . . so he was waiting for it all to make sense, like the men said.

However, instead of making sense, everything seemed to be going crazy. He was having dreams about everybody. Patrick's starting to look different. He lost his colors, the colors that floated around him every now and then. They use to be bright and happy, now they're slow, gray, or gone. What was going on with Patrick? It's something serious. Jackson decided to ask him.

"Hey Patrick, you busy? I need to talk with you. We need to talk, man."

"Hold up, don't come in here, I'll come to your room."

"I'm already here, what's wrong with you?"

"It doesn't make any difference, sooner or later you'll find out."

"Find out what . . . What? What's going on, man? "

Jackson followed behind Patrick inside his room to find Sherry Tucker, asleep, under the covers. Jackson turned his back because Sherry was naked."

"Baby, get dressed."

"I'll come back." Jackson turned toward the door to leave.

"No that's alright. She's got her robe on now."

"Patty, what's going on here? What's this girl doing?

220

Hi Sherry, what are you doing? Her clothes are hanging in your closet, how long has she been here? Mom's going to be pissed."

"Hey, you forget, Marianne is your mother, not mine. She's my sister, remember!"

"That's not going to stop her from kicking your ass, Patty."

"I know, but this is my woman. I'm taking care of Sherry, she stays with me."

"What you gonna say to momma? When she finds out, it's going to be bad. How did you keep this from Ms. Shirley?"

"Shirley knows she's here. Jackson, it's more to it than what you see. She's not pregnant or anything like that, but it's more to it. I love her."

Jackson started laughing. "Man when you do something you go all the way." Jackson gave Patrick a 'hi five' then turned to Sherry, "You know you're his first girlfriend. What did you do to this man?"

Jackson pulled up a chair and flopped down, he wasn't going anywhere; he wanted the full story. "If ya'll love each other, then go for it, but you need to tell momma before she finds out Sherry's here. How long you've been staying here anyway?"

"She's been here about a month."

"A MONTH! What about her folks, man? They must be worried. I know ya'll must have said something to them."

"Jackson, we're both 18, so we got married."

"Whhhaaaaaaaaaaat! You're kidding me."

"No I'm not kidding you"

Sherry raised her hand to show off her wedding ring. Jackson ran out the door.

"MOMMMM, MOMMMA, You need to come down here, quick! We got a situation and you need to know about this. MOMMMMMMMMMMMM, come here." Jacks ran to the door, to the hall and continued calling for Marianne.

Ms. Shirley ran in the living room mumbling under her breath. "Oh Lord. It's going to be some killing around here now."

She didn't want to be around when the action starts, so she gathered up her purse and headed toward the door, but Marianne stopped her before she got out the clear.

"What's wrong with that boy, hollering like somebody gone crazy? The house ain't on fire, is it?"

"Marianne, baby, you know I love you and those boys, love ya to death, I'll do anything for you; but right now, my name is less and I ain't in this mess." Ms. Shirley ran out the door to her house before Marianne could stop her.

Jackson, Patrick, and Sherry came out the room to face the music. Before anybody could say anything, Jacks started confessing.

"Mom, I know you're going to be a little upset, but first I want you to know that I had nothing, nottthhinnng to do with this. In fact, mom, I just found out myself a few minutes ago. Now, Patrick wants to tell you something. You better sit down first." Jacks pulled a chair up then waited for the action to start. "Mom you better sit down."

Marianne looked at Patrick then Sherry, her first thought was that Sherry was pregnant. She saw a little resemblance of her mother and immediately softened her stance. Her mind was going a hundred miles per hour. Marianne could see Sherry had an obvious disability; she felt a little sympathy and was waiting for the punch line.

"What's going on, Patty? Who's this pretty girl?"

"Well, Marianne this is Sherry and we decided we wanted to be together."

"Is that right? When did you decide that Patty? You

222

never brought a girl home before. This is the first time I ever saw this girl. When did you decide you wanted to be together? What do you mean, you wanted to be together?"

"Well Marianne, we met and fell in love, so we decided to get married. We got married three weeks ago."

"Is that right, Sherry? Ya'll are married?"

Sherry nodded then raised her hand to show Marianne her wedding ring. It had a nice little pear shape diamond with a little matching band. Patrick didn't have a ring on his hand.

"Well, I guess everything is done now. Are you pregnant?"

Sherry shook her head 'no'.

"What made you decide to get married? Why didn't you go together, like everybody else your age . . . sometimes when our feelings get involved we can rush into a situation; Patrick this is the first girl that you were serious about, people grow older and their feelings change. What's going to happen if in a couple of years, you don't feel the same? What if you out grow Patrick and want someone else, what then Sherry, have ya'll thought about that?"

"Marianne, I plan on being with Sherry the rest of my life. I'm going to take care of her."

"Okay then, I guess there's nothing else for me to say. I mean, the damage is done. We'll plan a reception and make an announcement, maybe put an ad in the paper or something."

"That's alright, Marianne. We're already married, we don't need a reception or announcement; we don't want all that. After school's out, we're going on a vacation; maybe go on a cruise or something, that'll be our honeymoon."

"You figured everything out, huh, I wish you would have discussed it with me." Marianne popped Patrick upside his head. "What do your parents say about all this or do they know?"

"They know, they haven't said too much."

"Well, let's make the best of it." Marianne turned to her son. "Jackson, if you ever do this to me, I'll break your little neck. You understand?"

"Mom, I'm the one that told you, remember."

"Patrick, we need to talk, you have a few things that need to be worked out." Marianne was thinking about Patrick's investments and savings. She couldn't help but think that this girl had tricked Patrick into marrying her, but she wasn't pregnant, so it couldn't be that. Patrick had enough savings to attend college comfortably . . . now what? She had so many plans for her handsome little brother, Uncle Charlie had his future set, and for him to do her like this was too much, so she decided to back up and let go before she got sick . . . Patrick married a crippled girl.

Marianne walked over to Sherry and gave her a hug. "Baby, I hope you know what you're doing. Are you comfortable in that room?"

Sherry nodded 'yes.'

"Well, you can stay here as long as you like. One day, you and Patrick may want to move into your own place, but for now, there's plenty room here. I want you and Patrick to continue going to school, get your education. That's important."

"Marianne, we decided that we're going to work for the restaurants after we graduate. There's plenty of work for us, a good living and everything, maybe later we can go to school, but now, we're going to work here; if that's alright?"

"Yeah Patty, it's alright. I need the help, it's time for me to take a vacation or something; maybe, I'll go on a cruise or go see Pali. I need a break, I'm tired." Marianne went to her room and didn't come out the rest of the day.

* * * * *

Dee wanted sex. It had been a while and she figured a

little bit won't hurt, not after all this time. She was cruising the block, looking for the convenience store she had shopped at earlier that week. There was a man that she wanted. He seemed to be Puerto Rican or from Cuba, something Hispanic. It was getting late and Dee thought the store would be empty, during lunch it was too busy.

"There it is."

Dee pulled into the little parking lot where only one car was parked. She hoped it belonged to the man working, not some customer. She walked in to find an elderly man shopping. Dee looked around trying to appear interested in the medicine aisles.

"Finally he's gone." Dee breathed a sigh of relief.

"Can I help you find something?"

He didn't have an accent. She was hoping he could speak Spanish.

"No, I don't see what I want over there." Dee walked to the counter and began undressing the man with her eyes. "You sure have a lot of muscles. Can I feel your arms?"

"You're a pretty little thing. What's your name and what you're doing in this neighborhood, this late at night?"

"I saw you the other day, I came back to get a better look. I wonder if you feel as good as you look. I told you I wanted to feel your muscles." She licked her lips, then started straightening her clothes.

Immediately the man walked from behind the counter and turned off the camera that was pointed directly at the cash register and him.

"You want to feel my muscles? I got a big muscle for you, you can feel that one."

The man walked to the door and locked it, then turned the 'open' sign over to display 'closed'. "I got something for you. I think you'll like it. I'll show you my big muscle."

Dee was happy and smiling, she was ready for a treat; but the man looked at Dee and got angry.

Another damn whore! He thought to himself as he reached for Dee's hand and led her to a back room where there was a television, a computer, a small couch, a table and chair. Once he closed the door, he grabbed her head; then let her hair down. The man started twisting her long hair around his hand so tight that he could forcibly maneuver her in any direction . . . he chose the floor.

"Oh shit, stop it, you're hurting me. Let go of my fuckin' hair you bastard. LET GO! "

The man grabbed Dee by her throat. "If I let go of your hair, then I'll grab your throat and choke you to death. You understand. Now, unzip my pants, bitch."

Dee nervously started feeling for his zipper while the man's two hands were wrapped around her throat. "You don't have to hurt me, I wanted it. I want to fuck you, just don't hurt me."

"Take it out and suck it."

Dee did what she was told, then the man pick her up, tore her pants off, then threw her across the desk. She screamed when she hit the desk, something cut her. The man took her head and hit it on the desk. "Don't you make another sound, you understand me. You're a sorry, low down piece of shit. I can't stand a low life bitch."

He continued to jab his muscle as hard as he could into Dee's vagina. "You wanted this didn't you. DIDN'T YOU! You little whore. You like it like this huh. Tell me . . . tell me you like it." He grabbed her hair and turned her over, he hit her in the stomach and threw her to the couch. He continued to fight her, making sure not to leave any visible marks on her face or body; that would be exposed. He kept up the abuse until he was ready to have sex again. After a few hours, it was all over.

226

Dee pulled as much of her clothes back on as possible, then waited for him to allow her to leave the room. She was afraid to make a sound, so she waited for him to open the door. They walked to the glass doors that led to her freedom, he unlocked it. She waited, careful not to start him up again.

"If you ever come here again, I won't be so nice." Then he shoved her out the door and gave her a look that dared her to ever show her face in his place again.

Dee was hurt. She held her stomach and sides and was sure her ribs were broke. It was hard for her to breath. With as little breath she could use, Dee thanked God for sparing her life. She had never gotten in trouble before, not like this. Usually the guys she picked up were okay. This time, Dee realized the kind of man she was just with; someone who could have easily thrown her in a dumpster . . . one who didn't care one way or another, what he did to her.

She couldn't go to work, not by tomorrow. She can't let Uncle Charlie see her like this; she has to hide for a couple of weeks. Dee arranged to have Victor stay with Uncle Charlie and Aunt Rosie a little while to give her time to heal. She was so hurt.

Dee decided she was changing her life. Picking up complete strangers is dangerous, just to have sex was crazy. This was the last time she would ever pick up a stranger. She had to change. The next one might really kill her. Dee rented a room so she could rest and take care of her wounded body. She wanted to talk with someone, her therapist, so she dialed her number then told her therapist everything that happened at the convenient store.

* * * * *

Det. Combs decided he was tired of chasing Marianne Robinson. How long had he been going down that path, it's been a couple of years. He'd been her flunky, sending all his friends and police there to get ribs and she wouldn't give him the time of day, unless she wanted something. Oh yeah, she calls when she wants something.

But on the other hand, her sister Dee, now that girl is different. She acts alive. Byron Combs contemplated changing his direction toward Dee.

"Yeah, she wants me. I know she wants me. I might as well go for it because Marianne ain't giving me any action."

Now all he had to do was let Marianne know, in a respectful way, that he was through chasing her picky ass . . . he wanted Dee, her friend or sister, whatever they are. Maybe she'll give him Dee's telephone number.

Byron decided that when he tells Marianne about his talk with Stevie Brooks, he'll just slip it in.

"I'm going to ask Marianne to hook us up . . . It serves her right. I didn't care if it hurt her feelings, shoot Marianne thinks she's all that." Byron discussed every detail with himself. "Ain't nobody gonna wait around for her like that. Wait till she see's what a good man I am, uh uh she'll see what she missed."

* * * * *

Juanita Williams had been driving around looking to see if she would see Jackson again. It had been a long time since she'd had a chance to see him. Now that she babysits her other grands, it's hard to stay in tune with Jackson Robinson. Both her twin girls had children now, a girl and boy a piece and they were a hand full. But it was something about Jackson, that boy is special. He should have known his father, and now since Reggie and Vanessa were divorced, Juanita was hoping Jackson would unite with their family.

She decided to talk with her husband again. It wasn't right that he would exclude Jacks from their lives. It wasn't right. Jackson was their first grandchild, and she felt deprived, being left out of his life; especially knowing that Jackson took after her side, her father and grandfather. She wanted to share his life; she wanted to be his grandmother in every way.

Mrs. Williams thought about the last time she had a chance to talk with Jackson. She stopped for him purposely because she had his younger sister in the car with her, Reggie's and Vanessa's only child, Alicia. It took every ounce of strength she had, not to introduce them as sister and brother, but it wasn't up to her. Shoot Reginald still didn't know about Jackson. They should know each other. Mrs. Williams decided she would talk with Marianne with or without her husband's knowledge or blessings.

"Hello Mrs. Williams, how are you?"

"Hello Jacks, I'm good, darling. How's Marianne and Patrick?"

"Mrs. Williams, we're doing great. My uncle, Patrick got married. That's all the action we've had. Mom needs a vacation. I think I'll work with Patty this summer so momma can take a long vacation. She really needs a break. You look wonderful Mrs. Williams. Come over here and have a seat; my mother will be here in a few minutes, give her ten to fifteen minutes. Can I get you something while you wait?"

"Jackson, a large glass of water would do me good."

Just then Marianne walked in the restaurant. When she saw Mrs. Williams, there was a little twang in her heart.

"Hi Mrs. Williams, it's good to see you again. How's the family?" Marianne turned to Jackson, "Did you get her order?"

"No mom, not yet, she just got here."

"Ummmm Marianne. I really didn't come to eat. I want a little talk with you if it's alright."

"This looks serious. Mrs. Williams, I remember the last time we had a serious talk. It took a long time for me to get

229

over it. I was broke up a while. I hope we're not having another talk like that."

"Baby, Please listen to me. All these years, I've been driving around the neighborhood, around the school, just to get a glimpse of Jackson. I've watched him grow from a distance, never having the opportunity to share his life. This isn't fair to me. I don't have many years left, I am his grandmother and just once, I would like to hear him call me 'grandma," Mrs. Williams started to cry. "But it's not my place to tell Jackson about Reginald. Would you please reconsider? Tell them. Let Reginald know he has a son. Jackson is a wonderful young man."

"Mrs. Williams, what about Vanessa, Reginald's wife? I'm not looking to start any trouble. Me and Jacks have been alright. If he ever asks me about his father, then I'll tell him, but he's never asked. Really, Mrs. Williams, I've been waiting on the right time to bring it up."

"Well, Marianne, I think it's the right time now. Reginald and Vanessa got a divorce a year ago."

"Oh, I'm sorry. What happened?"

"I don't know, but you talk with Reginald. He'll be here this week. Jackson has a little sister. She's fifteen, he's seventeen. Let those kids get to know each other."

"Mrs. Williams, can I ask you a question? Why haven't you told Reginald yourself about Jacks?"

"It wasn't my place. But hopefully, before I leave this world, he'll know."

Chapter 21

Tia didn't come to work. She didn't go to school the next day either. Her mother called Marianne to see if she was there.

"Hello, Marianne, this is Brenda, Tia's mom. Is she there with you?"

"No Brenda, Tia didn't come to work last night. She didn't call or anything."

"Is Jackson around, can you ask if he's seen her. When I see that girl, I'm going to kick her little butt. I try to give her some slack, let her have a boyfriend, she goes to work and she usually does good, but if she starts this Marianne, I'm going make her quit that job, I hate to do it but, she ain't gonna disrespect me like that. Tia knows I don't play."

"Yeah, I know, I hate to lose my little worker, she's usually so dependable. I'll have Jackson call you when he comes in."

"Thanks, girlfriend, I don't know what I'm gonna do with that girl. Give me a call if you hear from her before then, tell her to call home."

"I will, I will."

It had been a long time since Jackson had a vision or dream. He was in class when he saw Tia but he didn't know if he was dreaming. Tia didn't speak to him, she smile and waved; then walked off. Jackson wanted to catch her. But when he didn't move, he realized he was in one of his dreamlike states, dreaming or something. Still, he didn't know if Tia was real or a dream.

Jackson waited for Tia after school. He wondered what was happening with her, but seeing her in school made him uneasy. She waved and didn't wait for him. What was that about? On top of that, she didn't come to work last night.

231

Jackson knew it had something to do with Stevie Brooks, because Tia never missed work without calling and letting them know what was happening.

Jacks decided to have a real talk with Tia about this Stevie boy. She's going to have to let him go. Tia has always been a little sister to Jackson, but if he had to take up with her, and be a man to Tia, just to keep her away from Stevie boy, then he would do it. He figured that he could. There was nothing he couldn't do . . . once he made his mind up, he'd just make it happen. So he was taking Tia for himself. She couldn't be with that Stevie boy anymore, period.

Again, Tia didn't show up for work. Marianne was ready to give Brenda a call, to see if she made it home and to let her know she hadn't seen her. Jackson was pacing the floor getting angrier by the minute. They both worked without saying too much.

Marianne and Jacks quietly closed the restaurant. It was a quiet night anyway. Jackson had been going to Razz's club, delivering food by himself. Since Patrick was married, he hadn't been going gambling with him at all. He was happy for his uncle but he missed his company.

As soon as Jackson walked in the club, he heard Big Billy Joe Washington. Loud!

"Some coons can't, and some coons can!"

Jackson grabbed Big Bill and gave him a bear hug. But Big Bill wasn't ready for the new Jackson. He hadn't been around lately.

"Find you a stump to sit your rump, and I'll coon your can till you big booty jump." Jacks was quick to answer the challenge for a friendly card game; too quick for Big Bill.

"Razz what you been feeding this boy. You hear how he talks to his big daddy."

They grabbed a chair, sat at the table, unloaded a pocket

full of money, then they got serious about gambling. Everybody was around to see who would prove to be the better cooncan player. Jacks hadn't seen Big Bill in so long he had to ask.

"Uncle Bill, how did you get out the house? I know Michelle don't know you're gone." Jackson had everybody laughing at Big Bill.

Billy looked at Razz, "Man what ya'll been teaching this little grasshopper. He's talking big talk, making fun of Big Bill, acting like he knows how to gamble. Razz, man, don't be filling this boy's head with big dreams, thinking he can beat me. He's being disrespectful. I gotta show'em who's boss. They don't call me Big Bill for nothing. That stands for big dollars, boy!"

The first game was a draw. The second game ended in a draw too. Whenever there wasn't a winner, they both put another C-note in the pot. There was now three games and six hundred dollars on the table for the first clear cut winner. They both continued to block each other, making it again, another draw. Now there was eight hundred dollars on the table.

"You're getting nervous Uncle Bill? You know I can't let you take my money like that. I love you man, but not that much."

Big Bill started singing The Temptations and The Supremes song, *"I'm gonna make you love me, yes I will, yes I will . . . ,* cause all that money, right there, is mine." Big Bill was pointing at the stack on the table.

Right at that time, Jackson laid his cards down and said, "This is a beat a coon's ass tonight."

He caught Big Bill off guard.

"Sorry man, I would play you again, but momma's gonna be looking for me pretty soon. So I better get out of here. It sure was fun beating your ass tonight Uncle Bill. Can we do it again?"

Big Bill got up and gave Jackson a hand shake. "Tell your mom hello for me. I need to get over there. How's Ms. Shirley? I haven't seen anybody since Clarence's funeral."

As they both walked outside to their cars, Jackson gave Billy all the news. He told him that Patrick was married and taking over the restaurant off Fifth street. Uncle Charlie and Aunt Rosie aren't doing so good, Dee's taking care of them. Marianne's been thinking about putting them in the nursing home with Darlene because Rosie walked off a couple of times and Uncle Charlie's acting like his getting Alzheimer's too. Ms. Shirley is there every day, cooking as usual.

"Bill, you need to come by there and see Aunt Shirley. There's nobody to eat all that food she cooks anymore."

"Ummmmmmm, I think I will stop by." They were standing by their cars, talking, still catching up when Jackson popped the question.

"Hey Bill, Can I ask you something? I know this is gonna sound crazy, but . . . do you know who my father is, for real, man?"

"Marianne hasn't told you?" Big Bill was surprised because that didn't sound like the Marianne he knew, that's so detailed and never like anything left undone.

"Nawww, I've never asked her. I hate to ask, she works so hard taking care of everybody, I don't want to trouble my momma. Plus, I always had so many people around me, I never missed a father. You, Razz, Uncle Charlie, then when I was young I had Pali and Mr. White, then Uncle Clarence was there before he died. I never thought about my father. Just lately, I got a little curious."

"Jacks, I'll tell you what, ask your mother first. If she doesn't tell you, then I will. It wouldn't be right for me to say anything before she had a chance."

They shook hand and embraced before driving off. Jacks didn't want to ask Marianne. He'll just ask Razz next.

* * * * *

Nobody had seen Tia. She hadn't come to school or work in three days. Brenda called the police and listed her as a missing person.

Det. Combs got the missing persons report and came by the restaurant to talk about their little friend, Tia. Come to find out, Stevie haven't been home either in a few days. The police figured that they were together and would be back soon, but they would keep an eye out for the both of them. That didn't make Jackson feel any better. He was still planning on breaking up that union and taking Tia for himself.

* * * * *

Det. Combs finally asked Marianne for Dee's telephone number. Marianne was sooooo relieved. That meant an end to a lot of weaving and dodging the advances from Byron Combs. That meant all the excuses and lying about being too busy would end. But most of all, that meant, she could have a business relationship with the police department without feeling like she owed Byron something that she wasn't willing to pay. It was over.

She was glad for Dee and hoped Dee would act right with somebody that's really interested in her. She needed a real man that would take care of her and a police officer would be the right one, baby. She's so beautiful and Marianne wanted so much for her adoptive sister. Dee proved to be a shrewd business partner. She had so much to offer, she was so important to their business, but she didn't act like a person with her credentials. She didn't care about her reputation.

Marianne hoped and daydreamed for them. She got tickled just thinking about a wedding for Dee and Byron. She imagined Dee walking down the aisle in a white dress, Uncle

235

Charlie giving her away. She'd better hurry, Uncle Charlie can barely walk, as it is. They just got to hit it off . . . that shouldn't be too hard. Marianne continued to daydream about all the details of Dee and Byron's wedding. She even worked out the music and menu, her colors, everything that she, herself, always wanted. Then she started praying for Dee. She wanted so much for Dee to be finally happy. "Byron better treat my girl right."

* * * * *

It was late. Jackson was tired; he just come home from delivering food at Razz's and was too upset to stay and play a few hands of cards. That wasn't like him, he wanted to make a few dollars whenever he went to Razz, but today he couldn't get his mind off Tia.

He felt like him and Tia would always be friends, sister and brother if nothing else, but the thought of losing her was too much. He couldn't stop thinking about her. He already lost Patrick to Sherry, he barely saw him anymore, so he longed to see Tia and hear her smart mouth. He threw his socks in the corner and shouted "Tia hasn't showed up in four days."

* * * * *

He was sitting in his room, at his desk, looking in his opened closet at what he would wear to school the next day. He made a motion to get up but felt pressure as if someone had his shoulders and forcing him to sit back down. Then his head started spinning, the chair and room were all spinning.

The pressure on his shoulders was beginning to hurt so he relaxed and didn't fight against the pressure.

He heard a deep, powerful voice.

"Jackson, cover your eyes."

His hands automatically covered his eyes as he continued to spin. Jackson fell to the floor still with his hands covering his eyes, he wanted to see what was going on and tried to remove his hands but couldn't. Something held his hands in

236

place.   He tried again to move his hands from his eyes, but couldn't.

"Jackson, do you want to see what is happening?"

"Yes, please show me."

Jackson sat up on the floor with his back against the wall, and slowly removed his hands.   It was bright, almost too bright for his eyes, like watching lightning.   Then he saw Uri and Josias in ancient battle gear.   Uri is a very dark skinned, muscular African looking man.   He had two swords and was fighting fiercely with a man that Jackson didn't recognize. Josias also, was fighting a humongous man, hitting him with both a sword and a shield.   Josias is an olive skinned man, very handsome and athletic with thick curly black hair.   With every blow he shouted,

"In the name of Jesus the Christ, you will leave this place!"

As they continued to fight, electricity sparked and thunder sounded.   Uri looked at Jackson that made him want to back deeper into the walls.   He didn't know what was happening or why they were fighting?   Suddenly, it occurred to him.   They were fighting over him.   When this knowledge hit Jackson, he was scared.   He didn't want Uri and Josias to lose the battle.   He covered his eyes back so he couldn't see them fighting.   He screamed to God.

"Lord . . . Lord God.   Why God?"

"They fight for you, Jackson."

"Oh Lord, Help them.   Don't let them lose."

Then it happened, the words that seem to appear but then fade away before he had a chance to read or understand, where there.   He read it.   He read it.

"Before I formed you in the womb I knew you.   Before you were born, I set you apart.   I appointed you as a prophet to the nations."

237

Then it was over.

"What just happened?" Jackson asked himself. He wanted to talk with his friends Uri and Josias. He wanted to thank them, he wanted to understand; he wanted to know if it was real. He had seen the two men on several occasions and he knew they were real. Patrick and Tia saw them too. Jackson couldn't help but feel happy. He said to himself.

"They are angels and they fought for me."

Jackson thought about the words that he read. He thought about the powerful voice he heard, it said that he would always protect him, that he knew him before he was born? What in the world did that mean? Jackson realized that he needed advice. He needed advice from a professional, somebody who wouldn't think he was crazy. Who would he tell this to, who would believe him? Again, he thought about Patrick and Tia, they would back up his story about the two men. He was going to talk to Razz. Razz would believe him.

Is this what the angels meant, over a year ago when they told him that it would make sense to him, that his time is coming? They said he would understand what it all meant. Jackson almost laughed because, now, he was more confused than ever. Jackson went to bed peacefully. He knew his life would be alright and one day he'll understand everything.

* * * * *

It was a dreary, rainy day. Det. Combs drove in silence with his two passengers in the back seat, he hated what he was about to do. They stopped in front of the cute little house on Amber Street. He hated the thought of confronting the family inside. He opened the back door of the car and assisted Stevie Brooks and his father from the back seat. They all slowly walked together, in silence, to the door with their heads hanging. Mr. Brooks was ashamed and Stevie was sorry.

"Detective, please let me talk with Tia's mother." Mr.

Brooks asked with the little dignity he had left. The detective nodded in agreement and backed up behind Stevie and Mr. Brooks. Mr. Brooks knocked on the door.

When Brenda opened the door, she screamed. Seeing the police car, she realized the worst of her fears. She backed back inside her house, closed the door . . . crying.

"Noooooo, no no . . . please God. Don't tell me this." She opened the door again, but this time she ran out to get Stevie. She started hitting and kicking him. Nobody tried to stop her, not even Stevie. She fought him, they both were on the ground, Stevie covering his head, but didn't try to block her or refrain her. They let her fight and cry until she couldn't anymore.

"What happened to my baby? What did you do?" She could hardly talk.

"I'm sorry." Stevie was crying. "I'm so so sorrrrrrry. I didn't mean to do it. I just wanted her to listen to me. She was breaking up with me, all I wanted was for her to listen and give me another chance. I tried to stop her from leaving but she slapped me. I hit her back. I didn't mean to hit her hard. I didn't hit her that hard. She just fell . . . she fell on the steel corner of the bed frame, it hit her temple, it went through . . . then she died.

"Where's my baby? WHERE'S MY BABY?" Brenda was slapping his face with each word.

"We have her in the morgue, Ms. Houston. She's not in any shape for you to see her."

Mr. Brooks wanted to give his apology to Brenda Houston. "Ms. Houston, I want to formally apologize to you. There's not enough words to let you know how I feel right now. When my son came home, he told me what happened. Ma'am, she died a few days ago. Stevie had been in a hotel room with your daughter two days before he decided to bury her." Mr.

Brooks looked at Stevie with disgust. "He just came home today, it's been five days, ma'am, since Tia died."

Det. Combs took over the conversation. "Ms. Houston, we exhumed the body a couple of hours ago. Mr. Brooks called us and told us what happened and where we would find Tia. He was bringing Stevie into the precinct to turn him in, personally, but I told Mr. Brooks that it would be best if I came to pick him up. He requested to see you first . . . to apologize, personally."

"Ms. Houston, please forgive me. I loved Tia. It was an accident." Stevie's eyes were swollen and there wasn't enough fluid left for him to cry   .

Brenda Houston sat down on her steps, feeling defeated. Her head rested in her hands, she was shaking, not wanting to believe what she had heard. She must be dreaming.

"Is my baby really gone?" She asked Det. Combs.

"Ms. Houston, I sorry, but yes, it was Tia."

"Well, I guess that's it. All the plans I made for Tia is over. What do I do now? She was my little girl, and now, she's gone."

The news about Tia had spread through the school like a wild grass fire. Her funeral was set for the weekend; it would be a closed casket. Everybody was in mourning. Tia was popular, fun loving, and would be truly missed by her friends and classmates. Jackson was devastated. He felt he had let his friend down, that somehow he had neglected her needs. He felt it was all his fault.

"Jackson, baby, I know we made a huge mistake by not letting Brenda know that Stevie was fighting Tia. We'll probably feel guilty for a long time, but I do believe that it was her time to go. Her injury was an accident, a freak accident . . . for her to fall on the end of a bed frame, and for her to die from it, was an accident. Baby, when it's our time to go, we have to answer the call.

Jackson didn't say anything; he just listened to his mother and tried to understand why she had to go. Tia was his little sister, his best friend; and probably, would have been more if he had had enough time.

Then he thought about Josias and Uri, how they were always asking about Tia. He wondered if they knew all the time that she didn't have long to live. It was funny how every single time he saw them, they made a point to ask about her.

Then fear hit him, they told him to watch Patrick. It was something about Patrick. Jackson overlooked it, but he knew something was different with Patty, he noticed that his colors were long gone, even after he married Sherry, they never came back. He didn't want to lose his uncle. Jackson began to cry because he has this gift, and he didn't know what to do with it.

He decided he would have that talk with Razz tonight.

Chapter 22

"Hi Razz, how's everything?"

"Hey Jacks, man, we're fine over here. I'm sorry to hear about Tia. She worked for Marianne a long time. Ya'll were close, huh?"

"Yeah, Razz. We started working for mom when we were little runts. I'm hurt about that. I hurt real bad. Razz, I need to talk with you. It's important. Do you have time for me, Razz, man?" Jackson's voice quivered.

"Jackson, I'll make time for you. I feel like a father to you and Patrick, maybe more like a grandfather. Me and your grandmother, Patricia were good friends, we grew up together. Then I watched ya'll grow up to be good young men. You make this old man proud."

"Ahhh, you're not old, Razz."

"Why don't you come over now, before any customers get here?"

He was going to tell Razz everything. He needed to talk about his visions; he wanted to talk about Uri and Josias. He was going to tell him how Patrick is different, and most of all, he wanted to know what to do.

"This is going to sound crazy. I don't know where to start. Razz, when I was around ten years old, I started having these visions. It was pretty scary then because everything would turn dark, so dark that I couldn't see. Then I would hear a loud echoing blast . . . and all I could see was a bright flash. It would blind me for two to three minutes. After that, everything would go back to normal. I told mom about it, the first time it happened. She took me to the doctor and got me checked out . . . but like I said, everything went back to normal. Tia and Blue baby were with me the first time it happened."

"You say, a blast then a bright flash, huh?"

242

"Yeah, then these two men started coming around me. Razz, they're angels. I know this sounds crazy, but the other day, I had another vision or something . . . I don't know what it was, but they were fighting these monster looking men over me. They were in this ancient war gear . . . man, they were fighting with swords and everything."

"Man, you're serious aren't you?"

"Yeah, Razz, I ain't crazy . . . this happened."

"Why were they fighting over you?"

"I don't know, Razz. But they were fighting over me, cause then this voice told me that he'll always protect me. Razz, after that, I saw these words that said . . . hold on . . . let me say it right . . . it said, 'I knew you before you were born, I set you apart, to be a prophet to all the nations.'"

"Is that right?"

"Yeah, man, you see why I wanted to talk with you."

"Yeah, yeah, I can see why you needed somebody to talk to."

"Then Razz, the two angels were always asking me about Tia, every time I saw them, they would make a point for me to tell Tia hello, like they knew she didn't have long to be here or something."

"Jackson, man, you ever talk to your folks on the other side of your family."

"Naw Razz. I don't know'em."

"You don't know Rev. Williams and your folks on that side, come on, man?"

"Rev. Williams the preacher . . . that's married to Juanita Williams, you mean those Williams?" Jackson was shocked.

"Yeah, sounds like to me, you need to get with your father's side of the family. Your grandfather, that preacher with that big ole church over on Walker Avenue, ya'll need to talk."

243

"Who's my father?"

"Man, you don't know who your father is? Marianne hasn't told you."

"Nawwww. I can't believe this . . . that I'm related to the Williams. Mrs. Williams has always been around, when I was little, she used to always give me money. She came by the restaurant to talk with my mom, just the other day. She's my grandmother and my mom didn't tell me?"

"Ahhhh shit. I might have done wrong now. You go home and talk with Marianne. Then you talk with the preacher side of your family. You need to find out about these visions and everything. Don't go off with a hot head about the Williams. It's more important to find out your purpose in life; sounds like to me, the Man upstairs has some big plans for you, Jacks. So don't let you feelings get in the way of all that."

"Razz, I don't even go to church."

"That doesn't make you wrong. But you'll be wrong not to talk with them. All this stuff happening to you might have something to do with that side of your family. Go talk with them. It's important, Jacks."

Jackson had too much on his mind to talk with Marianne about his father. He decided to wait until after Tia's funeral, when he'll have time to think about how he would bring the subject up with his mother.

He felt sorry for his mother. All this time she took care of him and Patrick, she didn't finish high school because of Patrick, she never got married or even dated too much. Jackson could count the number of men that came to see Marianne on one hand. She never seem interested, her only concern was him, Patrick and the restaurants. She put her life on hold for everything and everybody. He often wondered how a woman as beautiful as Marianne, who had so much going on, would be without a boyfriend for so long. He figured that once he graduated and went to college; that she'll meet a man and she'll for once, have a personal life.

He wondered if she still loved his father. Is that the reason she never dated, because of him. Jackson wondered what kind of man he was to leave her while she was pregnant. For all he knew, he might have been a baby when his father left them. Jackson didn't want anything to do with the Williams. They're supposed to be preachers.

* * * * *

Tia's funeral was beautiful. The choir sang the song that she usually led in church. The school overflowed Redeemer Baptist Church, his grandfather, Rev. Williams facilitated the services.

Jackson wanted to focus on the services, but his mind keep slipping on everything else. He watched his grandfather; he listened to his message and thought him to be a hypocrite.

One by one, Tia's friends got up to tell their personal stories and memories of Tia. She was so very popular and loved. Jackson was on the program to be the last friend to give their remarks. Jackson stepped up to the podium.

"Tia Mae Houston, my friend, my sister. I love you Tia. I believe you are with God, right now. I will miss your smile, your laughter, your wit, especially, your smart mouth." Everybody laughed. "You made me a better person, in your life and in your death."

Jackson looked at his classmates, "We are young, but we need to be mindful of what's happening in each of our lives especially, while we're in school. If we see or suspect, something is wrong with one of our classmates, let's make a promise right now try to help each other out. It's going to take courage, but if it's the right thing to do, then let's do it and take care of each other. We can do that!"

Jackson began talking to his friend, "Tia, I have learned

from this tragedy. I will be a stronger friend from now on. May God continue to keep you now and forever."

Jackson went to her casket and kissed it. "Goodbye girl. I'll miss you so much."

Jackson stood at her casket not moving. He was crying now. Marianne got up and embraced her son, then walked Jackson back to his seat. The choir got up to sing again; then Marianne noticed it was Reginald Williams that sat behind the organ and began playing. The preacher held his hands up for everybody to stand, the funeral directors walked to the front of the church, ready for Tia's casket to be carried to her final resting place.

Most of Tia's close friends met at the restaurant after the service. Marianne and Jackson let Victor and Calvin work alone while they sat and reminisced with all their friends about the years and the fun they had with Tia. This was their first friend to pass. It was an experience they would never forget. They talked about the circumstances of Tia's death and the remarks Jackson made. They each made a promised to intervene, if it ever became necessary, they would do whatever it takes to help. They prayed that they wouldn't lose another classmate before they graduated from high school.

* * * * *

Blue Baby was ready to go home. He didn't want to bother Jackson, but he noticed Patrick and Sherry were getting up to leave.

"Patty, wait, can I catch a ride with you?"

"Yeah man, come on."

They got in the car and they were close to Blues' house when Sherry noticed Zetty car parked out front.

"Is that Zetty's car parked in front of your house, Blue?" Sherry asked looking puzzled. "Why didn't he go to the funeral? He's at your house." Sherry hadn't forgiven Zetty but

246

she tolerated him because of Patrick.

"Yeah, that's Zetty's car."

"What's he doing at your house Blue?"

"I don't know, maybe he's working on my mom's car." Blue didn't think too much about it. Zetty gives tune ups at a reasonable price. "She didn't tell me that she had car troubles, it's probably nothing much."

They parked and got out to go inside. Patrick hadn't seen Zett in a while, so he was going to see what's up. When they walked inside the door, they could see a shirt hanging on a chair. Patrick wanted to leave, but Sherry wasn't going anywhere.

"Come on baby, let's get out of here." Patrick whispered, tugging on Sherry to leave.

Blue picked up the shirt and went back to the bedrooms. He knocked on his mother's door. Then he heard the wrestling and hurried movements.

"Blue is that you?"

"Mom, who's in there with you?" Blue opened the door not wanting to see Zetty in his mother's bedroom, hoping it wasn't Zett.

Zetty was up and putting on his pants when Blue charged him. Blue hit him with his full body knocking him into the dresser. Zett caught him in a head lock and was trying to keep Blue from punching him. They were wrestling on the floor when Blue bit him."

Angie was screaming, "Stop it. Stop it Blue. I'm sorry. Please don't fight. Zetty please don't fight my baby. Ya'll stop it."

Zett threw Blue off and started punching. Patrick ran to the bedroom to stop the fight. It happened so fast that he was caught off guard. Patrick grabbed Blue Baby and was pulling him out the room but they weren't letting go.

"Let go of 'em, Blue."

"Tell Zett to let me go." Blue was breathing hard.

"Let 'em go Zett."

Zetty let go; he saw the perfect prints of Blue Baby's teeth in his side. Angie grabbed a towel and ice.

"Come on, Zett, I got to take you to the hospital. It's bad. You may need a shot." Angie didn't look at her son. She was embarrassed.

"Just get him out of here, Angie. I'll hold Blue. Ya'll just go." Patrick hollered while blocking Blue from getting to Zett again.

Once they were gone, Blue Baby started throwing everything everywhere.

"This is disgusting. Did you see that? That damn Zetty was fucking my momma." Blue screamed. "He was in bed with her, man. I came back here and he was putting on his fucking pants, man. I can't believe my mom would do this to me. She's messing around with one of my best friends. Hell, he only two years older than me."

Patrick and Sherry didn't say anything. They listened not knowing what to do or say.

"I'm not staying here." Blue grabbed a duffle bag and started packing.

"Where you gonna go?"

"I'll go stay with my father, man. I ain't staying here with that nasty bitch. She didn't even see if I was hurt. Did you see that? She don't give a damn about me."

"Man, I know you're upset, but that's no way to talk about your mother. Angie is a good person and she don't deserve you talking about her like that. Man, this isn't as bad as you're making it."

"I ain't hearing that bullshit, man."

"Where does your father live? I'll take you over there."

248

Blue chuckled, "Man, my father live waaay in Orlando. You gonna take me there?"

"Naw, so where are you going?"

"I don't know, but I'm not going back to that house with her."

"We got a room you can stay in for a while. But you should go on home. Blue, your mother is a beautiful lady. Everybody makes mistakes, so don't let this break you and your mother's relationship up. People do way more than that, in life. Believe me, people do terrible things and they get over it. She's human man. Shit Blue, you'll probably sleep with somebody's momma too, I know you'll do more than that before it's over. You wouldn't believe some of the mistakes I made. You got to forgive your mother, Blue."

"Patrick, I don't want to see her or that damn Zett again in life."

They drove the rest of the way in silence. Patrick thought about the huge mistake he almost made with Sherry. He thought about how much he loved her and he was about to throw her over a cliff. Now that was bad, that would have been final. No chance of fixing that. He was thankful that it didn't happen, and scared at the thought of how close he came.

The thought made him sick to his stomach. What Blue was going through was nothing. Then he thought about Sherry forgiving him and how much she must love him. Did he deserve someone like his wife? He was never going to leave Sherry. Never!

* * * * *

Earlier at church, when Marianne saw Reginald Williams, she nearly fell out her seat. How long had it been? She hadn't laid eyes on Reggie since he left nearly twenty years ago.

This was too close. She wondered if he recognized her.

She has to talk with Jackson before Mrs. Williams tells Reginald about him. She wondered if Reginald already knows.

The thought that Jacks was standing in church with his father was too much. She was going to tell Jackson all about him tonight, but she needed a drink first.

"Finally!" Marianne exhaled, once the last classmates left the building. It was Raven, who stayed to help Marianne clean up before she went home.

"How am I going to do this?" Marianne peddled around trying to think of how she would start the conversation.

"Mom, you ready to go home? I'm tired. It's been a long difficult day. Let's go home." Jackson turned the back lights off, locked the doors; then grabbed his mother to take her home.

"Jacks, baby, there's something I need to talk with you about."

"Can we talk when we get home? Let's get out of here."

"Yeah, I'm going to pick up a bottle of Hennessy first. Stop at the liquor store before we go home."

"Okay, I need a drink, too."

"Yeah, right!"

"Mom, I'm almost eighteen. You can send me to the military, but you can't let me have a drink with you?"

"I'll get you a wine cooler." Jackson smiled and thought about how much he loved his mom.

When they arrived at the house, Marianne reminded Jacks that they had to talk and it was very important.

"Okay mom, let me get us some glasses." Jacks was excited to be having a drink with her. He has a drink every now and then at Razz's, but this was different. It was his mom that was having a drink with him. It didn't matter that it was just a wine cooler.

"Mom, you're so cool and pretty."

"I don't know about all that." Marianne ignored her son's compliment. "Jacks . . . have you ever wondered about your father?"

"Yeah, but just recently; I figured you'd tell me when you were ready? Mom, don't worry. I know who he is. He's that preacher's son."

"How did you know that? Did Mrs. Williams tell you?"

"No ma'am. I just found out. But I was wondering, why didn't he marry you?"

"He doesn't know about you, not yet, anyway. Mrs. Williams is going to tell him, though, so I wanted to make sure you knew, before everything hits the fan. She's been getting on me to tell ya'll for years. That's why she came by the other day. She wanted to warn me that he's coming in town . . . to give me a chance to say something, and she wants you to know that she's your grandmother. That lady really loves you. Anyway, that's why I wanted to talk with you."

Marianne poured another Hennessy on the rocks; a big one. Jackson grabbed another wine cooler, this time he drank out the bottle.

"You know, he was at church today."

"For real? My father was at church today? Where was he? What did he look like? Did he say anything to you?"

"Naw, baby. I don't know if he saw me. He might not have recognized me. It was not the right time, anyway."

"Oh he recognized you, mom. You were looking good. But who was he?"

"Jacks, did you notice that man that came in late and sat at the organ, he was playing after you spoke?"

"Naw, I didn't notice. You think he'll come by here?"

"Yeah, he'll come . . . I want to be ready when he does. I don't want you to be surprised or upset with me or Reginald. He never knew about you because I was too proud to tell him."

251

"His name is Reginald?"

Marianne told Jackson about the summer she met Reginald Lamont Williams. He was so good looking and tall. She talked about them going to the concert, and they were so into each other, that they missed most of it.

She told Jacks that she didn't know she was pregnant until he had already left Kansas City. He had gone back to college and she was nearly four months when she found out, herself.

It was different times then. She didn't know how she was going to live her life, but thanks to all her friends, everything worked out fine. Ms. Shirley and Aunt Rosie were the grandmothers that he and Patrick would never miss. She told how they were in the delivery room, and they almost passed out when he was born. Jackson and Marianne laughed hard talking about that night because Marianne imitated them walking out the delivery room, holding each other up.

Marianne told Jacks how Big Bill wanted to be named as his father on his birth certificate, that's where he got his middle name of Williams, but it also was his father's last name too. Uncle Charlie wanted him to carry his name, that's were Jackson came from, and of course, he had to have her name. That's how he got to be Jackson Williams Robinson.

"So how did Mrs. Williams find out about me?"

"That was really a trip. You were about 2 years old and she came by the restaurant. You were running around, harassing the customers . . . you were really performing. She saw you, picked you up and knew that you were her grandson."

"But how?"

"Well, she recognized the birthmark on your leg. Her father and grandfather had almost identical birthmarks on their leg too. In fact, I got a picture that she gave me, showing her father sitting on a porch, with that birthmark looking just like

252

yours. You're his splitting image. She knew that Reggie and I were friends, so she put two and two together. That lady came to my restaurant talking about she can recognize her grandchild."

Marianne was getting relaxed.

"I know, ever since I was a little kid, she's been giving me money and rides whenever she sees me. She always asked about you. I used to see her at my school programs too."

"You're kidding. She came to your school?"

"Yeah, when I was little, she came around to my school. She was so nice to me. I thought it was because she knew you."

"No, that wasn't it. Anyway, I just went on with my life because your father was engaged and I didn't want to be a thorn between him and his wife. I didn't want anything from the Williams. When I found out he was engaged, I was too hurt to say anything else to him. My heart was broke!"

"Oh, my father's a player, he was messing with you and engaged to another woman."

"Yeah, that's about it. I don't think he was trying to take advantage of me. It was something that happened during the summer when we both was very young . . . hormones was jumping around." Marianne was very relaxed and happy to get this off her chest.

"I wonder why Mrs. Williams never mentioned me to my father? All this time, seems like somebody should have said something to Reginald."

"It was other circumstances. I really didn't want to start any problems with Reggie and his family. We didn't need anything from them. We had so many people around us that loved us just the same. It might have been a mistake on my part, by not contacting Reginald. Mrs. Williams gave me his information, to let him know, but she was trying to keep the peace, too."

"Well, I don't know everything, mom, but it seems to me something is missing from this story. Is there something you're not telling me?"

Marianne thought about her son, there's not a lot she could hide from him. He's so damn smart. Where does he get it from? But there was no way she would let him know that Rev. Williams didn't want anything to do with him. In fact, Mrs. Williams had to sneak and hide just to see him. She would never divulge that information, ever.

* * * * *

With everything happening on his beat, Det. Combs was too busy to give Dee a call. He was ready for a long vacation. He thought about it . . . a real vacation. How long had it been since he'd had a break from all the crime and dope peddlers? Where would he go? Usually when he took a vacation, he'd go to his family reunion in Tupelo, Mississippi. That was every year. Mostly because he had to help finance the affair and he wanted his money back.

He decided to skip the reunion this year . . . he was going on a real vacation.

"That's what I'm going to do. I'll get me some travel brochures and take them to Dee. I'll let her pick out where I should go, then see if she wants to join me."

Byron thought he was so clever to think of such a romantic and slick way to get to know Dee. "She'll melt in my hands when I pull this off."

Chapter 23

Mrs. Williams was cooking dinner and Reginald was helping by peeling the potatoes. He wanted to make the potato salad, himself. They were having a nice home cooked meal together. He loved his mother's cooking. It'd been a while since he had the chance to come to Kansas City. In the music business, there wasn't much chance of coming home. Reginald thought about how fast time flies, especially when you're getting old.

His parents would always come to Atlanta to visit him. After thinking about it, it had been almost twenty years since he came home. Where had the time gone? It didn't seem that long. He shook it off as being too busy.

"So mom, do you ever see Terry Sanders? Remember him. He used to direct the choir when we first built this church, then he would start drum majoring and dancing in the choir stand. Remember that?"

"Oh Lord, I had forgot all about that boy. I heard he joined the Navy. I thought him and that cute little Kim would end up married, but they didn't. She ended up marrying a lawyer, they're in Maryland last I heard. I haven't kept up with Terry. I haven't heard anything about him."

"I saw Marianne Robinson at church. Dang mom, she hasn't changed a bit. That girl is fine. I wonder who she ended up with. She was a really nice girl, back in the day. Now that's who I should have married."

"Why you say that, Reggie?"

"Aahh, it was nothing. I was just talking."

Mrs. Williams pulled up a chair and sat down, she thought about telling him everything, right then and there.

"Reginald, how close of friends were you with

Marianne?"

"We were close, mom. I liked Marianne. If I wasn't engaged to marry Vanessa, then I probably would have married Marianne. She was smart and responsible, very determined for her age. She intrigued me. But there was Vanessa, it's funny that we're talking about this. I always believed that Vanessa was going to be my wife. Now I realize that we weren't in love. We were never in love, not like you're supposed to be. We didn't have that crazy love. We never had it like that. I guess we were supposed to have Alicia, maybe that's it, because me and Vanessa had nothing in common."

"Oh Reginald, there's something you should know. You need to talk with Marianne. Go see her, better yet, give her a call and take her somewhere nice and quiet, so ya'll can talk."

"What are you talking about? Why should I talk with Marianne Robinson?" Reginald pulled up a chair to sit with his mother, he took her hands and held them in a reassuring way. "What's so important that I should take her somewhere quiet?"

"Reginald, let Marianne tell you."

"Wait a minute, you tell me what you are talking about."

"Baby, I can't. Your father will kill me."

"DAD . . . DAD . . . Can you come down here?" Reginald walked to the stairway and began calling for his father to come down stairs.

"Oh no, Reggie. Don't do that." Juanita Williams followed Reggie, pulling on his sleeve, begging her son. "Please son. Your daddy will be upset with me."

"Then you better tell me right now, momma."

"One day, about the time Vanessa was about to give birth to Alicia, I went to the restaurant where Marianne works. You should see that place now, that girl has really built that business up. She has three different locations now, Reggie. Did you know that?"

"Okay, okay, that's good, now get back to what you were saying."

"There was a cute little baby boy, running around, playing. Well, I couldn't resist the boy. So I picked him up, and took him to my table and was playing with him, then I saw you, the resemblance. I knew from the time I set eyes on that baby that he was by grandchild. I looked at his eyes, then there was that family birthmark on his leg, the one that my daddy and grandfather had . . . well, Jackson, Marianne's baby has the same birthmark."

Reginald jumped back in his seat. The chair fell over as he grabbed his head.

"WHAT!"

"I begged her all these years to tell you, but that girl is so stubborn. She didn't want to be a problem between you and Vanessa."

"Mom, why didn't you or dad tell me?"

"Your daddy can have poor understanding. You were getting ready to have Alicia when I found out and you know how your father is . . . he always think somebody's out to take advantage of us. He didn't want to hear anything about some girl having a baby, and saying YOU was the father, was like throwing gasoline on a fire."

Mrs. Williams started whispering. "He forbad me from talking about Marianne or Jackson anymore, period. I had to sneak around just to see the boy."

"Dad . . . Dad, can you come down here?"

"Please Reginald, your daddy is old and he's getting sick. Your father's not well at all. Please don't upset him."

"Mom, wait a minute. Did you know that Marianne dropped out of school to take care of her little brother? Did dad know that? She has sacrificed all her life, then to tell me, she was dealing with my son, without any help from me or my

257

religious family. What kind of business is that?"

"Son, your dad didn't want a bunch of mess going on between you and Vanessa."

"I lost twenty years with my son because dad didn't want it to be too messy between me and Vanessa? Me and Vanessa started out messy. We were trying to please ya'll, her family too. I can't believe this. You know what mom . . . right now I'm very upset and I'm very disappointed." Reginald stopped before he said something that he would later regret. "Me and dad need to have a talk."

"Reginald, I know you're upset. Now, I've never asked you anything before, but I'm begging you, son, don't do this. Your father just wanted the best for you. He is sick. Please don't make his last days ones that he'll regret. He's human, he makes human mistakes, just forgive him, son and don't bring it up. You have the rest of your life to get to know Jackson."

"Mom, I feel so bad for Marianne. She had to raise my son alone. She already had it hard. I let her down mom. I need to apologize to that lady."

"Baby, it's not too late for you and Jackson. He's a wonderful boy. You saw him the other day at that funeral. He was the young man that spoke, the last one that got up."

"That was him? Yeah, I remember seeing him. Marianne got up with him. So, that's my son?" Reginald took a paper towel and began wiping his face, eyes and head. "How can I ever make it up to Marianne? We really let her down as a family, mom. We should have been better folks than that. You have her number?"

"Yes Reggie, it's in my telephone book."

"You know where she lives now? Is she still living in that old house?"

* * * * *

Det. Combs set out looking for Dee like she was a

258

fugitive. He hadn't seen her in two or three weeks. She wasn't answering none of his phone calls or acknowledging any of his messages. He wondered if he was too late. Did she find some other man before he could sweep her off her feet?

Byron decided he would try another route. He would go by Uncle Charlie's house and ask to speak to her. Marianne told him that she was now taking care of him and his wife.

"She's probably so busy, I'll just go by there and see if she needs any help."

Dee was still recuperating from her last fling. She had been to a doctor and there were a couple of cracked ribs. The hospital police wanted to take a report for domestic violence, but she said she was running, not paying attention, then fell down a flight of stairs. She stated she didn't have a husband or boyfriend, so they didn't follow up with a police report.

Dee was so afraid of the man at the convenience store that she never wanted to cross his path, ever; so filing a complaint against him was not going to happen. That man scared her.

Byron had two days off and he was determined to talk with Dee. He went to her house and knocked.

"Just a minute." Dee opened the door, then stepped back behind the door. She hadn't expected company.

"Hello, Dee. Forgive me if I came at a bad time, I know I'm unexpected and all . . . I tried to leave a message for you, but you never returned my phone calls."

"I'm sorry, I've been really busy lately. How can I help you?" Dee thought the hospital police filed a report, without her consent and she wasn't reporting anything to him.

"Well, actually, I wanted to say hello. Marianne told me you were staying here and taking care of Uncle Charlie and Aunt Rosie, I came by to see if you needed any help."

"Detective, that's very nice of you. Thank you. Come

in. Excuse the mess, I had a little accident and I'm still really sore, so I haven't been able to clean up around here. Just move that stuff over . . . you can give those clothes to me. Here, have a seat." Dee motioned for Byron to sit down.

"You really hurt yourself. How did you do it?"

"It was a stupid mistake. I don't want to talk about it."

"If you're having a problem with somebody, just let me know, I'll straighten it out. All you have to do, is just say the word"

"Oh no no no, nothing like that. I had a stupid little accident, I hurt myself is all. But if I need your help, then I will call you Officer. I promise."

"Well, what can I do to help you right now?"

Dee's imagination went into overdrive. But she couldn't do anything now. She didn't want Det. Combs to see her body. He would think for sure, that she was beaten up. "No thank you. It's very nice of you, but no thank you."

"Dee, let me do something for you. Can I get you something to eat, anything? I know what, why don't I go in the kitchen and fix dinner while you clean up in here. Hey, that's what friends are for, to help out when you need them. Girrrrl, I can cook anything. Wait till you have some of my cooking."

Byron didn't take no for an answer. He went to the kitchen and started looking for something to cook. He decided he would bring out his travel brochures during dinner. Dee is so cute. Byron was going to enjoy his next couple of days off.

* * * * *

It was a beautiful day; the air was crisp and cool. Reginald was going to get out before it got too hot. Earlier, he called his office in Atlanta to let them know that he would be staying in Kansas City a little longer than planned.

Reginald drove by Marianne's house.

"Wow, that doesn't look like the old boarding house he

260

remembered." It was totally remodeled. The old sidings were gone. It now had the wood framed with stone and brick. Where her bedroom windows used to overlook the neighborhood, now had a beautiful stain glass decorative picture of birds. The house looked brighter. It was a really nice house. He wondered what it looks like inside.

Reginald smiled thinking about the last time he entered that house. Marianne probably got pregnant that night. He didn't stop like he had planned; he needed time to think about what he wanted to say. Maybe it would be a good idea to take Marianne somewhere quiet so they could talk.

He drove by all three of Marianne's restaurants, checking out her accomplishments.

"Now that's what I'm talking about. Look at my girl. She really stepped it up, I'm not surprised. I knew she would have it all together."

Reginald pulled over to look up a phone number for the restaurant, hoping somebody would let him know how to contact her.

"Uncle Charlie's Que Shop, how may I help you?"

Reginald recognized the voice immediately. "Hello, Marianne? How are you, this is Reginald Williams."

"Hello Reggie, I'm doing just fine. It's good to hear your voice."

"Listen Marianne, you know we need to talk. I'd feel better if we were able to go somewhere quiet and have a chance to talk without any interruptions. I don't know how I feel right now, I'm a little frustrated with my family and to be honest, I'm kind of upset with you, too. What were you thinking?"

"Reginald, truthfully, I don't know."

"Well, let me find us a place to talk. I would like to meet my son. When do you think that'll be possible?"

"He knows about you. We had our talk a couple of days

ago."

"When were you going to tell me? I just found out last night. Hey, look, let's just get together and we'll bring Jackson with us. We'll have an open and honest conversation." Reginald blurted out, "I can't believe I got a son."

"Reggie, he gets out of school at 3:30."

"Can you let him know that I want to meet him? I'll call you in about an hour, and let you know where we can get together. Man, I'm kind of nervous." Reggie laughed. "See you in a minute."

Marianne sat down at the counter with her head in her hands. She was wondering what was going to happen when they finally meet. She longed for this day, she dreamed about it year after year. She knew, one day it would happen, now it's here. She couldn't wait to see Reginald. Marianne thought about why she never told him about Jacks. Was it really because he was engaged, was it because she didn't want any problems between him and his wife, or was it because she wanted to make him pay for hurting her feelings. She was crushed after finding out that he was engaged. Then he left without saying a word to her. She wanted him to pay for all that, but she needed to be honest with herself, first, before they have their meeting.

Patrick saw Marianne looking down and so sad. He wanted to know what was happening with her.

"Marianne, is there a problem? What's wrong big sis?"

"Oh Patty, you'll never believe what's happening. I've been selfish. I was wrong."

"Marianne, that's one thing you can't ever be guilty of . . . you're the most generous and unselfish person, I'll ever know. Why are you beating up on yourself like this?"

"Patrick, Jackson's father came in town. I never told him about Jackson. He's pretty pissed with me. I can't blame him. I didn't want him to know about Jacks; I was wrong for that. They should have had a chance to get to know each other. What was I thinking?"

"Well, you must have had a reason, Marianne."

"Yeah, but that didn't make it right."

"So, who's his father?"

"He didn't tell you? His name is Reginald Williams, he's Rev. Williams oldest son."

"Whaaaaaaaaat? You're kidding, right? Aaahhh man! That's why Jackson has all those dreams and visions. He's a part of those preachers. Marianne, that's what's wrong with Jacks."

"That's what's wrong with Jacks? Boy, what are you talking about?"

"Jackson has these visions, remember when he was little; you took him to the doctor, because he blacked out. Well he still does it. Jackson always knows things, Marianne. He didn't want you to know about him blacking out, cause you'll worry. But Jackson knows about stuff he shouldn't know about. That's how he wins all that money at . . . " Patrick shushed up quick before he talked too much.

"Wins what money, Patty? What are you talking about? Now you got my attention . . . what money?"

"Oh it's nothing, we fellows play cards sometimes is all. So when can we meet Reginald Williams?" She didn't respond, she didn't say anything for a while.

"Marianne my father knew about me, and left us too. You're not running off all the men in the family are you?" Patrick wanted to get a smile from his big sister. "It's going to be alright? Just don't be holding no grudges against anybody, okay big sis, cause those grudges can stop you from moving forward in life. Let's just forgive everybody and move on, so we can be one big happy family."

Patrick was waving his hand around, trying to lift Marianne's spirits. He'll never forget or take for granted how his wife forgave him. What he did was so much worse than anything they could ever do. If they even knew how deep his transgressions were, but then, he realized that he had a special woman. She loved him.

"Marianne, Ole Blue is sure mad at his momma. He need's to forgive her. She's human like everybody else, we make big mistakes."

"Oh yeah, I've been meaning to ask you about that. What happened?

"Girl, Angie and Zett's been seeing each other."

"I know you're not saying, what I think you're saying."

"Sis, they've been seeing each other since we were in the 10th grade."

"Boy, shut your mouth!"

Chapter 24

Blue Baby called his father and told him eve-ry-thang! His father kept his conversation distant and didn't seem too surprised. He didn't criticize Angie or help his son degrade his mother and her young friend's relationship. In fact, he didn't have too much to say.

"Dad, I need to come there and stay with you. I can't be around her anymore. How can she have sex with one of my friends? We're damn near the same age, dad. I walked in on them. Man, I tried to kill that nigga. Mom had to take him to the hospital. We're not talking. I haven't said anything to her since, I moved out. I'm not going back, either."

"Blue, you don't have much time before schools out. Stay there, finish out this year, then I'll see about getting you here with me. You don't need to leave school . . . not right now. It's probably best to go on and finish high school there; you have only one more year, right?"

"No dad, I'll finish this year."

"Starting another school, especially in another state, might mess up your transcript, Blue. I don't think it's a good idea to move now."

"Man, did you hear what I just told you. I can't stay here. I need to be there with you. PLEASE DAD! Let me come there now. I don't want to see her again, period. Man, all my friends were there, they all know. Zet told everybody that they've been together three years now, since he was in the 10th grade. Everybody's talking about it. Man, this shit is embarrassing. I can't face my friends; I can't go back to that school."

"How long before school is out?"

"We have another three weeks."

"Let me check around, see what I can do."

"Dad, I can get all my school work and take it with me. I'll mail it back to school, I promise."

Blue Baby hung up the phone and knew in his heart that his dad wouldn't send for him. He remembered all the broken promises that he experienced throughout the years, when he was supposed to go there and stay the summer. He remembered all the excuses why it didn't happen.

Blue made a promise to himself that he would never leave his children. He was going to stay with them until they moved out the house. He would respect his kids. They would never worry about being ashamed or embarrassed.

He decided that he would join the Army. He's going to get his GED and leave Kansas City. He's never going back to that school. He hoped that he could stay with Jackson, at Marianne's house until he could leave. He decided he would work at making himself useful. He didn't want any reason for them to put him out.

* * * * *

When Jackson made it home from school, his mother was waiting for him with the arrangements his father had made to meet them at the Amador hotel, where he had reserved a penthouse suite. He ordered the best foods and drinks on the menu; he went all out for the meeting with Marianne and his son.

They finally arrived at the hotel to find a key waiting for them at the front desk. When they entered the room, Reginald was there playing the piano, trying to relax his nerves. They walked in and just listened until he was finished with the song.

"How did you like that? It's a new song that I'm working on. I haven't decided who I'll present it to; I need to finish it first." He walked over to Marianne. "Girl, look at you. I'm speechless! You're more beautiful now than when you

266

were a young dumpling." He turned to Jackson, he wanted to grab him and hug his son as hard as his arms would let him. "Jackson, I'm Reginald Lamont Williams, I very happy to meet you. I would love to hold you right now."

Reginald could see Jackson did have his eyes. Jackson had a lot of his characteristics. He remembered what his mother told him. He wanted to see the birthmark but he wasn't going to ask something like that . . . But later, for sure.

Jackson walked over to Reggie and held him. As they were there, time stood still, to let them enjoy the moment.

"Hello, I'm happy to meet you, sir." Jacks finally whispered.

Tears filled Marianne's eyes. This was exactly what she envisioned; how she hoped it would be, if she ever met her own father.

Reginald thought this meeting would be a lot of talking about the past, explaining this and that, but it wasn't. In fact, it was the opposite. They laughed and had fun catching up on each other's lives. They talked about everything and everybody. Reginald told Jackson about his little sister. They interrupted and laughed and talked all at the same time. They ate and talked more. It was a pleasant meeting.

Marianne and Reginald were still very attracted to each other. Reggie wanted to get Marianne a lone so he could find out what she's been doing all these years. Jackson could tell that his father wanted to talk more with his mother, he excused himself to give them space; Reginald had questions that Marianne still needed to answer.

"Mom, Reggie, I have to get back home. I have a lot of things to do, like homework. I really need to see about Blue. I got to check on the restaurant. I can tell you two still have things to talk about. Mom, this is a nice evening, why don't you get a room so you won't have to drive home tonight. Take a break. I'll take care of everything at the place."

"There's no need to get another room. It's an extra room in this suite. Jackson, I promise to take care of your mother." Reginald laughed at the thought.

It was amusing to Jackson too; the irony of the situation; his father trying to convince him that his mother is safe, in the hotel room, alone, with him.

"I thought that you and Marianne would want to stay here with me." Reginald explained. "She's more than welcome to stay. I mean, that's why I got this big suite." Reginald was almost begging.

"I can't stay. I'm sorry. I hadn't planned on staying here, Reggie. I have to be going."

"No you don't. Mom, stay and relax. I'm positive you and my father have more that you need to discuss. Plus, she needs to relax, Reggie. She works too hard. I'm leaving mom. Ya'll talk." Jackson didn't look back when he left.

Reginald was impressed with Jackson. "He's really an assertive guy."

"Reggie, he's been like that all his life."

* * * * *

Dee liked Det. Combs. He's very muscular. He's a little old for her taste, but he kept his appearance up in a vain way. She knew younger men that didn't have a hard body like his.

Dee didn't know how long she'd be able to keep Byron away. It's been close to a month and her bruises were still very visible. Whenever he came over, she couldn't react to the crippling pain that her body was feeling. She'd straighten up and walked right.

"Hey Dee, I'm getting off work, do you need anything? I'll be by your house in a little bit"

"No, thank you. How long before you're here?"

"Not long baby. I got a surprise for you."

This was so different than anything she'd been used to. So many times, she initiated the relationship. Actually, there wasn't a relationship; there's never been a relationship. It's always been sex. This was different. They had actually become friends. Because of her injuries, she was forced to calm down and they got a chance to know each other before she ruined everything, by sexing him first. This was better. This was definitely better.

* * * * *

Zetty and Angie decided that they were going to be open and honest about their relationship. No more sneaking around. If people didn't like it, then that's their problem. They truly loved each other. They were soul mates and had come too far and sacrificed too much. They had put everybody's feelings ahead of theirs for too many years. Blue should be old enough to accept his mother being happy. If he loved her, then he would accept Zett. Shoot, him and Zett were friends first.

Blue went to sign up for the military, that didn't work. He hadn't graduated from high school. He asked if he could stay with Patrick and Jackson at Marianne's house. He couldn't stay there either. Marianne didn't want to be in the middle of their situation. She told Blue to go home; he only had a few months to live with Angie.

Actually, Marianne thought Blue shouldn't disrespect his mother like he'd been doing. She had a real problem with that. Angie was wrong, she was very wrong; but still, that's his momma. Marianne couldn't identify with a woman choosing a man over her children, but she wasn't in Angie's shoes. She couldn't say what made Angie so determined to put her happiness before her son. Marianne didn't know so she didn't say too much about it.

"Honey, I think you need to make up with Angie."

"Ms. Marianne, she's still sleeping with Zett. If she thought about me, then she would stop. I told her how my friends are talking about her. What's going to happen when Zett finds somebody else, because she's old and wrinkled? What she's gonna do then? Marianne, my mother should love me enough to stop, but she don't. She'd rather let me be embarrassed . . . just to be with Zett."

"Baby, she wants to be happy. Now, I don't condone what Angie is doing. I think it's crazy . . . your mother should end this but she says she really loves Zett. Real love is dangerous; people don't think with their brains. Its funny cause very seldom do you find a family that likes their in-laws . . . very seldom. Families break up behind that all the time . . . and never get back together. This is hard, too hard for a young man, but can you deal with it, can't you, a little while longer?"

"Hell no, Ms. Marianne. It's crazy. Why my momma got to be the neighborhood freak? She's nearly twenty years older than Zett. Nobody else's momma is like that."

It wasn't long after that talk with Marianne that Blue Baby left her house. He didn't finish school and he didn't leave Kansas City. He stayed around town. Soon he met some new friends that let him stay with them.

* * * * *

Reginald decided to stay in Kansas City. He wasn't ready to leave . . . no time soon. His father, Rev. Williams was sick. His health was rapidly deteriorating. Reggie was the eldest son; the church needed him to help them and his mother.

Rev. Williams had a great staff. He had ministers that would step in whenever they had a chance to preach. There were some real guns waiting to take over. They were taught by the best, Rev. Williams.

Reginald thought he didn't have long to introduce his son to his father. He wondered how his father would receive

270

Jackson, after knowing he had blocked their relationship.

Marianne told him what happened. She told Reginald how she was willing to let Jackson be a part of their family, but his father wasn't willing to accept an illegitimate child. At first Reginald wanted to charge his father, he wanted to throw all the sermons his father preached in his face and condemn him to be a liar, but looking at him now, he couldn't. He realized he was a regular man; that was imperfect . . . once he left the pulpit.

"Dad, I got someone for you to meet."

"Oh yeah, tell them to come in."

"Jackson, come in. Dad, this is Jackson, my son. Jacks . . . this is your grandfather, Rev. Robert Earl Williams."

Rev. Williams sat up in his bed. "Come over here, son. I'd like to get a good look at you." Rev. Williams always wanted to take a good look at the boy. Yeah, he heard about him, but he didn't know for sure. He wasn't a naïve man, nooooo, there wasn't a naïve bone in his body. "Come here, boy." He sat up in the bed and looked deep in Jackson's eyes. He saw the strong resemblance to his father-in-law. He saw Reginald's eyes and stature.

"Yeah, that's my grandson." He laid back down in the bed, not willing to accept responsibility. It wasn't his fault.

Jackson walked closer to Rev. Williams and surprised him when he sat with him on his bed. Rev. Williams hurried and moved the blankets over, he straighten them out, to make a comfortable place for his grandson.

Jackson wanted time in private with the Reverend. He remembered what Razz told him to get with the preachers in his family, they would know about his dreams and visions. Jackson felt cheated because his grandfather wouldn't be here much longer. He didn't have long to pick and question this family legacy. He wanted to crawl in his bed and dig, question, examine and study.

271

"Can I have a little time with my grandfather alone?"

"Why?" Reginald wasn't sure about this.

"I need to talk with him." Jackson got anxious. He thought this would be his only chance. "Please, dad."

"He called me dad." Reginald's heart melted while he silently jumped at that the opportunity to be his daddy.

"Okay, let me know if you need anything." Reggie turned to leave the room. He wondered what Jackson would say that he couldn't say in front of him. He hoped that Jackson wouldn't be rasp with his father. He barely had a chance to know Jackson himself. Reginald was anxious; he worried leaving Jackson alone with his father, knowing there may be a little animosity floating around the room.

"Grandfather . . . I hope you can help me. I was told a few months ago to talk with the preacher side of my family. I didn't know I was related to preachers, until then."

Rev. Williams grabbed his glasses and took a drink of water. "Son, maybe we need to pray. I don't know what has you burdened, but if you want advice from me, then please lets go to the throne of grace, first."

Jackson didn't know the protocol for preachers to give advice, but he was glad to know that his grandfather prayed first.

"Father, God, We come to You, today, giving You honor and praise. We thank You for all Your blessing, including uniting us as a family and bringing young Jackson into our fold.

We thank You for our Lord and savior Jesus Christ. In your Son we have life, we have redemption. Lord, no words can express Your love for us so we just thank You so much.

Father, I don't know what has Jackson troubled, but we ask, in Your Son's name, Jesus the Christ, to open our minds and our hearts. Let us receive Your knowledge, let us receive Your instruction, and please, God, let us receive Your mercy. We want

272

to do what's pleasing in Your sight, Lord. Please grant us Your blessings as we desire to know Your will. Keep us in Your grace, lead and guide us, always and forever, in Jesus name, Amen."

This was the first time Jackson had an experience like this. He'd never prayed with anybody that knew how to pray. He was glad.

"Grandfather, I believe God has called me for something. I'm not sure, but maybe you can help me understand."

"Okay, I'll try. So tell me what happened to make you believe that God has called you."

"Well, it's a long story. I'm pretty sure He's called me. If this is, what I think, from God and all; then what should I do? That's why I need your help. I don't know what to do."

Rev. Williams was taken by Jackson's candor and honesty. He had questioned at first if he was truthful. He knew how some men wanted to become preachers for the prestige and honor. Sometimes people just wanted an audience to hold hostage while they talked forever.

Jackson proceeded to tell his grandfather about everything. It was like an unplugged waterfall; then released and everything came out all at once. He told him about the dreams and blackouts. He told him how he could see people's colors that floated around them. He told his grandfather that he knew people's intentions, that he could somehow read their hearts. Not everybody, but a lot of the times they were clear as a bell. He told him about the angels that were in touch with him for years and how they fought over him, and they were in ancient war gear. Then the voice that promised to protect him.

This was sounding a little farfetched to his grandfather, this old preacher.

Jackson continued to spew out experiences that dated

back over ten years ago. He told how Tia waved goodbye to him. Lastly, he told his grandfather about the words and what they said.

Rev. Williams was stunned. "Son, if what you're saying is true, then you will need to prepare yourself and prove yourself to be worthy. I don't know of anyone that has had so many signs; or was given so many gifts or fruits of the spirit."

"Well, Rev. Williams, grandfather, I hope you can help me to understand all this. What do you mean by prove myself worthy?"

"If you want to understand, then study hard. Study, study. study. You need to pray hard for understanding. Pray for the power of the Holy Spirit, because the Holy Spirit will help you understand and pray for power to stand against the attacks of the enemy."

"So, I need to prepare myself, how? Where would I go to do that? I don't know what to do."

"You'll need to go to a seminary college, study and pray. Learn the bible, learn the word. Study other religions so you won't be ignorant of different beliefs. I'm very excited for you, Jackson, and I'm proud to call you my grandson. Me, your father, and our church will help you. I'll make some calls to get you to the right school and get you some good mentors."

Chapter 25

Dee and Det. Combs were becoming very good friends. She'd never had a friend like Byron. He was so sweet. Anything she wanted to do, he was ready, willing and, gun ho!

She thought it was so cute the way he asked her to join him for a vacation. They were having dinner, and he brought out travel brochures from all over the world.

"Dee, I was thinking of going on a trip."

"Oh yeah, where?"

"I haven't decided yet. I got some brochures from all these places, I was trying to make my mind up where I'd like to go, but I can't decide."

"Let me see?"

Byron slid the brochures closer; there were six different luxurious descriptions of vacations from the Hawaiian Islands, the Caribbean Islands, the Cayman Islands, New York, Athens and San Francisco.

"So what do you think?"

"I don't know Byron, they all look really good."

"Well, where would you like to go?"

"Byron, I'd like to go to all of them."

"No kidding, all of them . . . Wow, I made a promise to myself that I would invite you to wherever you wanted to go, I didn't think you would say, all of them, Dee. I guess I'll just have to take you to all of them. Now tell me, where would you like to go first?"

"Oh Byron, you'll take me to these wonderful places? I'm a very lucky girl. Let me see, I think I want to go to one of the islands first."

Dee took the island brochures, put them behind her back, mixed them up, then told Byron, the brochure that's on top is where they'll go first. They were going to the Cayman

Islands.

"Now we'll go to these other places later, at least once a year. How's that?"

* * * * *

Marianne was sitting in the suite that Reginald had reserved for them so they could spend more quiet time together. She loved it. He'd call and asked if she wanted to get away for the weekend. He's so sweet and mature, so different from the last time they were together. She remembered how they, sort of, attacked each other back then. Now, they're older and slower; plus, they haven't decided if they wanted to be more than friends.

Reginald enjoyed his time with Marianne too, getting to know her all over again, the right way. They enjoyed sharing each other's past. He talked about is daughter, Alicia and she talked about Jackson and Patrick. What it was like with them growing up. They told about all the funny stories, the sad and the scary times. Reginald wanted to spoil Marianne, he wanted to make up to her, someway impress her in the most magnificent way his money could afford.

Reginald's gospel production company was one of the most lucrative music companies in Atlanta. He thought about branching out to the more popular sectors of music but decided to be true to himself, and produce his type of music that may cross over to the mainstream population, but stay gospel music.

Marianne educated Reginald on the restaurant and barbeque business. She told how she was able to open up two other restaurants, she told how Uncle Charlie's Q Shop became a Kansas City tourist attraction and now Dee, her sister, was running the sauce side of the business.

Reginald hadn't met Dee, so he asked Marianne where was she when they met?

"Dee came during the summers. She's Aunt Rosie's

276

niece. We spent the summers working for Uncle Charlie since we were in elementary school. When you were here, she did something to Uncle Charlie, I don't know what it was because she never told me, but he wouldn't allow her back for a couple of years. Whatever she did, it really pissed him off . . . cause Uncle Charlie is the sweetest man you'll ever know."

"So ya'll adopted each other."

"We had been around each other so long. I feel like she's my sister, my only sister. We've been calling each other sister since we were kids. I think when we realized that we loved each other; it started coming out that way, she was my sister. It was natural."

"You know, sometimes friends are closer than real family. I think that's what Jesus meant when he asked; who is my mother."

"Well, Dee has had her share of troubles. I feel I need to take care of her. I mean, she's had a hard life. She's had to get help, she still sees a therapist every now and then."

"A therapist . . . for what?"

"Dee has issues. But lately she's doing a lot better. She met a good man. Hopefully, he'll keep treating her right. It's been looking pretty good so far. Maybe one day, I'll be able to let go, I'm such a mother hen."

"That's what I admire about you Marianne. You take care of a lot of people. From what I can tell, you always have . . . I want you, I want you to take care of me. I want some of that love."

This was the first time in almost twenty years that Reginald Lamont Williams kissed Marianne Robinson. She'd wanted this so much that she never let herself get involved with another man, not for long. She didn't want to be tied up, if and when, he came back, she waited for Reginald. She hoped and prayed that one day he would come back to her. He's not that

277

beautiful, young rock hard man he used to be, he's lost most of his hair, he's gained some weight, but it's him and they kissed.

It was beautiful how Reginald took his time with Marianne. They got to know each other; they discussed exactly what happened when she got pregnant.

"I planned on getting on birth control, but something happened with the doctor, then you left, so after you were gone, I didn't need to see a doctor. Then I found out that I was already pregnant. I scheduled an abortion, but when I heard Jackson's little heart beating, it was loud; I couldn't bring myself to end it. I just couldn't."

"Man . . . I'm sure glad you didn't because I'm happy to have a son. If I had known that you were pregnant, I wouldn't have left you. I would have come back to you Marianne. You know, I thought about you over the years, and I believe you are the woman I should have married."

"You say that now, Reggie."

"I mean it. Vanessa is a good woman, she's a good mother, but we didn't have that kind of love you need in a marriage. She's alright. I told her about Jackson and she wants to meet him. I got to get him with Alicia, they're going to love each other."

"You sure Vanessa is going to be alright with Jackson?"

"Marianne, she's the one that asked me for a divorce. Marianne, our parents had us married when we were in diapers. I think we both grew up with so much of our parents influence, that we really thought we loved each other. Vanessa said let's try to be happy with the rest of our life, while we still can. So I agreed to a divorce and it was a relief."

* * * * *

Jackson went to Razz's. It's been a while since he'd been there; he wanted to have a little fun. He figured that he'd have a little fun before he made that drastic change or dedicated his life to his calling. He was going to play a few hands of Texas Hold'em and maybe a little Cooncan. He wanted to have a small drink with his friends while he could.

He'd been trying to prepare himself for the seminary college that his grandfather had suggested. He thought if he's going to be a preacher, then he should stop gambling. But he's not a preacher yet.

Razz was sitting with Darlene when he walked in the club.

"Hey girl, where has Razz been hiding you? I don't blame him Darlene, cause you look beautiful." Jackson kissed her then gave Razz a hand shake.

"Boy, you ain't changed a bit. You gonna always be my baby. When are you graduating? This year?"

"Yes, this year." Jackson nodded.

"Have you decided what college you're going to?"

"Naw, not yet."

"Make sure you let me know. Razz I got to get something for Jacks graduation. That's my baby, Razz and you got him in here gambling."

"He's good too. That boy has made me a lot of money. Ain't that right Jacks?"

Jackson didn't want Darlene to start so he was getting away while he could. He wasn't staying long anyway.

"Hey, who's upstairs? Is there a game going . . . I feel like robbing some of your customers today, Razz."

"They're up there playing poker. Go get'em."

Jackson went upstairs and sat at the table, he took a few hundred dollar bills out his pocket to tease his victims. They were playing Omaha Hi Low.

He called the first couple of hands but wasn't feeling it, so he quickly folded. Usually Jackson knew when to start playing hard. He waited for the right time. He called a few more flops so the other men and women at the table could relax; he wanted to throw them off guard before he launched his attack and take all their money.

They were dealt another hand; Jackson got an ace and king of diamonds; and a three and nine of spades. He checked. The flop came and it was a deuce of spades, a five of diamonds and a queen of spades. Jackson called the bet. The turn was a ten of diamonds. He had a good hand. This could be a hogger. He could win both the Hi and Low hand. This was going to be a big pot too, cause everybody called. He waited patiently. He couldn't start raising too fast, he didn't want anybody to fold. Then it hit him.

It was the vision that usually blinded him for two or three minutes. This was not the right time. There wasn't anybody with him that understood. He fell out his seat. The other gamblers stood up.

"What's wrong with the boy?"

"I don't know, get Razz."

Jackson watched the bright flash, then the sound of the blast. It was unusually real this time. Jacks could almost see through the darkness. It was somebody, who? He decided to stay there on the floor and not try to get up before it was over. Razz came up the stairs. He wondered if this is what Jackson was telling him about the other day.

"Hey now, you alright. Come on, talk to Razz . . . you alright?"

Darlene was taking his pulse, looking in his eyes, making sure it wasn't more serious.

"Man, it happened again Razz. I'm sorry. I didn't want to make a scene around here."

Jackson slowly got up. He took his money that wasn't in the pot and put it back it his pocket.

"I think I'd better go home. I'll talk with you later."

"You do that, Jacks. I want to hear from you."

Jacks decided he would focus on school. He's not meant to have fun like the rest of his friends. He had known a long time that he was different. All he wanted to do was gamble anyway . . . with the old cats. They talked in riddles and he liked it. *'All that glitters ain't gold and all that's good ain't gone'* or when they said *'The fruit don't fall far from the tree.'* Jacks turned that over and over in his head, before he figured out what they were saying. They talked in code. He liked those old cats.

He didn't want to think about being a preacher, if that's what he's really supposed to be. What would his life be like, what would he miss, who's going to be his friends now? School, he had to focus on school.

It was so different without Tia. Jacks was sure that Tia would have helped him figure everything out. She was his hanging buddy. It was a time when Blue Baby was the same way.

Blue was tripping. Jacks shook his head just thinking about Blue. He remembered the promise he made with all his class mates that they would look after each other and they would step in if one of their friends were in trouble. Well Blue was tripping hard. He's got some new friends, some real hard gangbangers. He saw Blue and called for him, but Blue wouldn't talk to him. Then he saw Blue a couple of days later, all dirty and beat up.

He wanted Blue to stay with them, but his mother wouldn't let him. Every time Marianne tried to get Blue to talk about his mother and try to get them back talking, he'd start calling her bitches or worse. Marianne wasn't going for that in her house, so he had to move out.

Chapter 26

Jacks finished his classes. He graduated and was lost; Jackson didn't have his close friends around anymore. It was ironic that it ended this way. It was just a few months ago, he was happily planning his life after high school. Tia and Blue still had another year before they would have finished, but nothing happened the way they had planned. Everything went berserk. Jackson wanted his friends back. He was lonely.

Patrick, Zett, Raven and J Rock had already determined how they were moving on with their life. Jackson was a little jealous that Patty's childhood friends were all still close and still around. They would see each other again.

Patrick and Zett were the only two that settled with a woman and they seemed very happy with their decisions. Raven and J Rock were in college. Patty gave them a little get together at the restaurant that he was running.

In his restaurant, Q2, it wasn't that big lunch crowd that went to the original place, so he wanted to change the dynamics a little by adding two pool tables and a bar. Marianne didn't fight against the changes, she remembered when she was Patty's age, she made changes too, changes that moved the restaurant to the next generation. Maybe this was the same with Patrick's Q2.

Patrick got Sherry some stacked shoes, beautiful clothes and jewelry; she looked so much better. She looked normal; you weren't watching her disability anymore. You saw a gorgeous woman, so beautiful. Now they seemed perfect for each other. Patrick wasn't making silent excuses for his decision to be with Sherry, they looked as they belonged together. Now, she glowed and she loved Patrick so much. At the get together, she danced and laughed so loud and long. Sherry was happily the rose that finally bloomed.

This summer, while they had a chance, Reginald wanted Jackson to meet his sister, Alicia. Jacks wondered what kind of girl she was, he asked Reginald for a picture.

"You got a picture of Alicia?"

"Yeah, I got a picture. This one is old. She's not even five years old in this picture. My mother has a picture. I'll bring you one."

"I have to come over and see my grandmother. You think we can have dinner or something with her."

"You know what, mom would love that. In fact, why don't I invite your aunts and uncles to come too; that'll give everybody a chance to meet you, Jackson."

Alicia was a cute 16 year old, very quiet and very athletic. She had very long red hair. Alicia was tickled to death to know she had a brother. She was naturally curious.

"I have a brother. Wow. Where did he come from?"

"He lives here in Kansas City. How about coming out here to meet your brother before you go back to school?"

"That sounds good to me. What's his name?"

"Jackson. His name is Jackson Robinson. He's really a nice young man. I'm proud to call him my son. I'll have to fill you in on the whole story. You and Jacks will be good friends. Just wait until you meet him."

"Wow, I can't believe I have a brother."

"I'll let you know about your plane reservations. Okay."

"Okay dad. How old is he?"

"He's 18. He'll be going to college this Fall, he'll go to a seminary school to be a minister. He doesn't seem like the type to be a preacher. I can't believe it, but he talked with dad, and dad says he was called to the ministry. So, you have a brother that's going to be a preacher, like your grandfather."

"I can't wait to meet him."

"We're having a dinner at your grandmother's house in

a couple of week. Your other cousins and everybody will be there to meet him too."

"Okay, daddy. Tell Jackson I said hello and I can't wait to meet him."

* * * * *

Rev. Williams contacted one of his fraternity brothers, Rev. Larry Foster and asked about a mentor for his grandson. Rev. Larry told about a young man by the name of Brett Reeves who lives in Kansas City.

"Brett Reeves is a dynamic speaker and considered a rising star around here. I hear he's conducting revivals in the inner cities, around Texas and Louisiana. He's one of those hip hop preacher. He's young, he wears those designer jeans to church, he has an earring . . . you know the type. They say he's leading these gangs to Christ."

"Is that right? Why haven't I heard about this young man?"

"I don't know Bobby, but the kids like him. He's a single man, and he rides a motorcycle to all his revivals. Brett's different, He's a stretch but that's what we need to reach these young men and women."

"You sure this man is somebody I need to introduce to my boy. He sounds a little rowdy.

"He comes off that way at first, but once you meet him, you'll realize he's a sincere man, very passionate about the Lord's business. Matter of fact, he doesn't want a wife until he can settle down. Now I thought that was a considerate decision."

"Why you say that Larry? These young preachers need to be married; you know how it is when a young girl starts on you. You need a woman, to be anchored down."

"Well, I know what you're saying, and I can understand what Brett is saying too, these young men and women are in

284

these streets and they need him. He attends Morehouse. Is that where your grandson will go?"

"Yeah, that's where he's going."

"Well, they can meet before they start school this Fall. I'll call Brett and see what his schedule is like."

"Okay. Thanks brother, as always, you've been a big help."

* * * * *

Marianne and Reginald had gone to a play. This was the first musical play Marianne's ever attended. It was Cats. Marianne was blown away and wondered about everything that she'd missed working like a slave in her restaurants.

She decided she was going to let more responsibility go to Patrick so she can play catch up with her life. She wanted to go on cruises and see more plays. Marianne had never gone to Vegas, there was so much she missed and this was the right time to live.

"Baby, I'm glad you enjoyed the play."

"I feel like I missed so much. I never was interested in going to anything like that. It never occurred to me what I was missing. I was missing it, wasn't I?"

"Yeah! My little workaholic, you'll be okay cause I'm going to enjoy myself and you will too."

They pulled up at Marianne's house and she noticed a man sitting in a wheelchair in front of her yard.

"Who's that in front of your house Marianne?"

"I don't know. Lord I hope these homeless people don't start standing around here."

They got closer and closer. The man's head was down and he appeared asleep. Reginald pulled up in the driveway.

"Hold on, I'll see about this man. You go inside."

"Be nice. Call him a taxi and give him a few dollars. You think I ought to get him something to eat?"

285

"Girl, he'll be out there every day if you start feeding him."

"Okay Reginald, be nice."

Reginald walked over to the man and tried to wake him.

"Hey . . . hey . . . what are you doing here? Can I get you something; you need a cab? You can't stay in front of this house, it's late."

"Is Marianne here?"

"Who are you?"

"Is Marianne here?"

"First tell me your name, then I'll let you know if Marianne's here. Tell, me, your, name?"

"I'm Lonnie, tell Marianne I want to see the baby."

"What baby you want to see? There's no baby around here."

"Where's Marianne?"

Reginald went in the house to get Marianne.

"That guy out there is asking for you."

"You're kidding, who is it?"

"He said his name is Lonnie."

Marianne flopped down in her chair. She was speechless. How could he bring his broke down ass here after he left them without a word in over twenty damn years.

"You got to be kidding me. He said his name is Lonnie?"

"Yeah, that's what he said. Who's Lonnie?"

"You remember when my mother died, oh you may have forgotten, but Lonnie's Patrick's father. He left at my mother's funeral and never came back."

"That's right, I remember that. My dad was going to marry them but your mother died. That's the guy? What is he doing coming around here now?"

"Ooooo Lordy, let me go out there and see what he

wants."

Marianne and Reginald walked outside to see what Lonnie wanted. When Marianne saw him, she couldn't believe he had the nerve to come there sick.

"Lonnie, what are you doing here?"

"Marianne . . . Marianne, is that you? Hiiiii, I just want to see the baby. Where's the baby?"

"His name is Patrick. Let me bring you in the house, Lonnie."

"How can we get him up the stairs?" Reginald was eyeing their situation. At first, they started taking Lonnie step by step up the stairs. It was hard.

"Marianne, we're not going to be able to do this. Maybe we can lift him and take him first, then take the chair."

Ms. Shirley was looking out her window. She's in her late sixty's now. Her babies were grown, there's nobody to cook and clean for; Marianne don't come home anymore. She was lonely.

"What in the wooorrld are they out there doing?" She watched as Reginald and Marianne struggled to carry Lonnie up the stairs.

"We need some help Reginald. I ain't gonna break my back carrying this man up these stairs."

"Let's call the ambulance; they'll help us get him in."

"Wait a minute, Shirley don't have all these stairs, let me see if we can take him over there."

Marianne started walking next door. Shirley hurried away from the window, she didn't want to be caught peeping.

"Shirley . . . Shirley" Marianne walked inside Shirley's house. She couldn't believe it; wait till Shirley hears this; that Lonnie Evans was outside.

"Girrrrrl you won't believe who's outside?"

"I saw that man sitting in front of your house. He's

been out there for hours. Who is it?"

"Girrrrl, you're not going to believe it, if I told you."

"Just tell me Marianne."

"It's Lonnie Evans."

"LORD HAVE MERCY! What does he want?"

"I don't know Shirley. He showed up on my door asking to see the baby."

"Is he alright? He should know Patrick's not a baby anymore."

"Shirley I don't know. I haven't had a chance to talk to him. He's sick. I can't believe he brought his sick ass over here. I guess we're supposed to take care of him, now. I ain't doing it. I'll send his ass over there with Darlene, somewhere . . . but he ain't staying here with me."

"So what? You want to bring his po black ass over here with me?"

Marianne started laughing. "I was just thinking it'll be easier bringing him here, we can find out later what he wants. Right now it's late and he needs to come inside. We can't take him up all those stairs."

"Call Patrick, let him do it. He can take Lonnie up those stairs. His friends can help."

"I'm gonna wait till Patrick gets off work before I tell him about Lonnie. He'll want to close the shop and he needs to stay there and work. He's just got liquor license and he needs the money."

"Well, bring his ass on over then!"

It was around 12 midnight, Jackson, Patrick and Sherry walked in the house together. Jackson was at the main restaurant and he decided to let Victor take the leftovers to Razz's. He still felt a little embarrassed falling out like that in front of everybody. Victor didn't mind, Razz would give him a couple of drinks for his troubles. So Jackson went to Q2, to hang out with Patty until he closed.

Marianne and Reginald were watching and waiting for the boys to come home. When they walked in the house, they could tell something was up. Reginald got up to excuse himself but Marianne told him to stay. Patrick and Jackson were concerned. They didn't want anything bad to have happened. Marianne looked so serious.

"We need to talk. Ya'll sit down . . . This is bad!"

They looked at each other not wanting to interrupt. She looked very serious. Jackson couldn't get her feelings. With some people, he could tell what they were feeling immediately, but his mother was something else. He could never tell with her. So he waited.

"Patrick, when me and Reginald came home today, there was a man sitting in front of the house in a wheelchair. It's Lonnie Evans, your father. He's sick, too. He asked to see you. I don't know how you feel about it, and I don't know what to do. I know how I would feel if my father suddenly showed up after twenty years. I would want to see him. But, to find out that he's sick, he looks like he needs to be in a hospital. Why he decided to come here, I don't know, but he's here. Now, what are we going to do about it?"

"My father's here? Damn Jacks, can you believe this. Both of us have a daddy now!"

Reginald kind of chuckled. He didn't want to make light of the situation, so he straighten up, quick.

"Where is he, mom?" Jackson got up to look around the house. "Is he here?"

"No, he's over Shirley's house. Like I said, he's in a wheelchair and we couldn't carry him up the stairs. He'll be alright with Shirley tonight. By now, they're probably asleep. You can see him tomorrow."

"Hey, I'm kind of glad he came. I always wanted to

289

meet the man. Can't he stay here with us?"

Marianne looked at Reginald. She knew Patrick would feel like that, but she didn't want any part of taking care of Lonnie. Then she didn't want to be mean about it, either.

"Are you going to take care of him, cause I'm not, he needs care. I was thinking we can put him with Darlene, at the nursing home. If he doesn't already have a place to go, then let Darlene take care of him. He may be just visiting. We didn't have a chance to talk with him yet. Po thang, Shirley said he was sitting out front of the house for hours."

"I'd like to get to know the guy; I want him here with me."

"I don't want to take care of Lonnie, not one day. You guys are grown now; you can do what you want. But don't expect me to help. I've done my part and I'm through."

Marianne and Reginald went to her room; Jacks, Patrick and Sherry went to Patrick's room. They all had a lot to talk about.

Chapter 27

Byron and Dee had a wonderful vacation in the Cayman Islands but they weren't ready to end it. They were at the airport and had a couple of hours before boarding their planes when Dee started complaining of going home.

"Byron, I had such a wonderful time. I hate to go back home to my boring life. I wish our vacation can last forever." Dee knew how to talk sexy and with a heavy accent where Byron couldn't resist her. "I want to be your little senorita forever."

"You do? We can fix that."

Byron was proud to have such a beautiful woman on his arms. He noticed how heads turned wherever they walked in a café or walked down the streets. He dreamed of introducing Dee as his wife at the next KCPD Christmas Ball. All his fellow officers would be jealous, and those booshy, stuck up women he dated in the past, the ladies that flock to police officers, trying to net one; they never gave him the respect or time he deserved. What are they going to say when Dee shows up on his arms; looking more beautiful and sexy than they could ever be . . . in a million years. And to top it off, she's a successful woman that owns a very profitable business.

Byron knew he was a good man, a great catch for the right woman, but none of the women he dated or tried to date appreciated him. Hell, he was an officer of the law, he protected their asses, and they treated him like shit.

"Hey, I got an idea, why don't we change our tickets to go through Nevada. We can spend a few days there, and let's get married while we're at it."

"Oh Byron . . . you are wonderful, my big handsome, strong police man. I do love you, I will make you a very happy man."

Dee was thankful for Byron. She was scared for so long, thinking that she wasn't good enough, thinking she didn't deserve to be happy, or a good man wouldn't want somebody like her, but then she met her new husband. He was the best man in the world. Byron would never let anybody hurt her again. She would be loved, but most of all, she would be protected.

* * * * *

Blue had a new family. He didn't care where he lived, as long as he didn't have to stay in the same house with his mother and Zett. Angie and Zett moved together once Blue moved out. It was disgusting to Blue. He felt his mother loved Zett more than him.

How could she? That was his mother, and she chose to be with Zett. He didn't care what happened to her. He didn't want to see her again. And his sorry ass father, that man never stepped up to the plate. He had lied to him, time after time, about coming to visit, about sending for him, he lied about sending money. Everything! There wasn't one promise that man made to Blue that he didn't break.

Blue laughed thinking about his life, how nobody was there for him . . . thinking about his friends. Jackson wasn't his real friend; he told him he had to leave his house. All the people that Blue loved had let him down.

His new family was there for him. They gave him a place to live. He had to join the family and make money for the family. That's expected from anybody. At least he had his pride and dignity still intact. One day soon, he'll have saved enough money to get his own place; he wouldn't have to sleep on the floor too much longer.

Blue saw Jackson the other day, he saw Jackson waving to get his attention; he wasn't trying to hear nothing that man wanted to say. That was his main man, his homeboy, and Jacks

292

made him leave when he needed help the most.

It was all Marianne's fault; she kept trying to get him to make up with his mom. Couldn't she understand? How many times did he have to say it. He didn't want anything to do with his mother, especially as long as she was living with Zett. But she kept trying and it just pissed Blue off.

"Blue Baby, what are you going to do? You'll be graduating next year. If there's a way that you could make up with Angie, I mean, if you at least try, then I think it's the best thing that could happen for both of you. You need to graduate and go on with your life. You think you could handle Zett until you graduate? Blue, don't let that situation keep you from finishing school." Marianne wanted Blue to think more about his future.

"Ms. Marianne, fuck my momma. I don't want nothing from her. She got what she wants. If she gave a damn about me, then she would stop fucking my friends. She's my mother; the bitch should act like it."

Marianne jumped up and started toward Blue. Jackson stepped in front of her, before she reached him, then turned to his disrespectful friend.

"Hey . . . hey . . . hey! Blue watch your mouth. You can't talk to my momma like that."

"Jackson, what's wrong with that boy? I can't have Blue talking like that to me. I don't care what his problem is with Angie, but he's gonna respect me, in my house. You better talk with your friend."

"Man, didn't I tell you to respect my mother? You ain't going to talk like that to my momma. You need to find someplace else to go. I talked to you before about that Blue. Then you do it again, and I'm standing here. I don't care what's going on with you and Angie. You can't take that shit out on us. Have your stuff ready when I come home from work."

The day Blue had to leave Jacks house was the second worse day in his life. He felt everybody had turn against him. Jackson said Ms. Marianne was making him leave, but Jacks could have said something to change her mind. Ms. Marianne said I disrespected my mother and she couldn't have that, well, what about my mother disrespecting me, what about me, nobody ever thinks about me.

"WELL I DO. I THINK ABOUT ME. Damnit!" Blue screamed but made sure nobody was around that could hear him. He had been living with his new family over two months. He walked all night long; his feet were hurting, but he had to make some money selling their drugs before he could go home and rest.

* * * * *

It was early Thursday morning, Patrick couldn't sleep, his father was next door. He wanted to meet the man. Marianne said he was sick. How sick?

"I hope he's not about to die or anything. I hope he will hang around a little while so we can get to know each other."

Patrick called Ms. Shirley to see what he was doing.

"Hello, Ms. Shirley . . . what are ya'll doing over there?"

"Hi baby. I'm here getting your daddy cleaned up. He didn't have no bags or clothes with him. Luckily, I still have Clarence's things in the closets. I couldn't bring myself to get rid of his old clothes. I got everything we need over here. They sure came in handy today. I'll have Lonnie ready in about an hour. You and Sherry come on over and have breakfast with us."

"Okay . . . we will. Jackson said he was coming too."

"That's fine. I'll see you in about an hour."

This was the longest hour . . . Patrick paced the floor. He wanted to see who he looked like. Everybody always told him that he looked like his mother, but had features like his

294

father. He was bright with green eyes like his father, but his face and dimples were like his mother. He just wanted to meet one of his parents.

They walked together over to Shirley's house. You could smell the fresh coffee and bacon. They walked inside and could see a frame of a man, in a wheelchair. Patrick felt sorry for his father.

"Hey, how are you? I'm Patrick, your son. You're doing alright?"

A weak voice spoke up. "Yeah, I'm fine. Step back so I can see you. Yeah . . . you're tall aren't you?"

"This is my wife, Sherry."

"She's pretty . . . looks like your mother."

Patrick stooped down to get a good look and hoping to see if he's alright. "How did you get here? Where do you live?"

"I live in North Carolina. I caught a plane, then a taxi brought me over here. I wanted to see you."

"Well, I'm glad you came. Will you be staying?"

"Staying where?"

"With me, you can stay here with me."

"Oh, you got to ask Marianne."

"It's okay, I'll take care of you . . me and Sherry will take care of you."

Sherry looked at her husband. She knew that she would be responsible for taking care of Patrick's father. She thought about all the years she took care of her parents. They daily drank and pee'd on themselves. They got sick and vomited, she washed, cooked, cleaned, every since she was five years old. She loved her husband, but she didn't want to take care of his father; another adult that didn't do the right thing with their kids.

Sherry didn't feel sorry for Lonnie Evans, she didn't feel

295

obligated to help, either. She'd been taking care of her parents all her life. There were going to be some rules. She's not doing this by herself.

Ms. Shirley looked at Sherry, she knew exactly what she was thinking. Ms. Shirley was feeling the same thing. She was thinking how she was getting out of this mess.

Jackson was there, listening and watching. He could feel what was going on. He knew what Patrick was feeling, he saw what Sherry felt, and he could read Ms. Shirley like a book, so he wanted to see what would happen, who's going to win this upcoming battle.

* * * * *

Dee called Marianne from the airport; she was so excited that she couldn't talk without going into Spanish.

"Maria, Maria, you'll never guess what happened. I can't wait to tell you."

"What . . . tell me, I can't play your guessing game, Dee."

"I'll be over in about an hour. Don't go anywhere. I have a surprise for you, something that will make you very happy."

"You hit the lottery?"

"Better than that."

"Okay, I can't imagine what would be better than that. Hurry up so I can see what you're talking about. You got to hurry cause I have a full schedule."

"Okay . . . okay. I'm coming."

"Hey Dee, I got a surprise for you too."

"You do? Yea! I'll hurry, I'm on my way."

Dee walked in the door with Byron slyly walking behind her. She didn't say anything, just walked with her hand extended sporting a two carat, marquis diamond sitting in the middle of a wide gold band. She walked around, prancing and waving her hand up and down.

"Taa-Daa! La dee daaaa. You know what this means, don't you?"

"I know you didn't do what I think you've done."

"You are now looking at Mrs. Police Officer. I am now a married woman." She hugged Byron and kissed him. "I will give you a hundred babies, a thousand babies."

"That's alright, let's just take care of each other."

"He's so sweet, Marianne. My strong handsome husband, look at his muscles. Can you believe them. He's got a mucho um um umm, too. I thought I was going to die. Look at him, he's so cute, he's blushing. Don't blush honey, you might hurt yourself."

Byron looked at Marianne, "What is she talking about?"

"I don't know." Marianne was tickled and happy. They were like little girls again. She took her ring off for Marianne to try it on.

"You got to get you one, okay sister?"

"Dee, now . . . you're ready for my secret?"

"Yes, of course. What is your secret, sister?"

"Girl, you'll never guess."

"That's right, I'll never guess."

"Lonnie is here."

"WHAT! Where did you get that gringo?"

"He showed up at my house. Dee, he's in a wheelchair. I don't know what he wants. You know Patrick wants him to stay."

"Aye yai yai!"

It was a very busy week, Dee coming home with a brand new husband, Byron Combs. He's been around for a while, but he's still a new addition to the family. Jackson always thought Byron was sweet on his mother, so he was happily surprised by his marriage to Dee. Jacks hoped Dee would be alright now. He knew about her.

Then Lonnie shows up at Marianne's doorstep, it was one exciting week. So Jackson decided to visit with Razz. In fact, Razz was the only friend he had left. He could talk with Razz about anything and everything.

"Hey man, it's been busy at our house. Do you know Lonnie Evans, Patrick's father?

"Yeah, I know him. I haven't heard that name around here in years. What about him?"

"He showed up the other day."

"No kidding?"

"Yeah, mom's tripping. You heard about Dee and Byron? They got married. They eloped. I think they're going to be alright. Dee's like a little tornado, she spinning around, happier than I've ever seen her in my life. We can't understand a word she's saying. She deserves to be happy."

"Yeah, you say they eloped. They may be too old for that."

Jackson and Razz laughed. Big Bill came in the club and they both gave Bill the news. Bill wasn't looking too happy.

"Hey Razz, can I talk with you?"

"Sure man, we can go in my office."

They walked upstairs and Jacks decided to get in on the hold'em game

"Razz I was wondering how's my credit with you?"

"Bill, you know you can always have credit with me."

Bill looked at Razz, giving him 'the look.'

"Why, what do you need?"

"Man, Michelle gone and borrowed some money from some people she ain't got no business messing with. Anyway, they're threatening to take the shop and still say we got to pay them all the money she borrowed, too, as interest. I didn't know she was messing around that deep. She always was the business man in our house. I trusted her, Razz. These people she's got caught up with will hurt you. Michelle started going to the casinos man, and she done lost her mind. I don't know if I can get her out of this."

"How much does she owe?"

"It's a lot. If we sell the house and shop, we'll still owe sixty grand."

"Whewww, are you serious? Who did she get the money from?"

"That family that owns that string of pawn shops, one is over on Eckhart, they do a little numbers running, they're into everything. You know who I'm talking about don't you?"

"Yeah . . . yeah, man. I don't know if I can swing that kind of money, Bill. They're some people I dealt with in the past; let me see if I can work something out. I'll let you know."

"Okay Razz, man, I'm sorry for coming to you like this, but I didn't know where else to turn."

"It's okay. Let Razz do his thang."

Razz was rubbing his hands together. He hated to hear about Michelle borrowing money from those loan sharks. They didn't play, especially if they could get inside your business, they'll take it over.

* * * * *

Jackson was playing his favorite game. He had a pair of eights. He betted and was called by everybody at the table. The flop came; it was a seven, an eight, and a Jack. Jackson caught trips on the flop. He betted again, everybody called, this time he was raised by another player. Jacks couldn't wait to call this raise. His hands were shaking, as he called the raise and placed the money up. He didn't want to give away his triple eights; he tried not to act so nervous.

When did he start doing this? All this shaking, Jacks had never gotten nervous playing cards or dice or anything while he was gambling, now he's shaking like he's on dope, and he's was sweating. What was that about?

He re-raised the bet. Players began folding their hands. It was just him and the one other player. Then he noticed that he wasn't relying on his intuition. He usually felt the surroundings before he began betting hard; maybe that's why he was shaking. He wasn't relying on his intuitions. Jackson felt confident he'd won, he betted all the money he had on the table . . . he was called again. They both revealed their cards; Jackson couldn't believe his eyes, the other player won. He had a flush. Jackson only had three eights. It caught Jackson off guard.

He pulled out more money; Jackson was the hot kid that beat everybody; today he was losing. He needed Patrick with him. He was tired of going everywhere by himself. He tried again and again. Razz was watching from his office window. Jackson wasn't in his game, he needed to stop and come back another day. Razz wanted to see if he would stop, he wanted to see how far he would go, how much he would lose before he stopped.

Jackson lost a lot of money that day. Razz finally walked behind Jackson and held his shoulders, he started rubbing and massaging, calming his protégé down.

"That's enough. You go on home. It's not your day."

"Razz, I just needed to warm up. I was cold all day. I don't know why I was losing like that."

"Then why didn't you stop. If you know it's not your day, then why didn't you stop? Why keep losing your money? Don't beat a dead horse."

Chapter 28

"Hallelujah . . . Glory . . ." She praised as she cooked.

Juanita Williams cooked for two days; the entire Williams clan was at her house to officially welcome Jackson to the family. This was the day she had waited on for nearly twenty years. Juanita always knew it would come; the day she would have all her family together. There was never a doubt in her mind that Jackson would be a welcomed member. After all, Jacks was her daddy's spitting image. This was her dream come true, her husband now accepts their grandson. Oh how she prayed, she always believed, so she waited. Now the day is here.

Everybody came from the Robinson's house too. Marianne, Patrick, and Sherry came, Ms. Shirley, Dee and her husband, Det. Combs were all invited to the Williams household. Vanessa, Reginald's ex-wife was there to meet and greet the long lost son. Vanessa was thankful that her daughter has a sibling, an older brother, and he's good looking, intelligent, seems to be a nice young man. She wasn't interested in the details. Somehow she felt she should have remembered Marianne, but she didn't. Vanessa tried and tried to remember meeting her . . . well, it doesn't matter. The boy does favor his father, there's no denying that.

Reginald's brother, Joseph, and his family, his sisters, Rosalyn, Sharon and Karen were all there with their families. It was a parrtay! So much food . . . and music!

Reginald played the piano, his brother Joseph was blowing a saxophone, one of the twins, Sharon or Karen were on the drums, the other had the guitar and Alicia's friend, Nikki was singing, throwing down Angela Winbush, 'Your Smile'. *Nothing means as much . . . like that special touch . . . from your smile . . . if anything I miss, how could I resist . . . your smile . . .*

Baby Smile!

Jackson couldn't resist. She was singing to him. Jackson worked hard trying to be calm and not get up and grab that girl, he decided to relax and enjoy every note she was hitting. He was kind of star struck by this little Nikki, girl. Marianne got tickled because Jackson was so thrown off his cool.

The Williams were showing love and affection that Marianne had never experienced, they all were dancing and singing in each other's face.

Marianne never knew people were really like this. She realized she had deprived her son by not contacting Reginald . . . a long time ago. She decided not to think about it, she would enjoy today. The Williams were extending a hand to everybody. Alicia had Dee dancing and singing, Byron was helping with the kids that were running around, climbing all over him, asking him police stories, and questioning if he'd ever shot anybody, then, have you ever killed anybody with his police gun.

All of a sudden, the base guitar started playing; everybody stopped in their tracks, looked at each other and grabbed a partner. They ran to the middle of the floor. Everybody started singing and dancing, *I know a place . . . ain't nobody cryin' . . . ain't nobody worried . . . ain't no smiling faces . . . Lying to the races . . . help me, I'll take you there . . . somebody help me now. . . I'll take you there.*

Jackson grabbed Marianne, Patrick and Ms. Shirley were up dancing too. Juanita Williams and Rev. William got up, doing their thang. This went on for hours, eating and singing and dancing and singing and eating and on and on.

The doorbell rang.

"Hold on daddy, I'll get it." Juanita lovingly calls her husband 'daddy'. Everybody in the house called him daddy, she was in the habit of doing it too, at church he was The Rev.

"Hey there, Larry, how are you, come in, we're having a little get together, ya'll come on in."

"Yeah, Robert asked me to come over today; he said ya'll were having a dinner over here. I'm sorry I'm so late. This is Brett Reeves, I was waiting on him to come in town; he just got here about an hour ago."

"Bobby's in there, why don't ya'll go in the kitchen and fix something to eat. We've had dinner I'll let Bobby know you're here. The restroom is right over there, if you want to freshen up."

"Okay, thanks"

"Yeah, just make yourself at home. There's an ice chest with sodas or whatever, I think a couple of beers are in there too. Let's see, there's turkey and dressing on the stove, ribs and brisket is there, covered up . . . let me see, there's salads in the fridge, look over on the table, there's everything else. Just make yourself at home. We got homemade ice cream in the freezer."

The Rev. Larry Foster and the young gun, Rev. Brett Reeves did what Juanita told them, they made themselves right at home. Bret had two plates, one for meats and gravies, the other for side dishes and salads. He was closing his eyes and making a humming sound with each bite. Brett lives on the road, eating fast foods, and he was so tired of fried chicken, this was a blessing.

"Man, you gonna hurt yourself, slow down, I don't want Bobby to think I brought an uncouth man in his house."

"You did. I'm as uncouth as they come. Now pass me a couple of them rolls over there, can you put some butter on 'em for me?" Brett was talking with his mouth full.

"Hey there, glad you could make it. Ya'll find everything you need?" Rev. Williams greeted his guest. He wanted to meet Brett Reeves before he introduced him to

Jackson. He trusted his friend Larry, but he still thought it best to talk with Brett, get an idea of his demeanor. This new generation; with their new ideas, are fine and dandy, but the gospel don't change. Rev. Williams wanted to make sure he was preaching the gospel of Christ; he wanted to get a sense of his doctrines before he introduced his grandson to the new style of preachers.

Brett Reeves put his fork down and stood up to meet the Rev. Williams.

"Hello sir, thank you for inviting me to your home. You have a lovely wife, and man, this food is off the hook."

"Thank you, glad to have you. Ya'll, go on and enjoy your meal, I'll be in my study. Larry, why don't you and Brett come in there once you've finished eating?"

Rev. Williams went to his study to meditate and pray before the other ministers joined him. It wasn't long before they came. Rev. Williams was blunt with the new generational preacher. Larry Foster got a little heated with Robert Williams, Brett was his friend, he knew the brother was on fire for the kingdom of heaven. Why was Robert questioning his integrity?

Robert Williams and Larry Foster go back a long way, Robert knows that he'd put his reputation on the line for anybody he formally referenced. They'd be top notch, so why was Robert being so silly. He was questioning this man's honor. He didn't bring Brett over to be insulted. But for some reason, Larry held his tongue.

Brett didn't seem insulted at all. He was standing toe to toe with the elderly preacher. They talked doctrine; Rev. Williams asked questions, asking Brett to explain his philosophy about God and other religions. He wanted to know if Brett was firm in his beliefs. Finally, Brett decided to tell Rev. Williams his story.

"Rev. Williams, for years I was the one selling that

304

poison on the streets, killing my own people. I was a big, bad bullying dope pusher. I was in and out of juvenile since I was ten. By the time I was fourteen, I had been shot twice, and on my way back to a cell. This time, they wanted to try me as an adult. I was looking at real time. I thought as long as I was underage, I could do like I wanted. Now they changed the rules on me. Somehow, I was given another chance. But, I wasn't finished yet; I still went back on the streets. So, I decided I had to be a little smarter, I couldn't risk the chance of being caught again, so I got me some little soldiers to sell my drugs, to do my dirty work. We were all riding bikes and selling more dope than anybody. If we got messed with, then we dealt with them, in a harsh way. I was raising little killers, just like me. By the time I was sixteen or seventeen, I was selling big drugs, making big money, paying all the bills for my family."

Brett took a deep breath, then continued his story. "My momma was on dope, I'm giving her drugs. What kind of man would do that? My own little sister and brother were selling and smoking crack like everybody else . . . anyway, I looked at my life and wondered if this is what it's all about. Seemed like to me, it's got to be something better than this, I was living in hell. I was helping my own momma kill herself. She looked like death, all day sucking on a crack pipe. Well, one day, I was walking down the street, detailing my life, tallying up everything I was doing, when I heard a car drive by and bullets started ripping my body into pieces. I got shot four times. Man, that night I died. I died on that ground, I was dead. I saw the light coming toward me; I jumped for it, like I was escaping something. I just wanted to go with it. It felt so good and peaceful, it was beautiful. I never wanted to leave that presence. I felt love like I've never knew existed. Then I heard this voice telling me that I wasn't coming yet, that I had work to do for Jesus now, and one day I would be with him. Rev.

305

Williams ever since I woke up in that hospital room, I've been chasing that light and that feeling of love. Whatever I have to do, sir, I'll do it for Jesus. I know what's it feels like to be with him, so I have to be obedient; I had to learn about this man called Jesus. I want everybody to know him, to experience, to have a chance, like I was given a chance. I don't know why I didn't die that day. So many others had died with far less injury, why he loved me, I was the worse of the worse, but he still loved me. So as long as I have air to breathe, a life to live, I'll work for Jesus Christ. I'll work, I'll study and preach; whatever I need to do . . . I'm willing." Tears were streaming down Brett Reeves face. Rev. William held his brother in Christ.

"Rev. Williams, I know I'm a little rough around the edges, I'm hardcore; I was raised that way. Maybe that's why Jesus saved me, because these kids today are hard, they're heartless, they're lost and they need that rough style to identify with their life and their stories. You can't be nice to everybody. Some of these girls walking around . . . need some raw gospel." Brett shook his head. "I want those kids to feel the love that I got when I came to know Jesus; I want them to be given a chance, like I was given a chance." Brett was just getting started.

Rev. Williams patted his back to let him know, it was enough. He was convinced.

"Thank you for being so patience with me, son. Let's call Jackson in here."

Jackson was sitting at the piano with his sister, Alicia and her friend, Nikki. Alicia loved her brother at first sight. Jacks planned on taking them both out, to the mall to do some shopping, and maybe a movie before they left town. He wanted more time with Alicia. She was so sweet, and her friend was so fine. Nikki had a voice that was deep, sultry, and sexy. Jackson told himself that he was giving that girl a couple of years to grow up; then he's coming after her.

Alicia thought Jackson was so cool, not like the boys she grew up with, he seemed so much older. But Jacks was only two years older than Alicia. He didn't dress like the other boys, Jacks wore slacks and had on this designer shirt. Her brother was sexy.

It was funny looking at him, Jackson looked so much like her father, but then he was different. His mother was cool, too. Alicia noticed that Marianne and her father were really close. They were laughing and talking all night. Her mother seemed really happy too.

"Are Marianne and my dad dating?"

Jackson choked. "I don't know for sure, why don't you ask them? I think my mom has loved Reginald a long time. I can't remember her ever having a boyfriend, I mean, a real boyfriend. She seems happy now."

"They both do. My mother is seeing another man. He's a judge in Atlanta. My dad got all fat. If he loses some of that weight, he'll be alright. I'll be happy if they were dating."

Everybody drifted to little corners of the room. Ms. Shirley left with Dee and Byron. They left Lonnie, Uncle Charlie and Aunt Rosie at the house with a caregiver. Shirley wanted to get home to see about them, before it got too late. She'd stay at Dee's house for the night, with the caregiver, that way Dee could stay at Byron's house. They needed some time alone.

Patrick, Joseph and most of the other men found a room where they could watch the pre-football game; and were getting a little loud. They talked football and basketball the rest of the evening, Patrick found some new friends. They lived on the other side of Kansas City in Missouri. They told Patrick to get a big screen TV and some sports channels; then they'll bring all their friends to his place. That's what going on now, the sports bars.

Rosalyn had the kids all rounded up and settled down, ready for bed. Sherry and the twins, Sharon and Karen were working hard, getting everything cleaned up. They told Juanita Williams to sit down, relax, and take a load off. She had worked enough.

Rev. Williams quietly asked Jackson to come to his study. He had someone for him to meet.

"Larry Foster, Brett Reeves, this is Jackson Williams Robinson, my grandson. He was called into the ministry. He doesn't know other ministers. I don't guess . . . Do you?"

Jackson shook his head "No sir, I don't"

"Well, Brett here, is attending Morehouse, where you'll be going this Fall. He seems to be a strong man in Christ. It's good to have other men that you can call on, while you're going through this process of becoming a minister, a servant. I hope you can be friends."

Brett shook Jackson's hand. His first impression of Jackson wasn't that good. He had a doubt in his mind about Jackson. Brett thought he looked too slick. He was a good looking guy. He might want to be one of these TV preachers.

"Glad to meet you, brother."

Larry Foster spoke up. "I think it might be a good idea for Jackson to go with Brett before school starts to one of his revivals. It's an experience . . . seeing the young men and women turning their lives to Christ."

"I would love to go. Where do you go?"

"Well, what I do is have revivals in the inner city streets, where the gang members and drug addicts hang out. I go where they are, cause nine times out of ten; they're not coming in the church, so I go to them."

"How does that work for you? I mean, how's the turn

out?"

"I have a little help. I'll promote the revival for about two weeks. Put up flyers and posters around the city and in churches. I have a band that travels with me; the tents are set up a couple of days in advance. I'll have them up so the people start going there, feeling comfortable, already. Sometimes people are just curious, they think it's a free concert or something. A few of the local churches help sponsor the event. Half the time, I don't know where the money comes from, but it's always there and it's always enough. By the time I arrive, they've been waiting and they're usually responsive to the word."

"That sounds awesome. I would like to go. When is the next one, where are you going?"

"It'll be in Little Rock. You can ride with me. I'm on a Harley or you can go with the band ahead of time, help set up, or I can meet you out there."

"I can help set up, help promote it. That's sounds like something interesting to do. I'd like to see how everything works."

Rev. Williams and Larry listened while they made plans to go to Little Rock for an inner city revival with the Evangelist, preacher, Brett Reeves. Rev. Williams thanked his friend Larry for introducing the two young ministers. They both nodded their heads in agreement.

"Well, let's make sure you two got each other's information. I think it's a good idea to thank the Lord for bringing these two men of God together." They all laid hands on each other and began to pray separately while Rev. Williams began praying aloud.

"Dear Lord, we thank You today for such a wonderful day. We had a glorious time with our friends and family. We thank You for the two young men here, willing to do Your work,

willing to tend Your sheep. We ask for knowledge and power in their lives. We especially thank You for Your son, Jackson. He's new to his calling and he's answered Your call. He's willing to do Your work. Give him grace, favor and mercy; let his mind and body receive Your blessing that Your Will is done in his life."

At that time, Jackson began feeling something warm on his head. It was a thick warm liquid slowly coming from the crown of his head moving slowly, dripping now onto his forehead. Rev. Williams watched in amazement. His voice was shaking.

"LORD . . . MY GOD, we see the anointment. We see the anointment, Father. Praise God . . . Thank you, Father."

Brett and Larry opened their eyes to see what was going on.

Rev. Williams started crying, and holding his grandson. Brett Reeve couldn't contain himself. He was walking around the room, talking in tongues. Larry Foster fell to his knees, he began prophesying. Jackson dropped to his knees, too; his head looking up toward heaven. He saw scriptures turning over and over, they were pouring into his mind. Jackson was in a total trance.

When Jackson woke up, they were standing over him, still praying and crying. Rev. Williams took his handkerchief and began wiping the oil off Jackson's forehead. Larry Foster and Brett took a cloth so they could have some oil too.

Brett picked his brother up, dusted him off.

"I'll be honored, Jackson, to have you come at my next revival."

Chapter 29

There was something different about Jackson; he could feel it . . . it was like breathing new air. He had confidence like he'd never had before. So strong and sure, he had a definite feeling of purpose. He was eager and excited, so excited. He couldn't wait to get started on this new journey in life. Jackson thought about Tia, he smiled, knowing she would be so proud of him. He wished she was here to share this experience with him. Jacks' grandfather asked him to start attending his church while he was still at home.

"You need to come to prayer and bible study, listen to the old hymnals so you can get a feeling of how grateful people were, back then. Study history son, history shows how the church has been very instrumental throughout the world. Oh, you'll get all that when you get to Morehouse . . . Jackson, Martin Luther King tackled racism with prayer. Prayer is a powerful weapon. Yeah, you come on this Wednesday night, get there around six. Son, I'm hoping that one day, this will be your church. I worried about who would continue to lead this congregation. Thank God I'm not worried anymore. I'm in my twilight years, I'm sick and old."

Jackson listened to his grandfather, but he remembered the lesson he learned. He had figured that nothing happens like you plan, so always keep an open mind. He wanted to tell Razz what happened to him. His grandfather was talking and planning his life, his mission, but he kept thinking about Razz.

"Wait till Razz hears about this anointing thing that happened." Jacks rehearsed everything so he wouldn't forget any details. Razz wanted to know details; he always told Jacks that hidden messages were in the details. He had to get to Razz.

* * * * *

Patrick was at Uncle Charlie's house visiting Lonnie.

He wanted to spend as much time as possible with his father. Patrick wanted to catch up, he felt that he didn't have a lot of time left to hear about his family and to get to know his father, and Lonnie was full of stories about his folk and their life in North Carolina.

Lonnie's voice was soft and strained, "Patrick, the Evans family has a lot of property there in North Carolina. That's what you are, an Evans, um, I got you down as the beneficiary, it's about 120 acres there, um, what last name you been using?"

"Robinson, Patrick Robinson."

"That's okay, um, you might have to change the name on the deeds. It shouldn't be a problem, um. (cough) um. You favor your mother, you got her smile, um she was pretty."

"Dad, why don't you lay down, I'll be back when I get off work tonight. Get some rest, okay."

"Okay."

* * * * *

Jackson was riding down the street, on his way to see Razz, when he saw Blue.

"Look at that boy, what's wrong with him?"

Jackson turned the car around, this time he drove up on Blue, riding beside him as he walked.

"Blue, man, what's wrong?"

"Ain't nothing wrong. What's wrong with you? You look like something's wrong with you, to me."

"Come on, man. Get your ass in the car."

"I ain't going nowhere with you Jacks. Kiss my ass."

"If I get out this car Blue, I'm going kick your ass. Now get in the car. . . . I'm not playing."

Jackson pulled to the curb, threw the car in park, and opened his door, leaving it opened and exposed to the street. He came around and grabbed Blue, opened the door and threw

312

him in the car.

"What's wrong with you, Blue? Why every time I see you you're all beat up, like somebody's done kicked your ass? Who did this to you? Look at you. You're all dirty - you ain't got clean clothes? Where's your clothes?"

"Hey, it ain't none of your damn business. I'm okay."

"You don't look okay. Who's been kicking your ass like this? Is this what you want? You want to live like this, like a bum, Blue? Let me help you. You come live with me. I got a plan, it'll work out. You just come stay with me."

"I don't need a damn thing from you, Jacks. You were my main man, but you threw me on the streets. Now I don't want nothing from your funky ass. Now let me out this damn car." Blue started kicking the dash and struggling with the door to get it opened, but Jacks had it locked from his side. Jacks popped Blue upside his head.

"Stop that, you ain't getting out this car. Are you on drugs now? You some kind of crack head now, Blue? When's the last time you talked to your mother?"

"I get so damn tired of ya'll asking me about my momma. Do I look like I talked to my momma? She told Zett not to give me any more money. I called her a few months ago." Blue started crying, "I asked her for a few dollars so I could get something to eat, but I heard her telling Zett not to give me anything. Can you believe that?"

"Well, I'm not taking you back to those streets. I'm gonna take you over to Ms. Shirley's house. You can stay there. She's never at home; I'll stay there with you for a few months, until I leave for school. You can stay there and get yourself together. I'll move in with you."

Blue was crying and nodding his head in agreement.

"You need to get cleaned up. You stink."

"Shut up, you stink."

313

They drove the rest of the way in silence. Jacks was thinking of what Blue could wear. He was so much smaller than him and Patrick. He didn't know what Blue's been doing this past year; he looked like a crack head. He wanted to leave him at Ms. Shirley's house while he shopped for clothes, but he didn't know Blue anymore, he might steal something from Ms. Shirley.

Jackson called Ms. Shirley to let her know that Blue was at her house getting cleaned up, and he was going out to get Blue some new clothes.

"Okay baby, if that's what you want to do. I'll be over here all day. Shoot, I might just stay here. It's so much easier with the caregivers helping me. They do all the work. I just tell them what to do. But I like to be here for Rosie. She's not doing so good. Yeah baby, whatever you want to do is okay with me. Let me know if you need anything."

* * * * *

Big Bill and Michelle were fighting. They had been fighting since Bill found out what Michelle had done with all their money, their property, and the business. Bill was ashamed that he had to go to Razz for help. He didn't want anyone to know about their mess, but he was desperate.

Razz contacted one of his sources and he was told that all their finances would be forgiven, but they still had to give up the house and the boutique.

"Damnit Michelle, don't you blame me 'cause you gambled away the house and business. Was I with you when you got that damn loan? Was I there? You damn right, I wasn't there, so I don't want to hear that bullshit come out your mouth."

"You wasn't home, either, Bill. I always have to go on my vacations by myself or with some girlfriends. Hell, I got a husband and you don't do anything with me. You spend all your

314

time at Razz's gambling. I wanted some fun too. Hell, I get tired of working all the time and all you have to do is play cards at Razz's."

"I make money playing fucking cards. Michelle, when have I ever taken money from you or this household? When did I do that? Now your sisters won't even speak to your dumb ass. They trusted you to handle their money. You ought to be ashamed of yourself, Michelle. How you gonna send your daughter to school? We can't get nothing because you wanted to play the slot machines?"

"If you had of just come to Vegas with me, then I wouldn't have done all that. You wouldn't come. I don't know why I did it. I thought I would make it back. Anyway, I didn't borrow all that money, they charged me interest. That's what happened, Bill."

"Michelle, some people you don't mess with. These were the kind of people that will kill you 'bout some money. I always thought you were smarter than that."

Michelle cried, "Where are we gonna go, Bill? Where are we gonna live now?"

"I don't know. I have to think about it."

Razz and Darlene were talking about their friends, Bill and Michelle. Razz couldn't believe what a mess they had gotten into. Razz hated to get involved, because those were the type, the kind of people, you kept at a distance. He wondered how Michelle borrowed that much money. That was part of the story she hadn't told.

But he knew one of the relatives and back in the day, they were friends, when Razz was able to move a few things.

One of Razz's homeboys from Wewoka had stolen a freight truck, one of those 18 wheeler trucks. They didn't know what was in it, they just took it. When they got to an open field they found it was full of whiskey. They called Razz.

"Hey man you want a truck load of whiskey for a few hundred bucks?"

"Hell yeah." Razz thought he could bootleg a little whiskey. He met his homeboys to buy the alcohol but when he saw it was a freight truck full, it scared him.

"Man, I can't do nothing with all this whiskey. That's waaaay too much for me. They don't have stamps on the bottles. I can't take that shit. Let me make a few calls, see if I can move it."

That's when Razz met this family that Michelle owed. They bought the truck of whiskey, and Razz moved it to one of their warehouses somewhere outside of Kansas. That was over twenty years ago. Razz was glad the man was still alive so he could get in a favor.

His nephew wasn't happy that Razz got in his business.

"You think this man is going to let it go, Razz?" Darlene was scared. "He was mad. I heard what he said."

"I ain't worried."

"But he was threatening you."

"Hey, hey, this is Razz baby, don't you worry. Have Razz ever let you down?"

"No baby. Never! I just love you and now we got these people talking crazy. They say you had to give them how much?"

"Nothing! I ain't giving them nothing. Now you don't worry about Razz's business. You hear me?"

* * * * *

Sunday morning Jackson was up and ready for church. His friend Blue was ready. His sister and Nikki would be there. Jackson couldn't get to church fast enough.

When they arrived in the church's parking lot they saw Marianne and Dee pulling up.

"Hi mom, hi Dee."

316

"Hi baby, where did you get Blue?"

"We're gonna be roommates, mom. I'll tell you about it later."

"Hello Ms. Marianne, Can I speak with you for a minute? I want to apologize for disrespecting you. You've always been nice to me and I shouldn't have talked to you like that. I'm really sorry."

"Baby, that's okay, as long as you're alright, that's all I'm concerned about. You okay."

"Yes ma'am."

They hugged and kissed. Dee was holding on to Marianne for dear life. She couldn't remember the last time she was in church. But now, since she's a married woman, she wanted to start going and doing everything right. She wanted her husband to be proud of her.

When they walked in, Jacks' grandfather motioned him to come sit in the pulpit with the other ministers. Blue couldn't believe his eyes. Jackson hadn't mentioned to him that he was going to be a preacher. Blue couldn't contain himself. He was about to burst with joy for his friend and brother. Why didn't Jacks tell him he was a preacher? Blue was absolutely thrilled. He couldn't wait to see more of this.

Church was good. The choir was great. The message was wonderful and inspirational. Jackson didn't look toward him or his sister. His head stayed focused on the preacher and he was taking notes. Blue wondered how he heard anything, being so busy writing. Blue was proud of his friend.

Then it hit him - that's what it's been all about. Ever since they were kids, Jacks had been seeing things. He remembered him and Tia talking about an angel that visited them when they were young. Tears started streaming down Blue's face. He saw his friend being a preacher.

"Yes, that's right Jacks. You were always the one. I'm

317

so proud of you." Blue took a kleenex from one of the ushers. "Thank you, ma'am." He continued to watch his friend sitting with the ministers, in the pulpit of this big church.

Church finally was over and Alicia, Blue, and Nikki waited for Jacks to come out, but he was busy. Rev. Williams introduced Jackson to all the other ministers. They went back to his office to talk more about Jackson's future.

"You want us to give you a ride home, Blue."

"Naw, that's alright. I'll wait for Jacks. I can see the resemblance with you and Jackson."

"Actually, he looks a lot like my dad. Grandma says he's the spitting image of her father. He was a preacher too."

"Man . . . my main man. Did you know he was going to be a preacher?"

"Yeah, my dad told me."

"He never mentioned it to me. I grew up with Jackson, all my life . . . we were best friends. I didn't know until now when he sat up there with Rev. Williams. I didn't know."

Alicia shrugged, she couldn't say anything about that. "Well, me and Nikki are leaving this evening. We're going back to Atlanta. It was nice meeting you. I'll probably see you again. Tell Jackson to give me a call, maybe I can see him before I leave."

Blue was sitting on the steps, waiting for Jackson when he finally came out.

"Everybody's gone?"

"Yeah, Alicia and Nikki just left. They said they were leaving for Atlanta this evening. Your sister is pretty man, but her friend Nikki is fine."

"I know; you should hear her sing. Man, I wanted to get with them before they left."

"You and Alicia look just alike, only she's yellow."

"It's weird isn't it? Blue, I'm gonna drive you home, I

got some errands to run. You'll be okay till I get back."

"Man, you don't have to babysit me. I'm good. Jackson. Why didn't you tell me you were a preacher? You had me in there crying like a little bitch."

"Blue, you gotta clean your trap around me. I'm a preacher now. "

Jackson took Blue home then raced over to his sister's room to catch her before she left town. He loved his little sister. He was eager to go to school in Atlanta, where he'd get to spend more time with her. Jacks couldn't get over how sweet and pretty she was. When he got to their room, they were eating. He got a little off each of their plates.

"I wanted to take you to dinner, you left before I could do anything with you, at least I'm able to tell you bye. Ya'll okay? You got a way to the airport?"

"Yeah, dad is coming to take us. When are you coming to Atlanta?"

"I'll be there in December. Our grandfather has everything all planned. I'm kinda of glad, because I didn't have a clue. I'll see you in a couple of months."

"Bye Jacks."

"Hey Nikki, you be good. It was nice meeting you. Ya'll take care."

Jackson kissed his sister and gave her a big hug, then left. It was getting late; he wanted to catch Razz before all his customers came in. He stayed with Alicia and Nikki too long.

"Wait till Razz hears what's been happening." Jackson raced to Razz.

Chapter 30

When Jackson got to the club, there were a couple of cars parked out front that Jackson didn't recognize. They were two matching black on black Cadillac's, with dark tinted windows and one red utility truck.

"I'm too late, he already has customers. It's only a few cars. Maybe they'll leave in a bit."

Jackson waited out front, hoping the customers would leave, but they didn't. He decided to go inside. Something was wrong. He peeked through the window. There were four men and one was arguing with Razz and pushed Razz in a chair.

Jackson could only catch every other word, but they were trying to force him to sign some papers. Jackson was watching through the little window, he tried to open the door but it was locked. Jackson knocked hard at the door.

One of the men got up and went to the door; he grabbed Jackson and pulled him inside. He pushed Jacks to the chair next to Razz.

"What's going on Razz?"

Razz was horrified to see it was Jackson; this was the last person he wanted to see. Not right now. He had to get him out of there. Razz had always been real cool. This was the time when he had to use every bit of cool he had in him. He couldn't let them hurt Jackson.

Razz got up from the table and nodded for Jackson to get up too. They walked toward the door as if nothing was wrong. Razz was still in control.

"You get on out of here. It's okay." Razz was rubbing Jackson's shoulders. Jackson remembered the last time Razz did that and asked him to leave. It was because he was losing a lot of money. Razz got him out that time.

The man that was arguing with Razz, the one that

seemed more in charge, motioned the other men to stop Jackson from leaving.

"No! He's not leaving here until I say he can leave. Nobody leaves until we settle our business."

"Razz, why are these men arguing with you? Who are these cats? You need me and I'm staying. I'm not leaving you here by yourself."

"Hey, man, this boy ain't got nothing to do with our business. We're talking."

Razz turned to Jackson. "I want you to walk out of here and whatever happens, don't you come back. You got that? You keep on walking and don't you look back, either. You understand me Jackson?"

Jackson was nodding, agreeing with Razz, but inside he was breaking down. Tears were streaming down Jacks face. He knew Razz was in trouble and he wanted to help. This was Razz, his friend, his hero.

"Hey and don't be calling the law to my place of business. You got that?" Razz was speaking loud so the men could hear and know that Jackson would do anything he said.

Jackson shook his head "Yes."

Razz was walking Jacks toward the door; he stopped and smiled at Jacks, looking at him in a fatherly way. He held Jackson's head in his two hands; he shook Jackson's head hard.

"Listen, listen! Don't, call, no, law, to my, place, of business . . . I need you to tell Darlene something for me. Let her know everything is handled and it's alright. Would you do that for Razz? Let her know. You get out of here; I want you out my parking lot."

Razz stopped just short of the doorway.

"You get out of here and do like I told you." The fatherly talk was over. "You hear me?" He was brass and stern.

One of the men started walking toward them, as if he had a change of heart. He wanted Jackson to stay.

"Hey, hey, wait."

Razz saw the man coming and raised his hand for the man to stop.

"Get out of here, Jackson." Razz pushed Jackson's head hard toward the door.

Jackson walked out the door and got in his car, he sat there contemplating what to do. His mind told him to leave, but his heart told him to go back inside.

"My God, what am I supposed to do? Help me." Jackson was begging. "Please God, help Razz."

Jackson got out the car and ran back inside the club, he screamed for Razz but no sound came from his mouth. He walked over to the men, ready to fight for Razz's life. He stood in front of Razz, trying to block him from the men . . . but they couldn't see him. Razz couldn't see him, either.

Jackson listened. This was about Big Bill and Michelle.

"Man, I'm not signing that. You do what you have to, but I'm not giving you my place of business."

"Before I leave, your signature or your brains is going to be on this deed."

Razz didn't care what they were saying. He was making peace with God and hearing very little of what was being said. He knew that they would kill him that day, regardless. Years ago, he decided never to run a club for somebody else to make all the money.

Razz felt that he'd already won. Jackson was gone; he would have signed anything to protect Jackson.

* * * * *

Jackson helplessly watched Razz, he saw the men. He saw everything but he couldn't do anything. They didn't see that he was there, with them.

Suddenly, Jackson started getting sick, everything started spinning and going in slow motion. Two men took their guns out; they stuck the gun to Razz's head . . . it was in slow motion like a movie.

Jackson screamed. He tried to fight.

"Noooooooooooooo!" His scream was in slow motion. Then it happened. The vision . . . the bright flash; then he heard the blast. But it was two blasts, two flashes of light. Jackson fell to his knees, he was sick to his stomach. This was it, the vision he witnessed since he was a child. This was it. He ran out the club. Jackson was crying.

"Lord what just happened to Razz. I'm not supposed to call the police."

Standing on the streets were Uri and Josias. This time they weren't smiling. Jackson looked in disbelief that they didn't help Razz.

They were there. They watched Jackson without saying a word. They saw that he was ready to give his life for his mentor.

They were commissioned to protect Jackson. They covered Jackson from the natural eyes of the men and Razz. They covered him until he was out and driving down the street, then they walked away.

EPILOGUE

It had been over six years since Razz died. Jacks often thought about that night and what he could have done different.

All his life he had experienced the visions with the blast and the flash haunting him. He wondered why he received the visions if he wasn't able to change the outcome.

One time he had a dream of Razz and Tia together. They were happy, the dream wasn't long. He thought Razz and Tia wanted him know that they were together and alright.

Jackson had a year left to finish the Masters program at Morehouse and he was preparing to get his PH.D., in Theology. He was now a married man. He met his wife, Dianna while she was studying to be a nurse. Jackson thought she was so beautiful and so serious about medicine; that he wanted to help her heal the world. She's real sweet like his grandmother, Juanita Williams.

His grandfather, Rev. Williams, Aunt Rosie and Uncle Charlie passed a few years ago. Everybody was leaving. Ms. Shirley and Lonnie were still hanging in there. Victor and Calvin still worked for the restaurant. Victor moved in with Ms. Shirley, faithfully helping take care of Lonnie. They all lived in Uncle Charlie's big house.

Lonnie was old as dirt, in his early 80's and doing a lot better than anyone could have imagined. He loved being around Patrick and his family. He and Marianne had a chance to bury a few hatchets.

"You know, Marianne, I always liked you. You were always smart."

"Why did you leave, Lonnie?"

"I couldn't take it. Um, Patricia dying like that. I felt guilty, like it was my fault. . . her getting pregnant. I went down to North Carolina to get my affairs in order, I was thinking of ending it, dying too. I thought I would disappear. Um . . . I had everything planned. After I got my Will done and got all those deeds in order, um, I thought I would fall in one of those abandon wells, but I couldn't bring myself to do it. (chuckle) "

"Lonnie, can I ask you a question? Maybe you will remember, I don't know. One day, when I was around 15 or 16, you were in my room, when I woke up, you were standing over my bed. What was that about?"

"Oh, um, I remember, I had bought your mother that ring. I was gonna ask her to marry me. I wanted you to, um, to see the ring, to see if you liked it. But, back then, you intimidated me. (chuckle . . . chuckle)"

"I'm so sorry, Lonnie. I was jealous of you."

"Um, your mother was the only woman that loved me. She, um, was the only woman, um, that um, I didn't have to pay for sex. Um (chuckle) That's something, isn't it?"

Marianne left the restaurants business to Patrick and Sherry. They were still in love. They had fraternal twin boys, Andolus and Andre. They'll be turning 4 years old, January 29th.

The first time Patrick heard Jackson preach, it was a sermon he couldn't shake. Jackson spoke of life; that nothing matters, except what we do for God.

One day, there will not be one person alive that will personally remember you. Who you were and what you stood for . . .

So knowing this, what is it in life that really matters? I can answer that. The only thing that matters in life is what you do for God. It will last because, God loves you and He will remember you, He knows you, He knows what you're about, He knows your people, where you come from. He will remember what you did on this day and that day, what you did on the job,

325

in that dark alley. God will remember you and everything about you.

Now some things we don't want God to remember!

But if we ask Jesus to come in our life, to cover our sins, God is just to forgive us. Then guess what, He forgets . . . that evil thing that you did will be removed from your record. That part about you, never to return in His presence again.

So, all that hard work you do today, well, it'll be gone. The people you love and work hard for will be gone. The people you try to impress, well, they will be gone too.

But what we do for God will be remembered throughout the ages because God remembers you. So why not make God happy? What you do for God is what counts. He will remember you, personally. It's through Him that you even arrived on the scene.

Give him a try? Confess your sins, and He'll be just to forgive you. Give your life, this day, to Him, Don't wait, God wants you now. He will remember you, love you, He's your only hope that you will live eternally as heirs with Christ. Be remembered. Put your trust in the only One that counts.

Patrick cried and asked Jackson to meet with him. He had something that he wanted to get off his chest.

"I have a secret that I've kept a long time, almost twelve years."

"What's up Patty? Nothing could be that bad."

Patrick nodded, "Yes it can; it's that bad. Jacks, you're going to be shocked, maybe more disappointed than anything."

"You heard the sermon didn't you? You don't have to tell anybody but Jesus . . . take it to Jesus, Patty and lay it at the throne of grace. Be honest, and he'll forgive you."

"You sure, Jacks?"

"Yeah, I'm sure. Hey . . . I'll pray with you. It'll be

okay."

"Jackson, I want to talk about it. I'm tired of having this secret eating at me, if I just talked about it, I've never talked about it to anyone, maybe this guilt, will leave me."

"Okay Patty, you talk about it, but once we give it to Jesus, you got to let it go and forgive yourself."

Patrick told Jackson the whole ugly story of the night he raped Sherry. How him and Zetty were planning to get rid of her body, but she woke up and he couldn't bring himself to do it. He told how Sherry forgave him and they had been together ever since. He admitted to Jackson that's why he loved her so much and he'll never leave her.

"Can you imagine somebody forgiving something like that? Sherry is special and she loves me, man."

"Yeah, I know love like that. Jesus loves everybody more, not just a selected few. I want you to read Psalms 32. Study it."

Tears flowed freely down Patrick's cheeks. He was letting the emotions and guilt release that plagued him for years. Jackson listened and prayed for Patty. When they finished, Jackson could see Patrick colors were faintly coming back. He was healing.

* * * * *

Dee and Byron are still together. She took it real hard when Uncle Charlie and Aunt Rosie died. She decided to make an effort to reunite with her mother. Dee and Byron took a couple of weeks to visit her side of the family, but they weren't all that happy to see Dee. She decided it would always be a distance between them. Anyway, she had a husband now, she had Marianne and everybody in Kansas City; they were her family. They loved her and it was okay.

* * * * *

Blue was a different man. He went back to school. He

327

got a degree in business and started helping Jackson and Brett Reeve with the Running For The Lord National Revival. He was their finance man, he married Alicia's friend, Nikki. They've been married about three years now. They had a beautiful wedding. At their wedding, Nikki sang her new single, My Forever Lover.

As much as he can, Jackson goes to Kansas City to preach at his grandfather's church and stay at their old house where Big Bill and Michelle are now living. Bill helps Patrick out at the restaurants and he works with Darlene in the evenings to help put his stepdaughter through college.

* * * * *

Michelle suffered a bout with depression. She got really bad for a while. Bill stayed with her, but he couldn't fix what happened to Razz. Dee tried to get her to see a therapist, but she wouldn't go. They tried to help her as much as possible, but Michelle's got to want help. She's been punishing herself for years now.

* * * * *

Darlene still works at the rest home, but she remodeled Razz's club. It's a high end jazz club called "Razz-Ma-Tazz" and Darlene is doing fine.

One day the men that murdered Razz came to visit her. They thought that she owed them some money, but she's a smart girl from New York City, and they weren't going to mess with Darlene.

"I understand that Razz crossed the line. I hate to disappoint you, but you won't get a damn dollar from me. Look around you; too bad you didn't pay attention. We had cameras all around this joint. You'll be surprised what I got on filmed. I'll make sure you a copy. If anything ever happens to me, if a fire or a robbery, if I trip and scar my knees, the films goes to someone I trust. That's a promise. Now please, get out of my place of business." They never came back.

* * * * *

Last year, Jackson presided over the wedding ceremony of Marianne and Reginald. It was a small affair with only a few guests. They left touring the states and Canada. They traveled through the Caribbean Islands, Mexico. They went everywhere. They plan on going somewhere every year.

* * * * *

Today, Jackson is filled with the Holy Spirit. He looked back on his life and he realized that it was only the grace of God that kept him. He used to love gambling, playing dice, and he loved hanging with the men in Razz's club, he wondered why God called him. Why not Zett or Blue, even Tia. He didn't know why, but he sure was glad it was him.

Jackson got his whole family and neighborhood prayed up and saved. Zett and Angie are faithful members of Redeemers Baptist Church. Jacks saw Stevie Brooks in prison, he was saved too.

Every few years, he could look out in his congregation and see his old friends and protectors, Uri and Josias; the angels that protected him since his childhood. He now looked older than his two angels. Sometimes they were smiling, then sometimes they were very serious and on guard. Then he wondered why, what was happening that he needed protection.

When he saw that they were there, ready to fight, he knew it was a reason. Then he would get louder, he would become bolder and he would preach the Word with all he had.

RAZZ

What can I say about a legend? My friend, George Coleman better known as Razz, was the epitome of cool, calm and class. When I met him in 2001, he started calling me First Lady. I love that nickname, it was something my Dad might have said.

I want to say thank you, Razz, for the friendship, love, and all the funny stories you gave me. You allowed me to use your name, but I wanted your style more. I tried to describe your smile and the way you received all your friends and customers. I hope I did you justice.

I don't know why I took so long to publish this book because it was finished in 2009. I guess because the fictional Razz would die at the end, but Razz sure was looking forward to seeing it published. He was excited about this book.

Well, this is it. Some of the real stories I altered because the book is fictional. But we sure laughed talking about these stories and what details I would include.

I know a few people will remember the old Shine rhymes that were told during my childhood. I have to give a shout out to my friend Ron, and my Uncle Wille Joe, and some of the other 'Ole Timers' that helped me put a few of those verses together, we sat at Razz's club and what we couldn't remember, we made up. Thank you too, Ron and Uncle Willie Joe.

Good bye my friend, my Razz-ma-tazz. He was a chapter that ended in Oklahoma on June 18, 2011.

www.ingramcontent.com/pod-product-compliance
Lightning Source LLC
Chambersburg PA
CBHW031234090426
42742CB00007B/194